Professional Training Institution

Copyright © 2010, 2012, 2013, 2014, 2016 2017 Professional Training Institution
2803 St. Joseph Ave Suite B
PO Box 6302
Evansville, IN 47720
Phone 812.422.4068 • info@ptischool.com

All rights reserved. No part of this book may be reproduced or transmitted in any form or by any means, electronic or mechanical, including photocopying, recording, or by any information storage and retrieval system, without written permission from the publisher, except for the inclusion of brief quotations in a review.

This publication is designed to provide accurate and authoritative information in regard to the subject matter covered. It is sold with the understanding that the publisher is not engaged in rendering legal, accounting, or other professional services. If legal advice or other expert assistance is required, the services of a competent professional should be sought.

Any laws and regulations cited in this publication have been edited and summarized for clarity sake.

We have tried to provide the most accurate and useful information possible. However, the content of this publication may be affected by changes in law or industry practice and information may become outdated.

Table of Contents

Insurance Basics for Life and Health 1
THE VERY BASICS 1
WHAT IS INSURANCE? 1
UNDERSTANDING RISK 2
MANAGING RISK 2
PERIL 3
HAZARDS 3
THE LAW OF LARGE NUMBERS 3
TYPES OF INSURERS 4
REINSURANCE 5
CONTRACT LAW 6
ELEMENTS OF A LEGAL CONTRACT 6
COMPETENT PARTIES 6
LEGAL PURPOSE 6
OFFER AND ACCEPTANCE (AGREEMENT) 7
CONSIDERATION 7
DEFINING TRUTH 8
INSURABLE INTEREST 8
CONSENT 9
WHEN DOES COVERAGE START? INTERIM INSURING AGREEMENTS 9
BACKDATING POLICIES 10
POLICY DELIVERY 10
UNIQUE CHARACTERISTICS OF AN INSURANCE CONTRACT 10
OTHER CONTRACT TERMS 11
INSURANCE LAW AND THE AGENT/PRODUCER 12
POWERS OF AGENCY 12
UNDERWRITING BASICS 14
WHY IS UNDERWRITING NECESSARY? 14
SOURCES OF INSURABILITY INFORMATION 14
AIDS, HIV AND UNDERWRITING 15

Selection and Classification Factors	16
Classification of Risks and effects on Premiums Charged	17
Gross and Net Premiums	17
Premium Modes	18
Premium Comparisons	19

The Need for Life Insurance 19
    Obligations at Death 19
    Methods of Estate Building 20
    Living Benefits 20
    Advantages as Property 20
    Needs Approach vs. the Human Life Value Approach 20

Chapter Review 22
    Terms to Know 22
    Sample Questions 25

Types of Life Insurance Policies 29
Term vs. Permanent Insurance 29
Term Life Insurance 30
    Level, Decreasing and Increasing Term 31
    Renewable and Convertible Term 32
    Maturity and Taxation 34
Whole Life Insurance 35
    Cash Value, Loans & Full Withdrawals 36
    Premium Obligations 37
    Maturity and Taxation 38
Adjustable Life Insurance 38
Variable Whole Life 39
Universal Life Insurance 40
    Premium Payments 41
    Loans and Withdrawals 42
    Waiver of Cost of Insurance 43
    Death Benefit Options 43
Variable Universal Life Insurance 45
Interest Sensitive Whole Life Insurance 45
Equity Indexed Life Insurance 46
Joint Life & Joint and Survivor Life 46
.... 48
Other Life Insurance Policy Types 49
    Modified Life 49
    Graded Premium 50

        JUVENILE LIFE 50
        CREDIT LIFE 51
    MODIFIED ENDOWMENT CONTRACTS (MEC) 51

Chapter Review 53
        TERMS TO KNOW 53
        NUMBERS AND TIME PERIODS 55
        SAMPLE QUESTIONS 56

Annuity Contracts 61
    PARTIES TO THE ANNUITY 62
    ACCUMULATION OR PAY IN PERIOD 62
        PREMIUM PAYMENT OPTIONS 63
        CASH VALUE GROWTH 64
        TAX CONSEQUENCES DURING THE PAY-IN OR ACCUMULATION PERIOD OF THE ANNUITY 64
        SECTION 1035 EXCHANGE RULES 65
    THE ANNUITY (PAY-OUT/LIQUIDATION) PERIOD 66
        LIFE ANNUITIES 66
        ANNUITY CERTAIN 69
        ANNUITY PREMIUM DETERMINATION 71
        EXCLUSION RATIO 71
    TYPES OF ANNUITIES 72
        FIXED ANNUITIES 72
        VARIABLE ANNUITIES 72
        EQUITY INDEXED ANNUITIES 73
        TWO TIERED ANNUITIES 73
        RETIREMENT INCOME ANNUITIES 74
        MARKET VALUE ADJUSTED ANNUITY 74

Chapter review 75
        TERMS TO KNOW 75
        NUMBERS AND TIME PERIODS 76
        SAMPLE QUESTIONS 77

Life Insurance Policy Provisions 80
    REQUIRED PROVISIONS 80
        ENTIRE CONTRACT/CHANGES CLAUSE 80
        INSURING CLAUSE 81
        PREMIUM PAYMENT CLAUSE 81
        INCONTESTABLE CLAUSE 81
        MISSTATEMENT OF AGE AND SEX CLAUSE 82
        GRACE PERIOD 82

- Reinstatement Clause 82
- Ownership Clause 83
- Assignment Clause 83
- Loan Values and Automatic Premium Loan (APL) Provision 84
- Time Limit on Lawsuits 84
- The Practice of Backdating 84
- Free Look Provision 84

Discretionary Provisions (Exclusions) 84
- Suicide Clause 85
- Hazardous Occupation (or Hobby/Avocation) Clause 85

Beneficiary Designations 85
- Primary and Contingent Beneficiaries 86
- Revocable and Irrevocable Designations 86
- The Estate as Beneficiary 87
- A Trust as Beneficiary 87
- Minors (Children) as Beneficiaries 88
- Applicant Control or Ownership Clause 88
- Uniform Simultaneous Death Act 88
- Naming Beneficiaries (per capita or per stirpes) 89
- The Spendthrift Clause 91
- Privilege of Change Clause 91

Chapter Review 93
- Terms to know 93
- Numbers and Time periods 94
- Sample Questions 95

Life Insurance Policy Options 97

Dividend Options 97
- Cash 98
- Reduction of Premium 98
- Accumulate at Interest 98
- Paid – Up Additions 99
- One – Year Term 100
- Paid – Up Life 100

Nonforfeiture Options 100
- Cash 101
- Reduced Paid-Up 102
- Extended Term Insurance 103
- Reinstatement 104

Settlement Options 104

Cash	104
Interest	104
Annuity Options	105
Living Benefit Options	106

Chapter Review 108

Terms to know	108
Numbers and Time periods	108
Sample Questions	109

Life Insurance Policy Riders 111

Multiple Indemnity/Accidental Death Rider	111
Guaranteed Insurability Rider	112
Cost of Living Rider	113
Term Riders	113
Waiver of Premium Rider	114
Disability Income Rider	114
Payor Benefit Rider	114
Accelerated Death Benefit Rider	114
Automatic Premium Loan Rider	115

Chapter Review 116

Terms to know	116
Sample Questions	117

Business Uses of Life Insurance 119

Key Employee Life Policies	119
Buy Sell Agreement	119
Split Dollar Plans	122

Chapter Review 123

Terms to know	123
Sample Questions	124

Qualified Retirement Plans 125

Qualified Versus Nonqualified Plans	125
Characteristics of Qualified Plans	125
Tax Treatment	126
Defined Contribution Plans versus Defined Benefit Plans	127
Defined Benefit Plans	127
Defined Contribution Plans	127
Common Types of Qualified Retirement Plans	127
401k Plans	127
403b Plans	128

- Keogh (HR-10) 128
- Simplified Employee Pension (SEP) Plans 128
- SIMPLE Retirement Plans 129
- **Individual Retirement Accounts (IRA's)** 129
  - Traditional IRA 129
  - Roth IRA 130
- **2014 Plan Limitations** 130
- **Plan Roll-Overs** 131

Chapter Review 133
- Terms to know 133
- Numbers and Time periods 133
- Sample Questions 135

Group Life Insurance 137
- Group Life Concepts 137
- Eligible Groups 137
- **The Group Contract** 138
- **Group Underwriting** 138
  - Experience vs. Community Rating 139
  - Contributory vs. Non-Contributory 139
  - Reduced Adverse Selection 140
- **Reduced Administrative Costs** 140
- **Life Conversion Privileges** 141

Chapter Review 142
- Terms to know 142
- Numbers and Time periods 142
- Sample Questions 143

Government Insurance – Social Security 144
- **Eligibility of Benefits** 144
- **Primary Insurance Amount** 145
- **Blackout Period** 146

Chapter Review 147
- Terms to know 147
- Numbers and Time periods 147
- Sample Questions 148

Health Insurance Basics 149
- **Definitions of Key Terms** 149
  - Insuring Clause 149
  - Consideration Clause 149
  - Free Look Provision 150

- Probationary (Waiting) Period 150
- Elimination Period 150
- Perils 152
- Deductibles 152
- Policy Renewal Provisions 153
- Preexisting Conditions 154
- Coinsurance 154
- Stop Loss 154
- Common Exclusions 155

Common Health Insurance Riders 156

Major Health Insurance Providers 158
- Stock and Mutual Companies 158

Chapter Review 159
- Terms to know 159
- Numbers and Time periods 159
- Sample questions 160

Medical Expense Policies 163

Characteristics of Medical Expense Policies 163
- Payment of Medical Expenses 163
- Assignment 164
- Insureds 164
- Deductibles 164
- Coinsurance 164
- Stop Loss 165
- Taxation 166
- Managed Care 166

Types of Medical Expense Plans 166
- Basic Plans 166
- Major Medical 167
- Supplemental Major Medical 168

Miscellaneous Issues 169
- Other Medical Expense Benefits 169
- Common Exclusions and Limitations 169
- Other Major Medical Concepts 170

Chapter Review 171
- Terms to know 171
- Numbers and Time periods 171
- Sample questions 172

Other Healthcare Providers 174

  BLUE CROSS BLUE SHIELD COMPANIES 174
  HEALTH MAINTENANCE ORGANIZATIONS (HMO) 175
  PREFERRED PROVIDER ORGANIZATION (PPO) 177
  POINT OF SERVICE (POS) 177
  AFFORDABLE CARE ACT 178
    THE INDIVIDUAL 178
    EMPLOYERS 179
    GENERAL TERMS 180
  MULTIPLE EMPLOYER TRUSTS (MET) 181
  MULTIPLE EMPLOYER WELFARE ASSOCIATION (MEWA) 181
  HEALTH SAVINGS ACCOUNTS (HSA) 181
  WORKERS COMPENSATION PLANS 182
  TAX TREATMENT OF HEALTH BENEFITS 183
  OCCUPATIONAL VS. NONOCCUPATIONAL COVERAGE 184
Chapter Review 185
  TERMS TO KNOW 185
  NUMBERS AND TIME PERIODS 186
  SAMPLE QUESTIONS 187
Disability Income Insurance 190
  CHARACTERISTICS OF DISABILITY INCOME POLICIES 191
    DISABILITY DEFINITIONS 191
    UNDERWRITING 193
    BENEFIT LIMITS 193
  OTHER DISABILITY BENEFITS 194
    WAIVER OF PREMIUM 194
    RETURN OF PREMIUM 194
    REHABILITATION BENEFITS 194
  TAXATION OF DISABILITY INCOME BENEFITS 194
  BUSINESS APPLICATIONS OF DISABILITY INCOME POLICIES ... 195
    BUSINESS OVERHEAD EXPENSE POLICY 196
    KEY EMPLOYEE DISABILITY INCOME POLICY 196
    DISABILITY BUY-SELL POLICY 196
    REDUCING TERM DISABILITY 197
    GROUP DISABILITY INCOME POLICIES 197
Chapter Review 198
  TERMS TO KNOW 198
  SAMPLE QUESTIONS 199
Accidental Death and Dismemberment (AD&D) Policies 201
  ACCIDENTAL MEANS 201

- **ACCIDENTAL BODILY INJURY** 202
- **PRINCIPAL SUM** 202
- **CAPITAL SUM** 202
- **MULTIPLE INDEMNITY** 203
- **ACCIDENTAL DEATH TIME LIMITS** 203

Chapter Review 204
- TERMS TO KNOW 204
- SAMPLE QUESTIONS 205

Limited Health Policies 206
- **HOSPITAL INDEMNITY POLICIES** 206
- **PRESCRIPTION DRUG POLICY** 206
- **DREAD DISEASE POLICIES** 207
- **DENTAL EXPENSE POLICIES** 207
- **VISION CARE POLICIES** 207
- **TRAVEL ACCIDENT POLICIES** 207
- **CREDIT INSURANCE** 208

Chapter Review 209
- TERMS TO KNOW 209
- SAMPLE QUESTIONS 210

Uniform Individual Health Policy Provisions 211
- **REQUIRED PROVISIONS** 211
  - #1 ENTIRE CONTRACT & CHANGES 211
  - #2 TIME LIMIT ON CERTAIN DEFENSES OR INCONTESTABLE CLAUSE 212
  - #3 GRACE PERIOD 212
  - #4 REINSTATEMENT 212
  - #5 NOTICE OF CLAIM 212
  - #6 CLAIM FORMS 213
  - #7 PROOF OF LOSS 213
  - #8 TIME OF PAYMENT OF CLAIMS 213
  - #9 PAYMENT OF CLAIMS 213
  - #10 PHYSICAL EXAM AND AUTOPSY 214
  - #11 LEGAL ACTION 214
  - #12 CHANGE OF BENEFICIARY 214
  - #13 GUARANTEED RENEWABILITY 215
- **OPTIONAL POLICY PROVISIONS** 215
  - #1 CHANGE OF OCCUPATION 215
  - #2 MISSTATEMENT OF AGE 216
  - #3 OTHER INSURANCE WITH THIS INSURER 216
  - #4 & #5 INSURANCE WITH OTHER INSURERS 216

- #6 Relation of Earnings to Insurance: Average Earnings 218
- #7 Unpaid Premium 218
- #8 Conformity with State Statutes 218
- #9 Illegal Occupation 218
- #10 Intoxicants and Narcotics 218
- #11 Cancellation 219

Chapter Review 220
- Terms to know 220
- Numbers and Time periods 221
- Sample questions 222

Medicare (Title 18) & Medicare Supplements 225
Medicare Eligibility 225
Enrollment into Medicare 226
Four Coverage Parts of Medicare 226
- Part A 226
- Part B, Medical 228
- Part C, Advantage 228
- Part D, Prescription Drug 229

Medicare Supplements (Medigap Policies) 231
Standardization 231
Core Benefits 232
Guaranteed Renewability 233
Nonduplication of Coverage 233
Policy Summary (Outline of Coverage) 233
Buyers Guide 233
Right to Return (Free Look Provision) 234
Open Enrollment 234
Pre-existing Waiting Periods 234
Replacement of Medicare Supplements 234

Chapter Review 235
- Terms to know 235
- Numbers and Time periods 235
- Sample questions 236

Long Term Care Insurance 238
Benefit Triggers 238
Types of Benefits 238
- Nursing Home Care 239
- Home Health Care 239
- Adult Day Care 239

- Respite Care 240
- **Minimum Benefit Period** 240
- **Preexisting Condition Limits** 240
- **Free Look Provision** 240
- **Inflation Protection** 241
- **Renewability** 241
- **Marketing the LTC Product** 241
  - Suitability 241
  - Outline of Coverage (Policy Summary) 241
  - LTC Shoppers Guide 241
  - Replacement 242
- **Partnership Plans** 242

Chapter Review 243
- Terms to know 243
- Numbers and Time periods 243
- Sample questions 244

Group Health 245
- **The Nature of Group Coverage** 245
  - Reduced Adverse Selection 245
  - Reduced Administrative Costs 246
  - Eligible Groups 246
  - Master Policy & Certificates of Insurance 247
- **Premium Rating Factors** 247
  - Group Underwriting 248
  - Experience vs. Community Rating 248
- **Establishing a Group Plan** 248
  - Probationary Period 248
  - Eligibility Period 249
  - Open Enrollment 249
  - Contributory vs. Non-Contributory 249
- **Key Concept of Group Insurance** 249
  - Occupational Losses 249
  - Maternity Benefits 250
  - Rights of Dependent Children 250
  - Changing Insurance Companies 250
  - Coordination of Benefits Clause 251
  - Preexisting Conditions Limitations 251
- **Portability Issues** 252
  - COBRA 252

- HIPAA 253
- **MISCELLANEOUS GROUP ISSUES** 253
  - 501(C)(9) TRUSTS 253
  - THIRD PARTY ADMINISTRATORS 253
  - BLANKET POLICIES 254
- Chapter Review 255
  - TERMS TO KNOW 255
  - NUMBERS AND TIME PERIODS 255
  - SAMPLE QUESTIONS 257
- Miscellaneous Government Healthcare Programs 260
  - **MEDICAID (TITLE 19)** 260
    - ELIGIBILITY 260
    - BENEFITS 261
    - FUNDING 261
    - ADMINISTRATION 261
    - SPOUSAL IMPOVERISHMENT RULE 262
  - **SOCIAL SECURITY DISABILITY INCOME BENEFITS (SSDI)** 262
    - DEFINITION OF TOTAL DISABILITY 262
    - ELIGIBILITY 262
    - PRIMARY INSURANCE AMOUNT (PIA) 263
    - TRICARE 263
- Chapter Review 264
  - TERMS TO KNOW 264
  - NUMBERS AND TIME PERIODS 264
- Final Test I 265
  - ANSWERS: FINAL I 276
- Final Exam, II 278
  - ANSWERS, FINAL II 291
- Glossary 294
- Index 305

PROFESSIONAL TRAINING INSTITUTION

Chapter 1

Insurance Basics for Life and Health

The better you know and understand the basics, the better prepared you will be for the exam.

A substantial portion of the questions on the exam will be over the basic terms and definitions. For that reason, you need to be familiar with these concepts. But, it is not just memorizing definitions; it is the comprehending of these terms and concepts and being able to understand them in the context of the questions. For a student new to the insurance industry, learning the terms and how to use them properly is much like learning a new language.

THE VERY BASICS

The understanding of the insurance industry begins with understanding basic terms and concepts that help define this industry.

WHAT IS INSURANCE?

Insurance is defined as the transference of risk. Every person lives with risk. **Risk is defined as the "chance or possibility of a loss."** In life insurance, an insured's risk is premature death. If a young man were to die unexpectedly early (prior to meeting all of his financial responsibilities in life to his creditors or to his family), his survivors would have to deal with the consequences. Insurance takes that large uncertain financial risk and for a relatively minimal fee, passes the responsibility to the insurer. Once the insurer accepts the risk, it then spreads that risk among other insureds with like exposure. The insurer will collect premiums from all of its policyholders, but only a small number will have a claim in a given year. Insurance then becomes the "many" paying for the "few."

If premature death occurs, the benefit is then available to the survivors in order to meet the insured's financial responsibilities.

UNDERSTANDING RISK

Risk has now been defined as the "possibility or chance of a loss." There are two different types of risk; one type is insurable, while the other is not. The first type is referred to as a **"pure risk."** In a pure risk, there is only a possibility of loss. If this happens, there is no opportunity for financial gain. These are the types of risks individuals always try to avoid. Death, sickness, and your house burning down are examples of pure risks. The second type of risk is called a **"speculative risk."** With a speculative risk, an individual has the chance to gain or lose. The individual may voluntarily choose to take this risk because there is a chance of coming out ahead. Investments and gambling are both examples of speculative risks. **The insurance companies never insure speculative risks; they only insure pure risks.**

MANAGING RISK

Risk is a part of life. Some risks are greater than others and may pose a greater threat to an individual. Managing risk is an important part of a person's life. Take Jill for example. Jill can manage her risk in several different ways. Jill's risk may be:

1. Avoided – If Jill chooses not to expose herself to the risk, the risk can be avoided. Some risk can be realistically avoided, but others cannot. For example, Jill might avoid the risk of dying in a skydiving accident by never jumping out of a plane.

2. Reduced – By reducing the risk, the chance of it occurring is less. Jill could decrease the likelihood of certain types of health conditions by living a healthier lifestyle which includes exercise and a healthy diet.

3. Retained – When Jill retains the risk or a portion of the risk, she is willing to pay for the loss, when and if it occurs. In health insurance, Jill may retain a portion of the risk by having a deductible on her health insurance policy.

4. Shared – When a risk is shared, Jill assumes a portion of the risk in relationship to her invested portion. An industry may join together to assume its own risk.

5. Transferred – Transference means that Jill takes the risk she is personally responsible for and transfers it to another party, who then assumes the risk.

When Jill purchases an insurance policy, she is transferring risk from herself to the insurance company.

Peril

A peril is defined as a cause of a loss. In Life and Health Insurance, the perils are accidents and sickness, respectively. Premature death, medical expenses, and disabilities are caused either by accidents or sicknesses.

Hazards

Hazards increase the chance of a loss. A hazard makes the risk more likely to occur. For example, ice on the road during a winter storm creates a more hazardous driving situation. The ice increases the risk or likelihood of an auto accident. In our example, the ice is not the risk; the accident is the risk. Hazards come in many forms. There are three different types of hazards:

1. Physical hazard – These hazards are physical in nature. You can see, touch or smell them. The ice in the above example is a physical hazard. Smoking is also considered a physical hazard.

2. Moral – A moral hazard is based on a person's values and ethics. A policyholder might attempt to create a loss on purpose in order to take advantage of the insurance company. This increases the chance that a company may have to pay a claim.

3. Morale – This hazard deals more with carelessness or irresponsibility. Someone who lives an unhealthy lifestyle or takes unnecessary risks may increase the chance of a loss.

The Law of Large Numbers

The law of large numbers is a concept that states the more numbers used to establish a statistic, the more accurate the statistic will be. The chance of heads turning up in a coin toss is 50/50. Tossing a coin twice and getting heads both times would not be a surprise. The statistic would be much more accurate after one hundred tosses.

This concept is critical to the concept of insurance. Because the insurance companies have access to statistics on large numbers of our population, they can adequately predict an insured's chance of death at a specific age or the chance that a house might burn to the ground. The law of large numbers is used to adequately predict and anticipate risk. It is the first step in establishing a rate for the product.

Types of Insurers

Lloyd's is a company that insures by **spreading risk over a group of investors**. Lloyd's of London is the original Lloyd's. Whereas a Lloyd's is not considered to be an insurance company (because an insurance company assumes risk and spreads that risk over its group of insureds), they do insure. A Lloyd's assumes risk and spreads the risk over a group of investors. They specialize in unique, hard to insure situations. Because of the unique nature of the need, there may not be the large numbers needed to properly spread the risk among others with the same need. The Lloyd's will use investors, who assume the risk individually, to properly spread the risk.

Stock companies are insurance companies owned by stock or shareholders. When a stock company makes a profit, the company may pay out that profit in the form of a dividend to the stockholders, who are the owners. The policyholder does not normally participate in receiving any divisible surplus that the company may have earned. Because the policyholder does not usually receive a dividend, both the product and company are referred to as **nonparticipating**. Stock companies do not generally pay dividends to the policyholder.

Mutual companies are companies owned by its policyholders. Since each policyholder has an ownership interest in the company, when the company makes a profit, it pays it out to the policyholder as a divisible surplus. When the divisible surplus is paid out, it is paid out as a dividend to the policyowner. Since the policyowner is receiving the dividend, this is referred to as a **participating** product or company.

The dividend from a participating product is defined as a **return of premium**. The policyholder previously paid a premium to the insurance company in exchange for coverage. If the insurance company has a favorable experience throughout the year, the insurance company will not need as much of that premium as it expected earlier in the year. Thus, the company sends back to the insured a portion of the premium paid at the beginning of the year. The **gross premium** of the insurance contract is determined by three sources; risk, interest and expenses. The formula for the gross premium is:

$$\text{Gross Premium} = \text{Risk} - \text{Interest} + \text{Expenses}$$

When an insurance company has favorable experience in any of the above areas, then the company may declare a dividend. For example, if fewer people had claims than the company expected in the current year, the company may not need as much as it collected and as a result has a divisible surplus. If the company's investment returns are better than expected or expenses are lower than anticipated, a similar result could occur. Since the dividend is actually a return of the policyholder's premium and since this premium was paid with previously taxed money, **any dividend returned to the policyholder will not be taxed**.

Also, keep in mind that since dividends are based upon three areas that cannot be precisely predicted, **the agent cannot guarantee a dividend** will be paid in the future. Dividends can be projected, but never guaranteed.

A Fraternal is a nonprofit entity that is organized under a lodge system. It has a large enough membership that the organization is able to provide insurance protection to its own members.

Reinsurance

Reinsurance is a form of insurance between insurers. Occasionally an insurance company (**ceding company**) will need to spread its risk beyond its own policyholder base. If a risk is larger than the company is comfortable with, it may seek out a reinsurer (**assuming company**). Reinsurance is when one insurer, for consideration, assumes the risk or part of the risk of another insurer. The concept of insurance is based upon being able to spread risk among large numbers. Reinsurance allows an insurance company to limit its exposure to a manageable amount. This allows risks of all sizes to be assumed.

A **reinsurance treaty** is the agreement between the ceding and the assuming company.

Contract Law

A contract is defined as an agreement between two parties. The agreement can be verbal or written. The policy the insurance company issues are a legal binding contract and must meet the requirements of contract law.

Elements of a Legal Contract

A legal contract is basically an agreement between two parties. It may be verbal or formalized in writing. The insurance policy is a legal and binding contract. As such, it must meet certain legal requirements. All contracts consist of four legal elements:

- Competent parties (Legal Capacity)
- Legal purpose
- Offer and acceptance (Agreement)
- Consideration

In order to understand the insurance transaction and the product itself, you need to understand each of the following terms.

Competent Parties

In a legal binding contract, each party must be legally competent. Examples of those who would **not** be competent include: one who is intoxicated or under the influence of drugs, mentally unstable, or under the legal age to transact business. Incompetent parties could not be held responsible for an agreement they entered into.

Legal Purpose

The intent of the contract itself must be for a legal purpose. A contract for an illegal purpose cannot be enforced in a court of law.

Offer and Acceptance (Agreement)

In order for agreement to occur, one party must make an offer and the other party must accept the offer. When both have occurred, agreement has occurred.

The offer can be made by either party, but **the offer is most typically made by the applicant.** It is an offer to buy. The applicant makes the offer with a completed application and payment into the plan (premium). The transaction is between the company and the applicant. The agent is not a party to the contract; therefore, the agent does not make an offer. The agent may present the plan or may assist the applicant in making the offer to the company, but this is not considered an offer. The offer is distinguished by the consideration. **The first party to offer full "consideration" as part in the transaction makes the offer.**

When the other party agrees to accept the first party's consideration in exchange for its own consideration, acceptance has occurred. **Agreement then results when an offer is made and accepted.**

Counter offers occur when an applicant submits an application and premium (his/her full consideration), but the company rejects the offer as submitted. Perhaps in the underwriting process the company discovers that the applicant has a heart condition. Due to this condition, the company is not willing to accept the business as applied for. The company will then reject the original offer and come back with a new offer. The new offer may say that the company will cover the applicant, but for a higher premium than was submitted. This new offer is made by the company and is called a counter offer. Once the applicant agrees to the alteration in terms or the additional premium, the offer has been accepted.

Consideration

In the insurance transaction contract, consideration is defined as **something of value exchanged** between each party of the contract. For a contract to be legally binding, each party must give to the other "something of value." In the insurance transaction the applicant gives two things of value:

- **Premium**, and

- **Information on the application**

In exchange for the applicant's consideration, the company gives the **promise to pay**.

Defining Truth

Warranties – A warranty is **a promise or a guarantee**. In life and health insurance, the statements made on the application are **not** considered warranties. The customer does not have to guarantee the information provided. An applicant could have a condition (cancer) and not be aware of it.

Representation – The statements on the application are considered representations. A representation is **the truth to the best of the applicant's knowledge**. It is what the applicant believes to be true. The applicant can only be held accountable for the knowledge he/she has.

Misrepresentation – A misrepresentation is a **mistruth or lie**. If an applicant lies about information that is considered material, the policy could be voided. A **material statement** is something that had the insurance company been aware of, the information would have affected how or if the policy was issued. In other words, it is important information to the underwriting process.

Concealment – Concealment is the **hiding or withholding of the truth**. Whereas this is not a direct lie (misrepresentation), it does mean that the customer is holding back information that may be important to the insurer.

The main difference between concealment and a misrepresentation has much to do with how an agent asks the questions to the applicant. If an agent asks direct questions (Do you have cancer?), the customer's answer is either the truth or it is a misrepresentation. If the agent's questions are vague (How is your health?), this opens the door to all kinds of vague answers and the opportunity for the applicant to conceal important information. The applicant could tell the agent about his high blood pressure without mentioning that he/she has cancer. The applicant has not lied; he/she just has not told all of the truth.

Insurable Interest

Insurable interest is the **financial or emotional interest** one person has in another's life or health. Insurable interest must exist in order to buy insurance on another person's life. An employer could have an insurable interest in a key salesperson or executive. A bank has insurable interest in someone that it loans money to. You have an unlimited interest in your own life. A husband has an insurable interest in his wife.

Insurable interest must exist at the time of the sale. It is the insurance company's responsibility to see that this interest exists. Insurable interest may or may not exist at the time of the claim. This is why consent is so important to the application process when purchasing life insurance on another person's life.

Consent

In order to buy an insurance policy on the life of another person, the owner must obtain consent from the individual being insured. This is just as important as having insurable interest. To be able to buy insurance on the life of another person without his/her consent would not be considered to be in the best interest of the members of our society. In fact, insurance without consent could create an incentive for some pretty undesirable behavior.

Consent is established by obtaining a signature on the application. In the case of one adult buying insurance on another, the owner (who is the person buying the policy) would sign the application and the insured (who is the person giving consent and being covered) would also need to sign the application. A child, of course, could not sign the application as a minor, so the company requires the signature of a parent or guardian.

When Does Coverage Start? Interim Insuring Agreements

Based upon contract law, a contract does not go into effect until after the agreement is complete. Agreement is not complete until the offer has been accepted and each party has exchanged consideration. In the insurance transaction, this would mean the policy would not go into effect until after the money is paid, the application is submitted, the policy is issued and the policy is delivered. This total process may take over a month to complete. In our industry, this may not be acceptable. The client expects coverage as soon as the premium is paid. The unexpected will happen eventually. The agent will have cases where a client buys a product and experiences a loss within days of purchasing the policy. Thus, there is a need for the **interim insuring agreement**.

An **interim insuring agreement is an agreement for the company to provide coverage on the client while still completing the underwriting process.** The purpose of the agreement is to speed up the effective date prior to the contract law situation. There are several different agreements that a company may use. Two methods commonly used include:

- **Conditional receipt** – This receipt states that coverage will begin either on the date of the application or the date of the physical (if required), whichever is last, **if** the applicant was insurable on that date.

- **Binding receipt** – Coverage begins the date of the application, until the applicant is notified otherwise. The binder could be replaced by the policy, it could expire, or the company could cancel the binder with one days notice.

Notice that these agreements are given in the form of a receipt. In other words, it is going to require the applicant's full consideration before the company will make this acceptance. Without payment, coverage would not begin until the transaction is complete (contract law).

BACKDATING POLICIES

The agent is allowed to back date the effective date of the life insurance policy. Backdating is done to save age. An agent can backdate the application up to **6 months**. Backdating the policy would accelerate the cash value growth in a policy but most other waiting periods (suicide clause and incontestability period) would be based upon application date. Premium renewals would be based upon the date that the application was backdated to.

POLICY DELIVERY

Once a policy is sold, underwritten and issued, it is then sent to the agent for delivery. This is an excellent opportunity for the agent to see that any of the insured's questions are answered and that the insured is comfortable with the coverage. The agent may be asked to get a "**statement of good health**." This is when the agent checks the health status of the applicant one more time prior to the delivery of the policy, to make sure nothing has changed since the date of the application. The statement of good health is requested from the company to insure the risk has not changed since the application date. The agreement is not complete until the contract is delivered. If the agent finds that the health of the applicant has changed, the agent may be directed to return the policy and avoid deliverance.

UNIQUE CHARACTERISTICS OF AN INSURANCE CONTRACT

We earlier stated that the insurance policy is a legal binding contract. As a result, it must meet some standard characteristics of a contract. The industry is unique in many different ways. In fact, the policies (contracts) issued have unique characteristics themselves. The following is a list of some of the unique characteristics:

Conditional – The insurance contract comes with conditions that will be spelled out in the policy. For example, certain events must occur (sickness or death) before the insurance company will pay its claims.

Valued, Reimbursement, and Service contracts – There are a variety of products on the market. Insurance policies may be distinguished by how they pay:

- Valued contracts pay a specified amount that may or may not be related to the extent of the loss. Life insurance and disability policies typically pay an established amount.

- Reimbursement contracts are designed to reimburse the insured based upon the extent of the loss. Major medical policies pay a percentage of the actual bill.

- Service contracts are prepaid coverages that provide protection in the form of services rather than benefits. Health Maintenance Organizations (HMO's) provide the healthcare services as well as the protection.

Unilateral – The insurance contract is considered to be a unilateral contract. Only one party in the contract can be held to a promise. The insurer makes a promise to pay if a claim occurs. The policyholder is not obligated to pay a premium.

Adhesion – One party (the insurer) is responsible for the wording of the contract. Since the contract is written by the insurance company with no input allowed from the insured, if the contract wording is "**ambiguous**" or unclear, any challenge would be interpreted by the courts in favor of the insured.

Aleatory – An aleatory contract is a contract of **unequal exchange**. One party stands to receive more than the other. In insurance, the insured may pay premiums for years and never file a claim. On the other hand, the insured could file a claim immediately after paying the first premium.

Other Contract Terms

Waiver – Waiver means to **voluntarily give up a known right**. The insurance company has the right to collect the premium in a timely fashion. If a policyholder paid a premium beyond the acceptable time period, the company would have the right to cancel coverage. If the company chose to accept this late premium without consequence, then the company has waived its right to cancel and reinstate by accepting the late payment.

Estoppel – Estoppel means to be legally stopped from being able to enforce one's legal right. In the above example, the company chose to accept the late payment without consequence. If this happens year after year, then a precedent has been established. If a claim occurred between the premium due date and the date that the policyholder normally paid a premium, the company might have normally had the right to refuse the payment of that claim due to nonpayment of premium. The court could force the company to pay since its history shows that it had accepted late payments and all indications are that it would have accepted this one also, had there not been a claim.

Fraud – The definition of fraud includes three main points: Fraud is **lying** with the **intent** to **gain**. Both the agent and the insured can commit fraud. If the insured commits fraud, the policy may be voided. Attempting to falsify a claim is a way insureds are often found guilty of fraud.

Insurance Law and the Agent/Producer

An agent is defined as the **representative of a principal** (insurance company). This makes you, the agent, an extension of your insurance company. This agreement is established through the **agency agreement**. The agency agreement is the contract between you and your insurance company.

You as an agent also need to understand your responsibility with your insurance company. Because you are considered an extension of your principal, the **agent's knowledge is deemed to be the knowledge of the company**. If an applicant discloses material underwriting information to the agent, the agent has the responsibility to disclose it to the company.

You also need to also understand that your actions and statements may extend the company's liability or responsibility to the client. If an agent were to imply or state that coverage exists when the contract states otherwise, the company could find that it is liable for a claim that it should never have been responsible for. You, as the agent, must understand your role, relationship and responsibility with your principal.

Powers of Agency

As a representative of your insurance company, you will have certain powers or authorities. When discussing the "powers of agency," there are three different categories of power:

- **Expressed** – These are the powers and authorities expressed in the agency agreement. They are clearly spelled out as the powers that you have when representing your insurance company. For example, the agent may have the power to use company material and name.

- **Implied** – These powers are not spelled out or expressed by the company, however the powers are allowed and may even be expected by the company. The company is aware of what the agent is doing and does nothing to deter the agent. The company may even encourage the agent to continue these actions. For example, the company may not tell the agent to assist the client with claims, but allows the agent to do so, since it is good business for the company and the agent.

- **Apparent** – This authority, unlike the two previous ones, is not a "real" authority. Due to the licensing authority with the state and with the company, the first two are considered "real." Apparent authority looks "real" from the client's perspective, but it does not actually exist as a "real" authority. For example, a client enters an insurance office to purchase an insurance policy. The person behind the desk at this office designated as an insurance office may not be licensed and would not have the "real" authority of a licensed agent. But to all appearances, this person may look licensed. Insurance companies and agencies must be careful about what this person says and does with the client.

When an insurance company provides company material, applications, or brochures to an unlicensed person, a **presumption of agency** may exist. This could also occur when an unlicensed person is explaining coverage or acting as an agent without proper licensing. Presumption of agency is the appearance of agency from the client's perspective.

Underwriting Basics

The underwriting process involves the company gathering and evaluating the information of a prospective insured in order to determine the applicant's risk. Once the underwriter understands the risk involved, he/she must decide to accept or reject the risk. If the risk is accepted, it must then be classified for rating.

Why is Underwriting Necessary?

There is a direct relationship between the risk assumed by the company and the premium charged to the customer. Each insurance company prices its product based upon the risk assumed. If the risk is greater than expected or priced for, the company could find it difficult, if not impossible, to meet its financial obligation to the client. In order to meet the needs of the client, the company must work within its established risk parameters. The primary responsibility for underwriters is to select risks their companies are designed to handle.

Sources of Insurability Information

In order to properly evaluate the risk, the first step is to gather the relative information. The insurance company has many sources to gather information from:

Application – One of the first and most obvious sources of information is the application itself. It includes personal, medical and other insurance information. The application is the written "offer" signed and made by the prospective insured. If there is a mistake on the application and it needs corrected, it is the applicant who is responsible for the correction. Even though the agent is involved in the presentation of the product, the application is the applicant's statement of information and **an agent may not change the information** that has been stated by the applicant. **The applicant will designate the correction by initialing any change made** on the application.

If an application is submitted without complete information, it is the responsibility of the company to obtain the missing information, if it is important. **If the application is approved and accepted without complete information, the applicant cannot be held responsible for that information after the policy is issued**. An applicant cannot be accused of misrepresentation or concealment, if the question was never answered on the application in the first place. The company may request the information prior to issuance or may reject the coverage if the information is not obtained. For this reason, agents need to see that the application is completed as required.

The agent and the applicant are both required to sign the application. These signatures are important to the application process. When the applicant signs the application, he/she is stating that the information given is his/her representation of the truth. The applicant's signature may also be necessary to properly gather information for underwriting purposes. When you as the agent sign the application, you state that you have asked the questions on the application and the answers are true and complete to the best of your knowledge. Both parties have a responsibility to the information on the application.

Agent/Producer's reports – The agent's report allows the agent to share information and observations with the insurance company concerning the applicant.

Medical information and exams – The insurer may choose to gather more detailed and current medical information on the applicant. One source of medical information is the applicant's personal physician. Through an **Attending Physician's Report (APR) or Attending Physician's Statement (APS),** the company can gather the past notes and observations of the applicant's attending physician. If the company needs further information, they may require a **physical** from the applicant. Depending on the company and the risk being assumed, companies may ask for several different degrees of physicals.

Medical Information Bureau (MIB) – The MIB is a source that subscribing companies use to share application information. These companies do not share the underwriting results, but they do share basic information from the application. This allows companies to check and verify information gathered.

Credit reports – Sometimes the company will include a prospect's credit report in the underwriting process. The **"Fair Credit Reporting Act"** is federal legislature designed to protect consumer information.

- The act requires that the applicant knows who is gathering the information

- The applicant has the right to see the information, in order to verify its accuracy

- The applicant has the right to have any misinformation corrected, if necessary.

Inspection reports – A report concerning the financial, moral, physical or any other relevant information concerning the applicant.

AIDS, HIV AND UNDERWRITING

Acquired Immune Deficiency Syndrome, or AIDS, is a factor in the underwriting of an insurance policy. Blood tests to determine HIV is necessary in some cases to properly underwrite the risk. However, laws have been put in force to protect the applicant against unfair discrimination and privacy.

- The insurer may perform an AIDS test, at the company expense, for underwriting purposes.

- The applicant always has the right to know and approve any test being given.

- The insurer may not underwrite or ask questions concerning sexual orientation or anything that might be discriminatory in nature.

- Any prior testing done by the applicant may not trigger the need for an AIDS test to obtain a current policy.

- The test result must be kept confidential.

- Companies may only report "abnormal blood test results" to the MIB

- Companies may deny coverage when AIDS is detected during the underwriting process. If AIDS develops after the policy is issued, it is covered like any other sickness.

SELECTION AND CLASSIFICATION FACTORS

Along with health conditions, other factors will be evaluated during the underwriting process. These factors may affect whether the application is accepted or denied. If the application is accepted, these factors will affect the rating as well.

- **Age** – As people age they become more prone to various health conditions.

- **Gender** (sex) – Men and women face different health issues at different ages. Women tend to live longer than men. As a result, a woman might pay a lower rate for life insurance.

- **Tobacco** usage – The rates for a smoker would probably be higher than the rates of a non-smoker. A smoker is susceptible to more health conditions and has a shorter life expectancy.

- **Occupation** – Some occupations are higher risk than others. A skydiving instructor might be a higher risk than a clerk in a supermarket.

- **Avocation** or hobby – The underwriter is also interested in the applicant's hobbies. The application may ask about hobbies like skydiving, rock climbing, kayaking, repelling or other high risk activities.

Classification of Risks and Effects on Premiums Charged

Once the underwriter has gathered and evaluated the information concerning the applicant, it is time to accept or reject the application. If the risk falls within the parameters of what the company is able to accept, the underwriter may choose to accept the business. Once the decision is made to accept the business, the risk has to be classified. Most companies have at least three categories for risk classification:

- **Preferred** – This is a better than average risk. These individuals may be in exceptional health. They are less likely to have a claim and as a result they will receive a lower rate than average.

- **Standard** – The standard rate is the normal rate. These individuals fall into the category of average and will pay accordingly.

- **Substandard** – If a client falls into this category, the underwriter has determined that based upon the information, this client is more likely to have a claim. This policyholder will pay a higher premium as a result of the higher risk.

It is possible that after reviewing the information gathered, the underwriter has determined that the applicant is a greater risk than the insurance company can accept. Instead of accepting and categorizing the risk, the underwriter may choose to **reject** or **decline the risk**. If this occurs, the offer made by the applicant will be rejected and the premium submitted will be returned.

Gross and Net Premiums

Gross premium is the premium the applicant pays. It is the full, total or gross amount paid. There are three factors that make up the gross premium.

- **Risk** – Risk was defined earlier as the chance of a loss. When each policyholder pays a premium payment to the company, a portion of that payment has to be available to pay the claims that will result that year. This is the risk factor of the premium. Every policyholder pays a small amount into the company and a few will take out a large amount for the claims experienced.

- **Interest** – The premium is always paid in advance. This means that the company will have use of this money prior to paying out the claims that they will be responsible for throughout the year. The more interest earned on the money prior to using it to pay claims, the more it will reduce the amount that the company will need to collect from the policyholder.

- **Expenses** – Companies must collect enough to cover operating expenses. The company has office space to pay for, payroll, utilities, advertising, and many other responsibilities in order to do business. This is sometimes charged in the form of a "load" fee.

Gross premium is sometimes expressed as a formula. The formula for gross premium is:

Risk – Interest + Expenses = Gross Premium

Net premium is the true cost of insurance. Net premium includes both risk and interest, but does not take into account expenses; therefore, the formula for net premium is:

Risk – Interest = Net Premium

A company may offer additional amounts of insurance on a net basis. The expense of adding or changing coverage could be limited on an existing insured.

PREMIUM MODES

The mode of premium is how often or frequent the payments will be made. Most premiums are calculated on an annual basis. Sometimes, the client may choose to break the payments down into smaller, more frequent amounts. For example, a policyholder could choose to pay quarterly instead of annually. The more often the payment is made, the more expensive it will be over the year. For example, an annual payment of $1,000 broken down into two payments (semi-annual) might cost $550 per payment or $1100 a year. If that payment was broken down quarterly, the payment might cost $300 every 3 months.

There are two reasons why the payment will cost more for the policyholder if the payment is broken down:

- Loss of interest or investment opportunity – The Company calculated an annual premium it expected to receive up front, in advance of its claim responsibilities. This gave them the opportunity to invest, which in turn would have reduced the payment. That opportunity is gone and must be made up by charging a higher rate.

- Added expenses – Because the payment is broken down, more expenses will result. Now a statement must be generated more often, processed and mailed. This takes time, manpower and supplies. This added expense will result in a higher rate.

Premium Comparisons

Two common methods used to compare premiums between different policies include:

- Net Cost Method – This method averages the number of years in the period evaluated. It then averages the cost per thousand for a policy surrendered for its cash value at the end of the period.

- Interest Adjusted Cost Method – This method provides an estimate of the policyowner's average annual out of pocket outlay, adjusted for time value of money.

The Need for Life Insurance

When an agent presents the life insurance product to a prospective client, the need for the protection must be established. The life insurance product has many features that make it advantageous to the insured.

Obligations at Death

The primary reason most people purchase life insurance is for the death benefit. This death benefit is provided when funds are needed most. The death benefit can then be used to meet the obligations that exist at time of the insured's death. Most of these obligations can be categorized into three main areas:

- **Immediate needs** – Funds are used to pay off debt (mortgage, car payments, student loans, credit cards, etc.).

- **Final expenses** – These are expenses resulting from the insured's premature death. This could consist of funeral expenses or unpaid medical bills.

- **Future needs** – These include income needs for survivors and college expenses for surviving children.

METHODS OF ESTATE BUILDING

Life insurance is defined as the **creation of an immediate estate**. The two main points to this definition are the terms creation and immediate. Life insurance is only one way to create an estate. Other ways include saving over time and investing. The potential problem with saving and investing is both of these methods require time and risk. In contrast, life insurance is immediate. Once an insured dies prematurely, an estate is created immediately (not over time or subject to investment risk) to provide funds needed by the survivors. With life insurance, the owner knows that the beneficiaries will receive the funds to take care of the immediate, final and future needs premature death creates.

LIVING BENEFITS

A living benefit is any benefit that can be utilized while an insured is alive. Even though the primary reason for buying life insurance is the death benefit, life insurance policies provide benefits that can be used while the insured is alive. Most living benefits are generated by the cash value whole life policies. Living benefits will differ with different policies.

ADVANTAGES AS PROPERTY

Because life insurance can be owned and controlled, it is considered property. After an insured builds up cash value in a policy, it can be used as equity to secure a loan. A policy can also be sold to another person, given away, or transferred to another person.

NEEDS APPROACH VS. THE HUMAN LIFE VALUE APPROACH

While presenting the need for life insurance, the agent will need to discuss with the prospect an appropriate amount of death benefit. How much life insurance will it take to meet this prospect's specific circumstances? There are two different methods used to establish an amount, the needs approach or the human life value approach.

Needs Approach – The needs approach asks the question: **"How much death benefit would it take to meet the needs of the beneficiaries, if the insured died today?"** When determining the need, the assumption is always based upon premature or immediate death. The needs approach takes into consideration three areas of need:

- **Immediate needs** – Funds are used to pay off debt (mortgage, car payments, student loans, credit cards, etc.).

- **Final expenses** – These are expenses resulting from the insured's premature death. This could consist of funeral expenses or unpaid medical bills.

- **Future needs** – These include income needs for survivors and college expenses for surviving children.

Human Life Value Approach – This approach looks at the worth or value of the individual that is being insured. This method asks the question: **"if the insured died today, what potential value would the family lose?"** This method looks at earnings expectations and potential. It would look at the number of years of potential income. From this information, a value is established. This would determine the amount of protection purchased.

Chapter Review

Terms to Know

Insurance

Risk

Insurer

Insured

Pure Risk

Speculative Risk

Risk Management Techniques

Peril

Hazard

Physical Hazard

Moral Hazard

Morale Hazard

Law of Large Numbers

Lloyd's

Stock Company

Nonparticipating

Mutual Company

Participating

Gross Premium

Fraternal

Reinsurance

Competent Parties

Legal Purpose

Agreement (Offer and Acceptance)

Consideration

Counter offer

Warranties

Representation

Misrepresentation

Material Statement

Concealment

Insurable Interest

Consent

Interim Insuring Agreement

Effective Date

Conditional Receipt

Binding Receipt

Statement of Good Health

Conditional

Valued, Reimbursement, and Service Contract

Unilateral

Adhesion

Aleatory

Waiver

Estoppel

Fraud

Agency Agreement

Agent

Broker

Expressed

Implied

Apparent

Adverse Selection

Application

Agent/Producer's Report

Attending Physician's Report

Medical Information Bureau (MIB)

Fair Credit Reporting Act

Credit Report

PROFESSIONAL TRAINING INSTITUTION

Inspection Report

Preferred

Standard

Substandard

Declined

Net Premium

Premium Modes

Uses for Life Insurance

PROFESSIONAL TRAINING INSTITUTION

SAMPLE QUESTIONS

1. Which of the following is not an essential component of a legal binding contract?
    a) Competent Parties
    b) Consideration
    c) Agreement
    d) Incompetent Parties

2. Which of the following is gross premium?   R − I + E = GP
    a) Net Premium + Investment Return
    b) Chance of a loss − Interest + Load
    c) Mortality − Load + Interest
    d) Risk − Load + Investment Return

3. In the insurance transaction, unequal values are exchanged; one side of the contract receives more. This characteristic describes which type of contract?
    a) Aleatory
    b) Adhesion
    c) Unilateral
    d) Conditional

4. Which term is defined as "the chance of a loss?"
    a) Risk   chance
    b) Peril   Cause
    c) Hazard   increase
    d) Loss

5. In the law of agency, the agent represents:
    a) The insured
    b) The broker
    c) The principal
    d) The insurance agency

25

6. The answers the applicant gives on the application are called:
    a) Misrepresentations
    b) Representations
    c) Warranties
    d) Concealment

7. Which type of insurance company is owned by its policyholders?
    a) Lloyds
    b) Stock — Stockholders
    c) Mutual — Policyholders
    d) Fraternal

8. Which of the following is not considered an insurance company?
    a) Lloyds
    b) Stock
    c) Mutual
    d) Fraternal

9. When a client withholds important information crucial to the underwriting process, it is called:
    a) Misrepresentation
    b) Concealment
    c) Fraud
    d) Representation

10. Not official authority that is assumed by the client based upon circumstances created by the principal is called:
    a) Express Authority
    b) Implied Authority
    c) Apparent Authority
    d) Binding Authority

11. Underwriters use which law to accurately predict losses?
    a) Law of Adverse Selection
    b) Law of Large Numbers
    c) Law of Underwriting
    d) Law of Accurate Predictions

12. In life insurance, when must insurable interest exist?
    a) At the time of the sale and at the time of the loss
    (b) At the time of the sale
    c) At the time of the loss
    d) At the time of the beneficiary's death

13. In life insurance, the peril covered is death. A peril is defined as:
    a) The chance of a loss
    b) Increases the chance of a loss
    (c) The cause of a loss
    d) The chance and cause of a loss

14. When the insurance company makes the insured whole, no more, no less, this is the concept of:
    a) Insurable Interest
    b) Adverse Selection
    c) Insurance
    (d) Indemnification

15. Which type of insurance company is owned by its shareholders?
    a) Lloyds
    (b) Stock Company
    c) Mutual Company
    d) Fraternal

16. An insurance company is able to insure:
    (a) A pure risk only
    b) A speculative risk only
    c) Either a pure or speculative risk
    d) Neither the pure or speculative risk

17. Which of the following companies typically sell participating policies?
    a) Stock
    (b) Mutual
    c) Lloyd's
    d) Fraternal

18. Who typically makes the offer in an insurance transaction?
    a) The applicant *to buy*
    b) The agent
    c) The insurer
    d) The policyholder

19. A substandard risk would cost:
    a) More than average
    b) The same as average
    c) Less than average
    d) A substandard risk would be unacceptable

20. Upon delivery of the policy the agent may be required to check the health status one last time. This would be a:
    a) Delivery receipt
    b) Statement of good health
    c) Conditional receipt
    d) Condition of coverage

21. Under contract law, coverage does not begin until the transaction is complete. What is typically used, to speed up coverage for the applicant?
    a) Coverage always begins the date of the application, nothing needs to be changed
    b) Coverage will begin the date of the application, as long as the premium is paid up front with the application
    c) An interim insuring agreement can be used to speed up the effective date
    d) Coverage will begin the date of the physical. The sooner the physical the sooner coverage goes into effect

22. All the following would be sources of insurability, EXCEPT:
    a) Application
    b) Producers report
    c) MIB
    d) Fair Credit Reporting Act

Answers: 1.d 2.b 3.a 4.a 5.c 6.b 7.c 8.a 9.b 10.c 11.b 12.b 13.c 14.d 15.b 16.a 17.b 18.a 19.a 20.b 21.c 22.d

PROFESSIONAL TRAINING INSTITUTION

Chapter 2

Types of Life Insurance Policies

One of the real challenges the consumers face is determining which type of product best fits their needs. The agent is critical in assisting the client in this decision making process. The better the agent understands the different products available to the consumer and each of their advantages and disadvantages, the better the agent is able to assist the client. Doing the best job for the client is all about placing the right product in the right situation. This is accomplished by understanding the products. The more the agent knows about the products, the better agent he/she will be.

TERM VS. PERMANENT INSURANCE

All life insurance products fall into one of two categories: term or permanent. Within each category, a variety of products with unique features are available. Both categories have their own advantages and disadvantages. Once you understand the differences between them, you can learn to appreciate how each can be used in different situations to benefit different clients and their needs.

The following is a comparison of term and permanent insurance products.

Term	Permanent
Temporary coverage for a temporary need (raising children, debt protection, etc.)	Permanent coverage designed to cover a need that one cannot out live (estate planning, business continuation, wealth transfer, etc.)
Protection (death benefit) only, no cash value or living benefits available.	Protection (death benefit) with internal cash accumulation (living benefits or cash value)
Low cost due to lack of cash value accumulation	Higher cost due to build up of equity within the product

TERM LIFE INSURANCE

Term insurance provides large amounts of death benefit for a reasonably low price. It has two primary characteristics: **low premium** and **temporary coverage**. Term provides no "living benefits." It only provides death protection. So, it is first characterized by its low premium. As the insured gets older, risk increases and it becomes more expensive to insure the individual. Eventually term expires or the premiums become so expensive (due to age) that the insured is forced to drop the coverage.

A client purchases term with the understanding that it is not intended to be kept indefinitely. Typically, a young family has much financial responsibility with limited resources. For a few hundred dollars a year, a breadwinner might be able to purchase hundreds of thousands of dollars of protection to see that in the event of his/her premature death, the survivors are able to pay bills, living expenses and future education needs. While the family is young, they need a low and affordable premium. Once the children grow up and establish themselves, the need for this protection may disappear.

Another common use of term insurance is to protect an outstanding debt. An individual may finance a home over 30 years. If the breadwinner were to die prior to paying off this debt, the survivors could find it difficult, if not impossible, to maintain the payments on their home. As long as there is a mortgage on the property there may be a need to protect it. Term insurance, also referred to as mortgage insurance in this situation, may be used to protect the home until the loan is paid in full.

LEVEL, DECREASING AND INCREASING TERM

One way the term insurance product can be characterized is by the type of death benefit that it provides. There are three different types of death benefits available: level, decreasing and increasing death benefit products.

Level term has a death benefit that does not change throughout the term. If Jim purchased a $300,000 20 year level term policy at age 25, the death benefit would be consistent at $300,000 over the term of 20 years or until the insured is age 45. Once the term is over, the policy and protection end. If Jim dies within the 20 year term, his beneficiaries would receive the death benefit of $300,000. If Jim lives beyond the 20 years, the policy ends and his beneficiaries receive nothing upon his death.

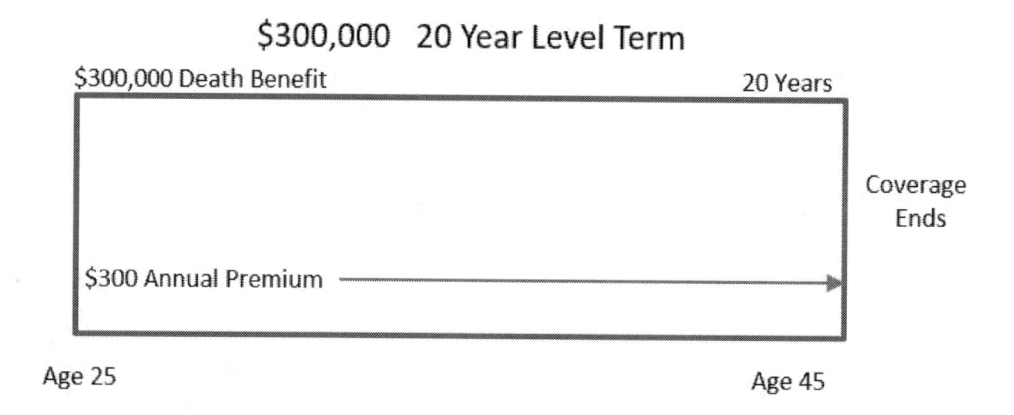

$300,000 20 Year Level Term

$300,000 Death Benefit — 20 Years — Coverage Ends

$300 Annual Premium

Age 25 — Age 45

Decreasing term has a death benefit that decreases throughout the term of the policy. Decreasing term is a good product to use to protect a debt. As payments are made on the loan, the balance reduces over time and the amount of protection needed lessens as well. If Jim has a mortgage of $300,000 and wants to protect his home in the event that he dies prior to paying it off, he might want a decreasing term policy. Jim could buy a $300,000 20 year decreasing term policy to cover his decreasing obligation; he would be covered throughout the term of the loan, 20 years. Each year that he lives, his death benefit decreases. If he lives beyond the 20 years, his death benefit would have expired. Once the loan is paid off, Jim no longer needs the protection.

$300,000   20 Year Decreasing Term

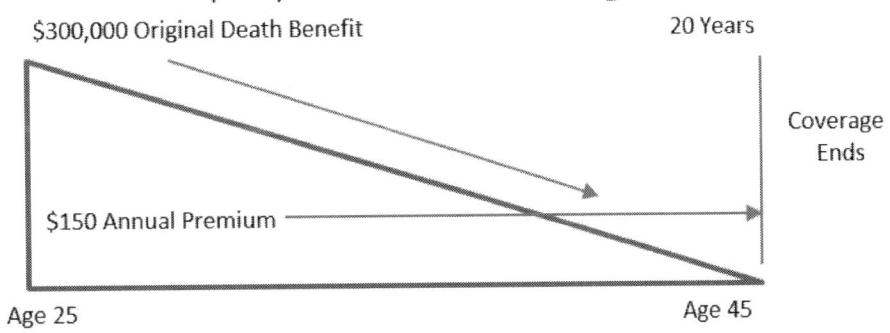

$300,000 Original Death Benefit   20 Years

Coverage Ends

$150 Annual Premium

Age 25   Age 45

These two products, level and decreasing term, have both similarities and differences. Both of our examples begin with and are designated as $300,000 policies. Both the premium payments and protection end after 20 years. Also, each policy has a level premium payment throughout the term. Even though the products are similar in some respects, they definitely have their differences. If Jim dies 8 years into the plan, the level product will still pay the full death benefit of $300,000. The level provides more protection throughout the term. On the other hand, the decreasing term would pay significantly less if death occurs after 8 years. In our example, the decreasing term will have a lower premium than the level term.

Increasing term insurance works just the opposite of decreasing term. Instead of a reducing death benefit, this death benefit increases each year throughout the term. Increasing term is not as common as the other two, but it is used for specific reasons. It may be used as a "return of premium" or "return of cash value" rider. If the insured died within the term of the rider, the death benefit of the rider would be designed to match either the amount of premium payments to date or the cash value growth within the product.

RENEWABLE AND CONVERTIBLE TERM

Term may also be renewable or convertible. These features are not always included in all term policies. Never assume they are included automatically. If these features are included in the product, it will be stated in the policy. So, unless otherwise stated, always assume that a 10 year level term policy will end after 10 years.

Renewable term products will be clearly identified in its title. For example, Sarah bought a 10 year renewable term product. At the end of 10 years, she would be able to renew this product for another 10 years.

Renewability could be limited by age. Sarah could have a 10 year renewable term policy to age 65. In this case, if Sarah is 35 when she buys the policy, she will be able to renew it two more times, at age 45 and then again at age 55. Since the policy is renewable up until age 65, she will no longer be able to renew her coverage.

One of the primary advantages of renewable term insurance is that **insurability** does not have to be established or proven in order to renew the term. Sarah may buy the 10 year term with the intent of using it to cover a 10 year debt obligation. However, if 8 years into the policy, she discovers she has a serious health condition, she will be able to renew the policy and maintain coverage, no health questions asked. Since she now has a serious health condition, she may have a hard time obtaining coverage on a new policy. The renewability feature of this product will help her maintain protection, despite her health condition.

Even though the company will not ask any health questions or ask Sarah to prove insurability, her rates will still increase when she renews the policy after year 10. When her policy renews for a new term, the rates will be increased based upon her **attained age**. From ages 35 to 45, Sarah paid a level premium of $600 per year for her coverage. When she renews at age 45, a new term will begin based upon the age that she has now obtained. Her rate may go to $1100 for the next 10 years. If she renews the term again at age 55, her rate will experience another increase based upon her attained age.

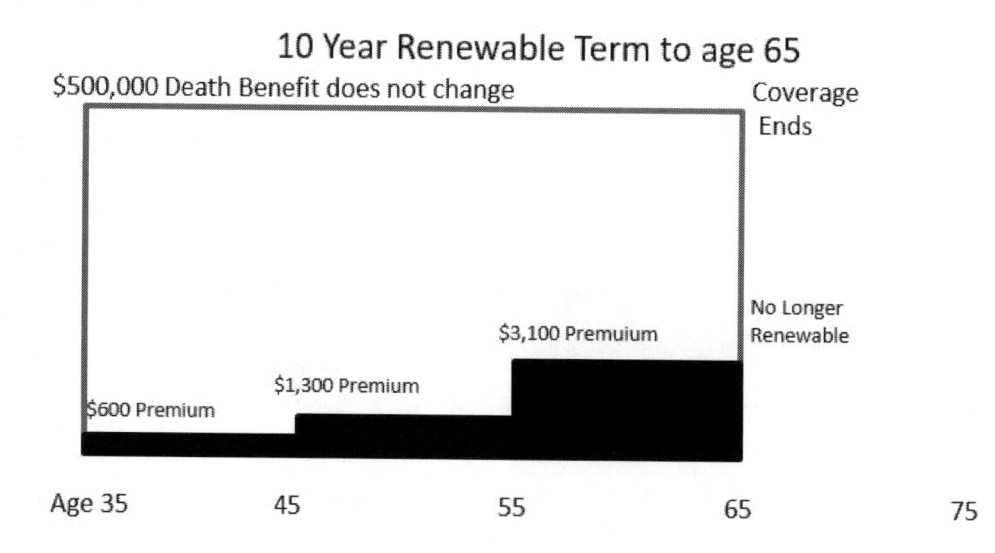

10 Year Renewable Term to age 65

$500,000 Death Benefit does not change — Coverage Ends

- $600 Premium (Age 35)
- $1,300 Premium (45)
- $3,100 Premuium (55)
- No Longer Renewable (65)

Age 35 — 45 — 55 — 65 — 75

With any term longer than one year, the insurance company will average out the premium over the period of the term. This is referred to as a "**level premium term**" policy. **The premium of the term is always level throughout the term** and will increase based upon attained age if a new term is renewed. Five year renewable term will have a level premium throughout its term of 5 years and then will increase if renewed for the next 5 years. Level premium term products come in a variety of terms as determined by the company selling them. Examples would include 5, 7, 10, 15, 20 or even a term to a certain age, like age 65.

If the term is one year, the product is referred to as **annually renewable term.** It is renewable and will increase its premium each year when a new term is purchased. This is done each year based upon attained age and without an increase in the death benefit. This product is not considered to be a level premium product.

Convertible term is a product that can be converted from term to permanent **without proof of insurability**. Hosea purchased a 15 year renewable and convertible term policy with the intent of dropping it after 15 years. He has been paying a premium of $400 per year. After 13 years, Hosea's needs have unexpectedly changed. Hosea finds that he would like to keep his protection for estate tax purposes. This means that he will need permanent insurance instead of term insurance. Since his policy is a convertible term policy, the company will allow him to convert his term policy to a permanent policy, with the same amount of death benefit and without asking him any health questions. This would be to his benefit because he now has some health conditions and could not prove insurability if he tried to buy a new product today.

Of course, since Hosea is converting his policy from term to permanent (which will include cash value build up and guarantee coverage for life) he will have to pay a higher premium since he is changing to a higher premium product. If Hosea converts at the **attained age rate**, he will also have to pay a higher premium because he is now 13 years older than his original purchase age. His new premium in our example is $2,000 per year.

If the company allows, Hosea could be given the option of renewing at **original age rates**. In this case, Hosea would be allowed to convert to a permanent insurance policy using the age that he originally bought the term insurance at 13 years ago. Obviously this would give Hosea a lower annual premium. Let's say the original rate was $1,500 per year. This is a savings of $500 per year for the rest of his life. In order for Hosea to qualify for this rate, he would have to make up the difference between his new premium rate ($1,500) and what he has been paying ($400) since the original purchase date (13 years ago). If Hosea will make an initial payment of 13 X $1,100 or $14,300, the company will give him a product based on the original age or a premium of $1,500.

MATURITY AND TAXATION

A life insurance policy is said to **mature when it pays out its death benefit**. When a life insurance policy matures and pays out the death benefit, the benefit is not considered to be income to the beneficiary; therefore, **the death benefit is income tax free.**

WHOLE LIFE INSURANCE

Whole life insurance derives its name from the fact that it provides protection throughout one's whole life. Regardless of how the plan is paid for, limited payments or throughout one's whole life, the plan provides **permanent protection with level premium payments**. In order for the insurance company to be able to offer this type of protection, there must be a buildup of value within the policy in order to be affordable at the later ages. This build up of value is referred to as the **cash value**. As the cash value grows, it offsets and reduces the risk that the company is responsible.

For example, the following illustration shows that a policy purchased at age 25 will provide a consistent death benefit up until age 100. As the insured ages, the risk of death increases. Since a portion of the premium is being set aside as cash value that accumulates at a **guaranteed growth rate**, its value can be used to offset the reducing risk. This gives the insured a level death benefit consisting of both risk and cash value accumulation.

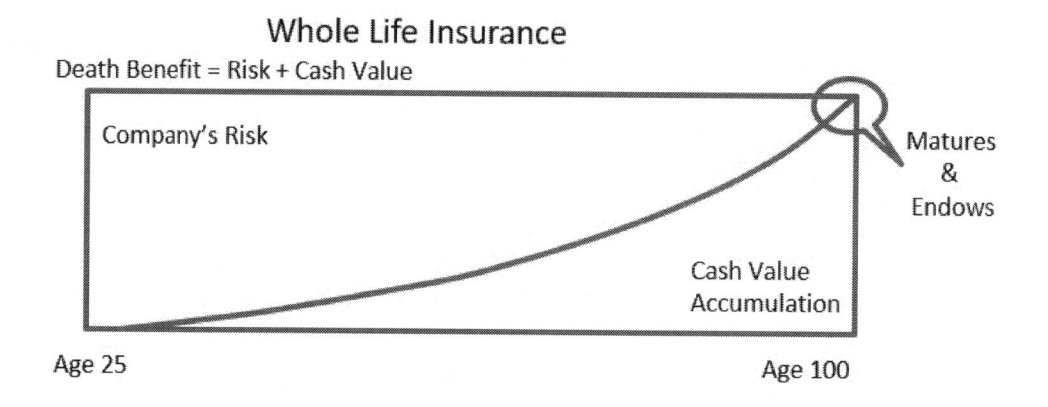

Whole Life Insurance
Death Benefit = Risk + Cash Value

Company's Risk

Matures & Endows

Cash Value Accumulation

Age 25   Age 100

Notice that the **risk the company assumes is greatest at the onset** of the policy and reduces as the individual ages. Whereas the risk is greatest at the beginning of the product, the **cash value accumulation is the greatest at the end**. At age 100, the cash value accumulation is designed to equal the death benefit. This means that there is no longer any risk being assumed by the insurer. Since there is no longer any risk, and insurance is all about spreading risk, the policy is said to mature and endow. In other words, it ends and pays out its death benefit, even if the insured is still living. If the insured does live to maturity, the policy benefit paid out is still considered a death benefit and is not income taxed.

CASH VALUE, LOANS & FULL WITHDRAWALS

The cash value accumulation is the equity within the policy. An insured is able to borrow money against the equity in his/her policy. The amount of money that can be borrowed on the permanent life insurance policy is based on the amount of the cash value.

Sue buys a $100,000 whole life policy. She is 25 when she purchases the plan and her premium is $600 per year. At age 45, Sue has accumulated $14,000 of cash value. If Sue died at this point in her policy, it would still pay a death benefit of $100,000. The death benefit consists of the company risk ($86,000) plus the accumulated cash value ($14,000).

Sue could also choose to use her cash value in the policy while she is living. If Sue chose to end her coverage, she could take the $14,000 in cash value at this point and end the coverage. Instead, Sue might choose to keep her protection but borrow some of her cash value from the policy in the form of a loan.

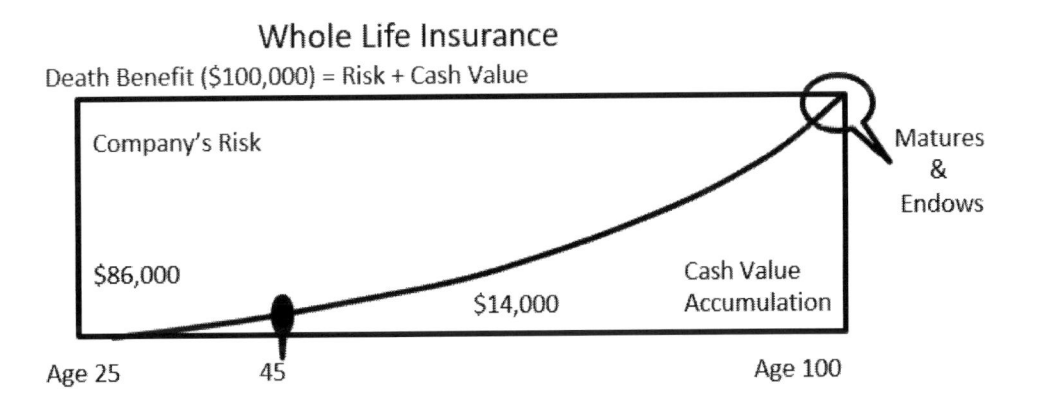

Whole Life Insurance
Death Benefit ($100,000) = Risk + Cash Value

- Company's Risk
- $86,000
- $14,000
- Cash Value Accumulation
- Matures & Endows
- Age 25 — 45 — Age 100

The maximum loan amount Sue could borrow from her cash value would be a little less than the full cash value. Sue must leave enough behind to cover the interest for the loan. If the loan plus the interest on the loan ever reach the full value of the cash value accumulation, the policy will end. At this point, it is no longer considered a loan, but a full **withdrawal** which ends the coverage. **As long as the transaction is considered a loan, it will not be income taxed.** Basically, the insured is stating the temporary use of the money with the intent of putting back into the life insurance policy to be used as it was intended to be used, as a death benefit. **If a full withdrawal is made and the policy is ended, then there may be a tax consequence.** Anything above the insured's **cost basis** will be considered earned income and taxed accordingly.

For example, if Sue cashes in her policy for $14,000, she has a cost basis of $12,000 (she has paid $600 annual premium payments for 20 years). She has made a profit of $2,000 and will pay taxes accordingly.

What are the consequences if Sue chooses to borrow $10,000 from her life insurance program? First of all, when the company issued Sue's policy, their intent was to use the funds Sue put into the program to help pay claims each year. Since Sue paid her premium in advance, the insurer reduced her premium because they expected an interest return on the money prior to using it to pay a claim. Sue has now taken some of the funds out of the company's possession. **This means the insurer must make up this loss of funds by charging interest** on the loan. Second, Sue must account for this loan in one of three ways:

- Sue could pay the loan back at once or in payments over time with interest

- Sue could allow the loan to grow over time and have the balance deducted from the death benefit at the time of maturity. If Sue dies at age 50 without making any payments on the loan, her **beneficiaries** would receive a reduced death benefit.

- Sue could end the policy by taking the cash value minus the loan and its interest. Sue chooses to end her coverage one year after taking out the loan. The loan has grown to $10,600, while her cash value has grown to $14,700. The insurer will send her the difference of $4,100 and end the coverage.

PREMIUM OBLIGATIONS

The premium on the whole life policy is a fixed premium. It must be paid each year or the policy could end. The amount is constant, it will not increase or decrease as the years proceed. It is sometimes referred to as a **level premium**. There are several ways that the insured could pay the premium. Regardless of how the premium is paid, the protection is for life.

Continuous premium or **straight life premiums** are paid each year up to age 100. This payment method will have the lowest payment per year. Since money goes into the plan at a slower rate, the cash value will have the slowest build up.

Limited pay whole life limits the payment to a designated period of years but still provides lifetime protection. Examples would include 20 pay life, 30 pay life or life paid up at age 65. These plans will cost more per payment period. Since more money is going into the plan earlier the cash value will accumulate at a faster rate. Even though the premiums are higher, the insured doesn't have to pay premiums his/her whole life, which is an advantage.

Single premium plans make one payment into the policy and pay up the protection for life. This product has the highest premium, but accumulates the quickest cash value growth.

Which of the above would be the least expensive assuming it was purchased and the insured died within the year? All three would pay the same death benefit, but the continuous premium would reflect the least money put into the plan to receive the death benefit, since only one payment was made on each of them.

Which of the above would be the most expensive assuming the insured lived a full life expectancy and then some? Since the single premium provided more funds to the insurer earlier, the insurer was able to use more money for a longer time. Since interest reduces the insured's premium, this would have provided a significant discount for making full payment up front. The single premium would be the lowest premium paid out. The continuous premium would then be the most expensive.

MATURITY AND TAXATION

When the whole life policy matures, either at death or at age 100, **the policy pays out its death benefit income tax free.**

As long as the cash value is accumulating within the policy, taxes will not be required. **Cash value is said to grow tax deferred.**

Loans are not taxable income, since the intent of a loan is to repay the funds that have been taken out of the product.

Withdrawals are taken without the intent to be repaid. **Any amount in excess of the cost basis will be taxed** the year the funds are withdrawn.

ADJUSTABLE LIFE INSURANCE

The key feature of the adjustable life policy is, as its name implies, that it is an adjustable whole life policy. This product allows the insured to make changes in his/her contract over time without purchasing an additional policy. The adjustable life policy allows the insured to increase or decrease the amount of protection. The insured may increase or decrease the premium payment. The insured may also alter the period of protection.

Typically changes that increase the risk and exposure of the insurance company will require proof of insurability. If the insured requested an increase in the death benefit, the insurer would ask health questions.

In effect, it allows the insured the options of moving from a term like product to a permanent product and vice versa. The insured may alter premiums as financial needs and objectives change. Because of its flexible nature, the adjustable life product may have a higher expense ratio built in.

Variable Whole Life

A variable product is any product that takes the cash value in the product and invests it in a **separate account** chosen by the insured. **The insured then assumes the investment risk** with the potential for gain or loss on the investment.

In order to sell this product the representative must be dually licensed. Since it is an insurance product the representative will be required to have an insurance license and will be regulated by the state Department of Insurance. This product has investment risk in it also, and must be sold by a securities licensed representative licensed through the **Financial Industry Regulatory Authority (FINRA)** and regulated by the **Securities Exchange Commission (SEC).**

The investment risk differs from the traditional whole life product. In the variable product the policyholder assumes the investment risk. With the traditional concept, the insurance company pays their policyholders an interest for the use of their money. The funds are then intermingled in the company's **general account** where they will use it with other premium dollars to invest as they choose. If the company's investment fails, the insurer pays the interest to the policyholder regardless. It is the insurance company that takes the investment risk.

In a variable product, the consumer maintains control of the funds by choosing to place them in a separate investment account very similar to the mutual fund concept. It is now the policyholder who is making the investment decision and assumes the investment risk.

Traditional Whole Life	Variable Whole Life
Insurance License Only	Insurance & Securities License
Regulated by the Insurance Industry	Regulated by FINRA and Insurance
Investment Risk Assumed by the Insurer	Investment risk Assumed by the Insured
Company General Account	Separate Account

UNIVERSAL LIFE INSURANCE

Universal life insurance is a unique product due to its **flexible** design and options. It is a form of permanent life insurance in which the owner of the policy has the choice to modify the frequency and amount of the premium payments, which in turn periodically changes the death benefit amount. Premium payments are made into a premium account and all expenses and mortality charges are disclosed to the policyholder and are deducted from the premium account. The unused balance remaining in the premium account draws interest tax deferred and make up the policy's cash value.

To understand the policy design and structure of this product, there are two aspects of the policy that needs to be looked at and understood. The two aspects are the premium structure and the death benefit options.

Premium Payments

One of the unique characteristics of the universal life policy is how the premium is managed. As premium payments are made into the cash value account, two postings will be made on a monthly basis.

First, the insurance company will deduct or debit from the account the cost of protection for that month. This is the risk factor in the plan. Each month there is a chance of premature death (risk) and this cost is what is being deducted from the account.

Secondly, the company will credit the account with an interest payment reflecting current interest rates. The **current interest rate will consist of a guaranteed minimum plus excess interest**. Guaranteed minimum rates are set when the policy is issued and remain in force for the duration of the contract. This is the least amount of interest the company will ever pay. It is a guaranteed minimum rate. The company hopes to do well with its investments. If so, it will be able to pay over and above the minimum rate guaranteed. The amount over the guaranteed minimum is the excess rate. This means the client receives **cash value growth on an interest sensitive basis**.

Typically, the insurance company will charge its insureds for the managing the account. This can be done one of two ways. Some companies will charge a load or fee each year, while others will use a back end cancellation fee or penalty. A back end cancellation fee is a charge for early withdrawal.

Universal Life Premium Payments

Flexible Premium Payments → [cash] → Cost of Protection (Risk)

Current Interest = Guaranteed Rate + Excess

It is the owner's responsibility to assure there are always adequate funds in the account in order to pay the cost of protection that is being deducted. As long as there are adequate funds to cover this cost, the policy stays in effect and coverage continues. This means the insured can adjust the premium payment into the policy over time. The insured could even skip a payment. If the funds are not in the account to cover the cost of protection, then the policy owner would either have to make an additional payment or the plan will go into a grace period and lapse.

This plan gives the customer complete control over the payment plan. Based upon what the client wants to accomplish with the policy, the agent will suggest a target premium. The policy could then be paid over a lifetime. It could be paid over a limited amount of time. The insured could switch from one payment plan to another mid-stream, or any number of strategies could be utilized with this program.

Loans and Withdrawals

Just like any other permanent policy, the universal life policy has the option to borrow on the cash value account. The loan is not taxable and must be accounted for by either payment, deducted from the death benefit or deducted from the non-forfeiture value. The policyowner must remember though, that as money is taken from the cash value account, less is available to cover the cost of protection.

Another option available to the owner of the universal life policy is a withdrawal. Whereas a loan commits the insured to paying the money back, a withdrawal is just a reduction of the cash value account.

Bill overfunded his universal life policy premium account. When he purchased the policy his original intent was to pay high premiums up front in order to avoid payments during his retirement. Fifteen years after he purchased the policy, Bill has found himself out of work and in need of cash. Since he overfunded his plan early, Bill has funds available in his account for withdrawal. He opts to withdraw an amount that can be utilized today. He understands that the consequence will be the extension of his payments beyond retirement.

By withdrawing the money instead of borrowing it, Bill does not have to pay it back; it is not a loan. Since it is not a loan, he will not be charged interest and the amount withdrawn will not reduce his death benefit or non-forfeiture value. Although Bill will not be charged interest, he might have a tax consequence if he is above his cost basis.

Waiver of Cost of Insurance

Later we will discuss a common rider available on most life insurance policies called "waiver of premium." This rider is not available on the universal life policy. Instead, this policy has available a "waiver of cost" rider. The intent of this rider is to maintain the policy in the event that the policy owner becomes disabled and cannot afford to keep the policy in effect. In universal life, the premium paid is flexible and may be more than needed to keep the policy in force. **The waiver of cost rider waives the cost being deducted each month from the cash value account in the event that the insured becomes disabled.**

Death Benefit Options

The second unique feature of the universal life policy is the death benefit options. Universal life allows the insured to purchase one of two options: Option A and Option B. **Option A is referred to as the "level death benefit." Option B is the "increasing death benefit."**

Option A is designed to provide a level death benefit. Like the traditional whole life policy, the death benefit consists of risk plus cash value. The risk is greatest at the beginning of the policy and is designed to reduce over time as it is offset by a growing cash value account. Since both the interest rate and the payments into the plan are flexible in this product, the company cannot with certainty determine the outcome of the account. It may grow quicker and higher than anticipated.

To maintain the integrity of the insurance product the insurer must assume a risk at all times, up to age 95 or older. If the cash value account were to reach the face amount or get too close to that amount prior to age 95, this would become a taxable product. It would no longer meet the definition of insurance, which is transferring risk.

To protect the product, a **risk corridor** is established. The risk corridor is designed to satisfy the IRS and the definition of insurance. Even though this product is designed to have a level death benefit, if the cash value account grows quicker than expected, this product could end up having an increasing death benefit in later years.

Option A, Level Death Benefit

Death Benefit = Risk + Cash Value

Risk Corridor

Risk

Cash Value

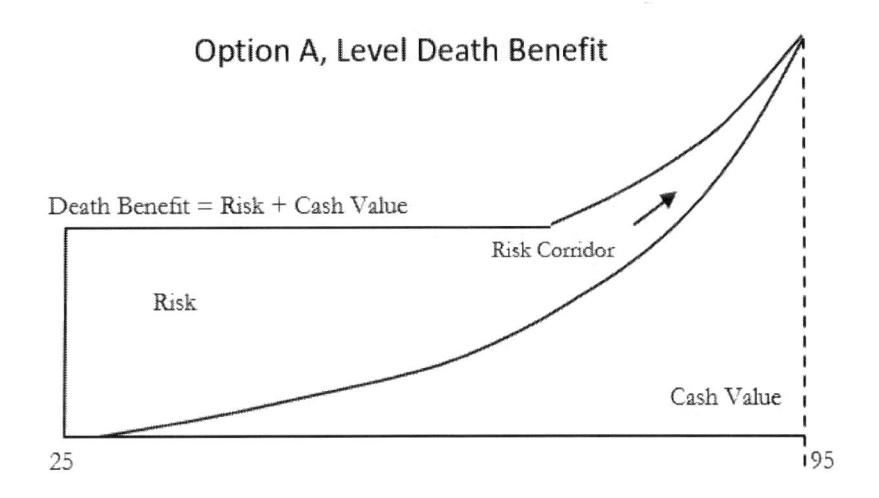

25 — 95

Option B is designed to provide an increasing death benefit. The risk in Option A is designed to decrease as the cash value increases. In contrast, the risk in Option B stays constant. The risk never changes from the original death benefit amount purchased. The death benefit is now equal to the cash value plus the original face amount.

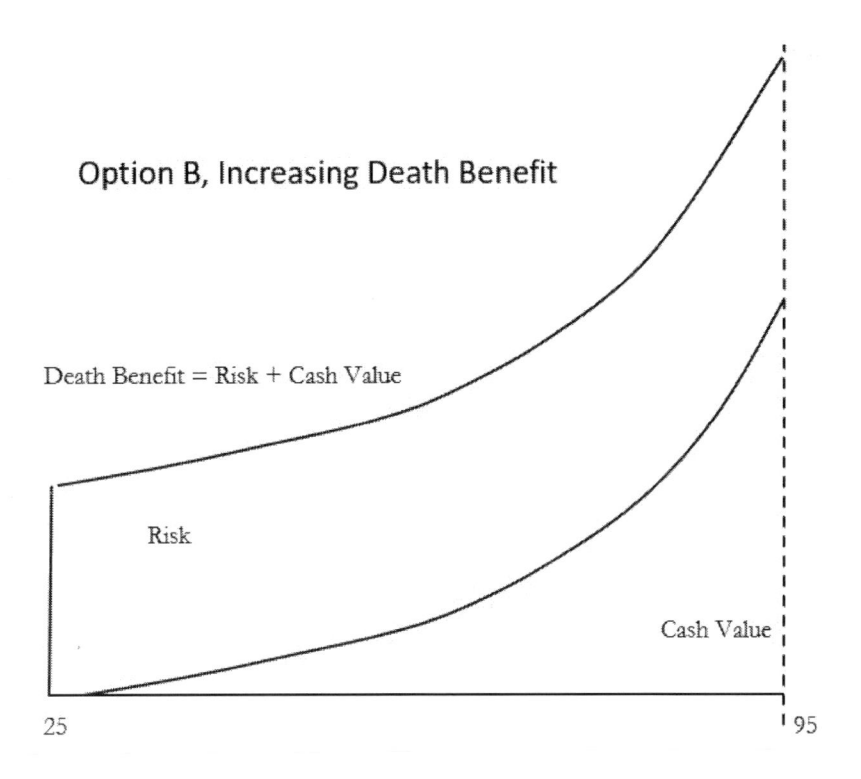

Option B, Increasing Death Benefit

Death Benefit = Risk + Cash Value

Risk

Cash Value

25 — 95

Variable Universal Life Insurance

A variable product is any product that takes the cash value in the product and invests it in a **separate account** chosen by the insured. **The insured then assumes the investment risk** with the potential for gain or loss on the investment.

In order to sell a variable product, the representative must be dually licensed in securities and insurance. Since it is an insurance product, the representative will be required to have an insurance license and will be regulated by the state Department of Insurance. This product also has an investment risk, and must be sold by a securities licensed representative licensed through the **Financial Industry Regulatory Authority (FINRA)** and regulated by the **Securities Exchange Commission (SEC).**

The investment risk on a variable product differs from the fixed universal life product in that the policyholder assumes the investment risk in a variable product. With the traditional concept, the insurance company pays its policyholders interest for the use of their money. The funds are then intermingled in the company's **general account** and used with other premium dollars to invest as the company chooses. If the investment fails, the insurer pays the interest to the policyholder regardless; the company must pay the insured the guaranteed minimum rate. So in the fixed concept, the insurance company takes the investment risk.

In a variable product, the consumer maintains control of the funds by choosing to place them in a separate investment account very similar to the mutual fund concept. It is now the policyholder who is making the investment decision and assumes the investment risk.

Interest Sensitive Whole Life Insurance

The interest sensitive product takes the predictability of the traditional whole life policy and the investment return advantages of universal life and combines the two. At the inception of the policy, it looks very much like traditional whole life. It is a permanent policy with cash value growth and a fixed premium. The difference is, the interest credited to the cash value account is not a fixed interest rate. The interest rate is based upon the company's investment experience along with a guaranteed minimum. Because the cash value growth can no longer be precisely predicted, if it grows greater than anticipated, it will have an impact on the policy in one form or another.

Some products will recalculate the premium as time goes by, allowing the insured to benefit from a lower premium since as cash value increases, risk transferred to the insurance company is reduced.

If premiums are not decreased, then the product could re-evaluate the death benefit. If the original risk expected is covered but the cash value is greater than anticipated, this will have an impact on the total death benefit by increasing it.

Equity Indexed Life Insurance

The equity indexed product takes the cash value in the product and pays an interest based upon the change in a particular equity index. This product also has a flexible interest rate. This flexible interest rate is directly tied to the movement in an equity index fund such as the Dow Jones Industrial Average or the Standard and Poor 500. As the index changes throughout the years, the product will reflect an interest rate based upon those changes.

Today there are multiple types of equity index products on the market. They differ based upon how the insured's growth is determined, which index fund the product will be tied to, caps or limited rates credited, and the percentage of change credited to the account. The similarity between all equity indexed products is that the greater the change in the underlying index fund, the greater the interest credited.

Since the insurance company takes the investment risk and not the owner, if the index drops over the designated period of time, the policy never shows an investment loss.

This policy has an upside potential gain based upon the company's investment experience without the downside risk for the consumer.

Joint Life & Joint and Survivor Life

The joint products **insure multiple lives but only pay one death benefit**.

Joint Life (First-to-Die)

The joint life policy is designed to cover two or more lives. The policy pays out the death benefit after the first insured's death. The premiums charged by the company will be based on the average age of both insureds.

Fred and Wilma purchase a joint life policy to cover both of their lives. Fred names Wilma as his beneficiary and Wilma names Fred as her beneficiary. They purchase this plan in order to provide an income to the survivor, after the first insured dies.

Joint Life or First – to -Die

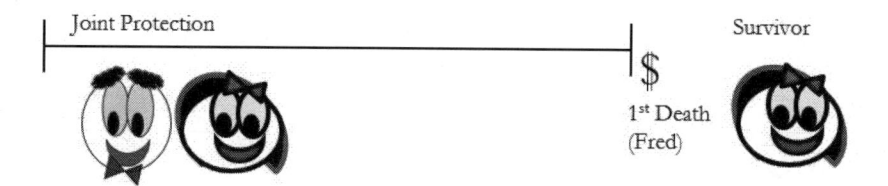

Joint and Survivor (Last – to – Die)

The joint and survivor policy covers the life of two or more insureds. When the first one dies, the policy pays nothing. The protection continues until the last (survivors) death. At that time, the death benefit pays out to the beneficiaries.

Marlin and Margaret buy a survivorship policy to help pay their estate taxes upon the last death. The money will be used to pay taxes in order to conserve the estate value for the children.

Joint and Survivor Life or Last – to - Die

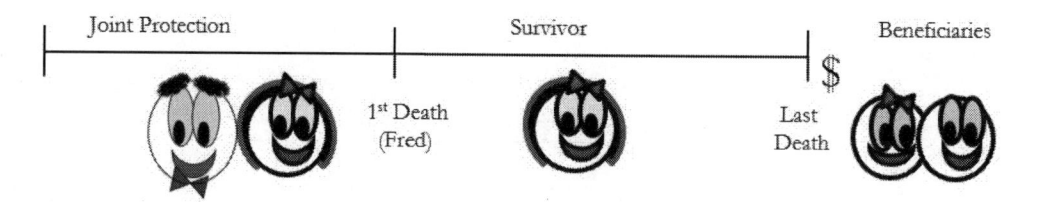

Family (Protection) Policy

The family policy is the one policy that provides **multiple death benefits for multiple insureds**. This policy, sometimes created with the use of a rider, **covers each member of the family**. The policy provides a death benefit for the breadwinner and a separate death benefit for the spouse and each of their children. The **breadwinner receives permanent protection** and each of the **dependents would be covered with convertible term**. The convertible term provides temporary protection and allows the protection to be converted to permanent if the dependent came off of or lost dependent status. For example, dependent status could be lost due to divorce, death or age.

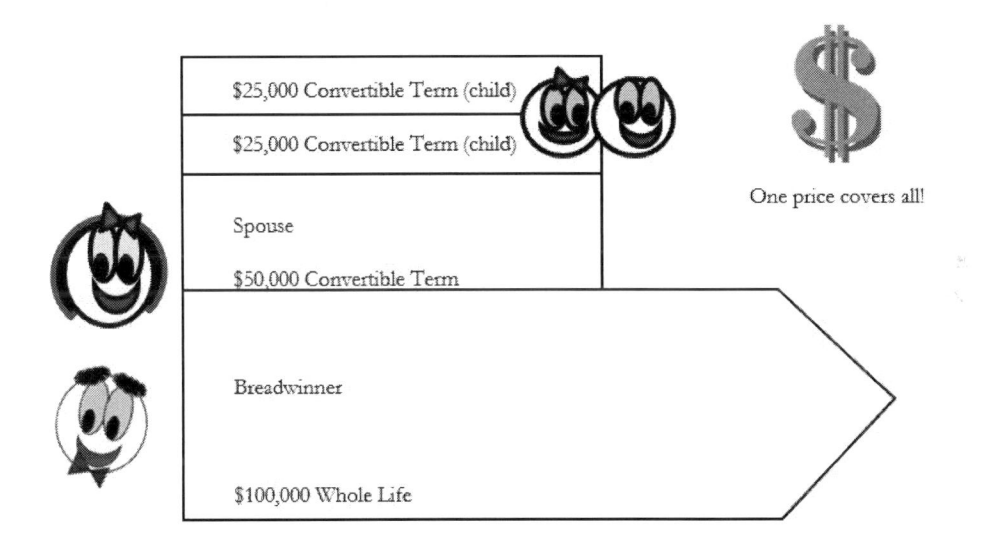

```
$25,000 Convertible Term (child)
$25,000 Convertible Term (child)

Spouse
$50,000 Convertible Term

Breadwinner

$100,000 Whole Life
```

One price covers all!

Sometimes this product is sold in **units**. In the above example, one unit would be $10,000 on the breadwinner, $5,000 on the spouse, and $2,500 on each child. The client has purchased 10 units.

Newborns and adopted children are covered automatically. There is a **14 day** waiting period before coverage takes effect. The date of placement would work the same as the date of birth for adoption.

The premium charged for this type of product is one price for all insureds.

OTHER LIFE INSURANCE POLICY TYPES

MODIFIED LIFE

The modified life insurance policy is an insurance policy that makes a **modification in the premium structure** in order to make the product more marketable or easier to purchase. This product begins with a low premium structure, and after a period of time (typically 5 years), the premium increases and then levels off. This product is a cash value product that begins accumulating after three years.

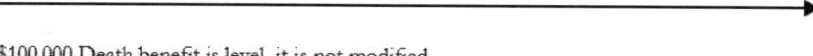

$100,000 Death benefit is level, it is not modified

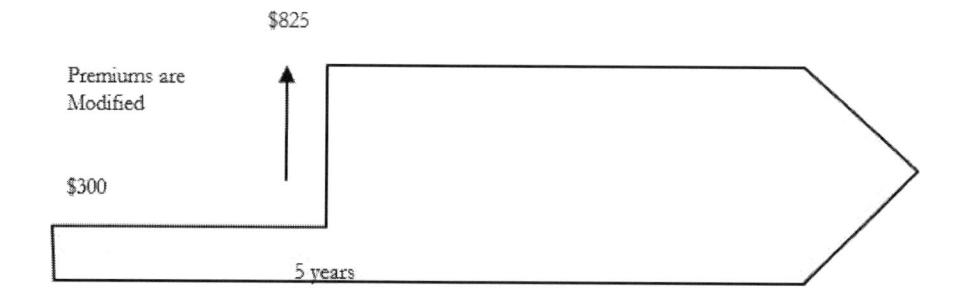

$825
Premiums are Modified
$300
5 years

Barbara is just beginning a new career. She just graduated from college with much debt; therefore, she has a large financial responsibility. For the next few years, Barbara cannot afford much premium, but she wants to purchase a $100,000 whole life policy. The modified life policy would allow Barbara to purchase a permanent policy at a low rate ($300 per year). Her premium will then increase in five years ($825 per year). At this time, she expects to be more established and able to handle the full premium.

GRADED PREMIUM

The graded premium accomplishes the same objective as the modified policy, but in a different way. Instead of the premium making one dramatic jump after a few years, this product will **gradually increase each year** until it finally levels off after 5 years.

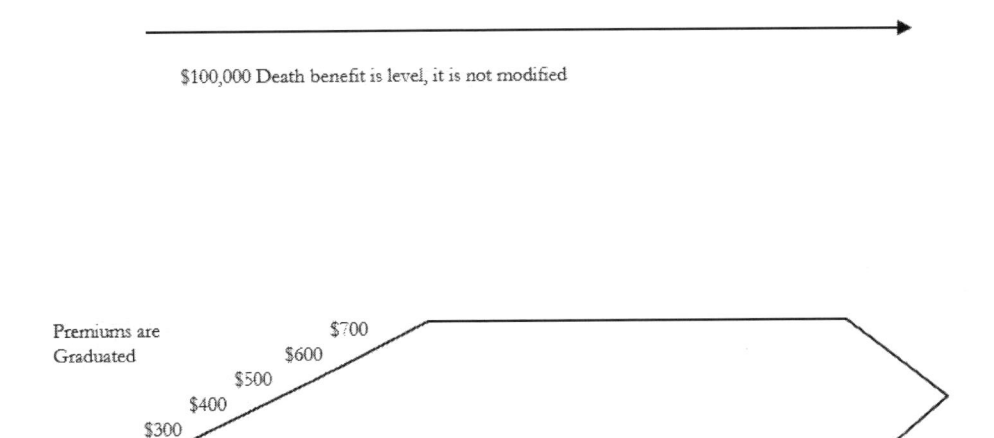

$100,000 Death benefit is level, it is not modified

Premiums are Graduated — $300, $400, $500, $600, $700

Year   1   2   3   4   5

JUVENILE LIFE

A juvenile life policy is any product created specifically to provide **coverage on the life of a child.** Many different companies provide a variety of policy types. One of the original juvenile policies is the "**jumping juvenile**" policy. This policy provided a death benefit for the child up to age 21. At age 21, the benefit increased, or jumped, 5 times its value without increasing the premium.

The juvenile policy may include a "**payor rider or benefit**." Since this policy is providing coverage on a child, typically an adult or parent pays the premium. The payor rider protects the policy in the event that the payor cannot pay the premium due to death or disability. If the payor dies or becomes disabled, the premium will be paid up until the child is old enough (typically 21) to take over the premium payments.

Another benefit common to the juvenile policies is the "**guaranteed insurability rider.**" This rider guarantees the right to purchase additional amounts of insurance at certain ages (typically every 3 or 5 years, up to a certain age) without proof of insurability.

Advantages of the juvenile policies include:

- Low premiums due to age

- Guaranteed insurance with the possibility to purchase additional amounts without proving insurability

- Protection for the child, if the parent or guardian dies or becomes disabled

CREDIT LIFE

Credit life is insurance used to pay off a debt, in the event of the insured's death. Credit life is usually written in the form of decreasing term. When credit life is used to cover a mortgage loan, it is referred to as mortgage insurance. The creditor (bank or financing institution) is the owner and beneficiary. The person (debtor) borrowing the money is the insured and pays the premium.

Regardless of the amount of the death benefit, the creditor can only collect up to the balance of the loan at time of death.

MODIFIED ENDOWMENT CONTRACTS (MEC)

In the market today, there are several different types of permanent policies that allow the insured to pay a substantial amount of money into the policy upfront into the policy. Since the cash value accumulation is tax deferred, the policy could be considered an attractive area to place funds in order to avoid current taxation. The life insurance policy was designed first and foremost to be a product that protects against premature death. The MEC rules were established to protect the intent and purpose of the life insurance product.

If too much money is deposited into a life insurance policy too early, the product could be considered to be a MEC. The **7-pay test** is used to determine if too much was dropped in too early. The 7-pay test states if the accumulated amount paid under the contract at any time during the first seven years exceeds the total net level premiums that would have been paid on or before such time if the contract provided for paid-up future benefits after the payment of seven level annual premiums.

The penalties for a MEC are based upon the usage of the cash value. Any funds distributed from a MEC contract are distributed on a LIFO (last in first out) basis. Anything above the cost base will be considered taxable income. If the owner is younger than 59 ½ and withdraws funds from the cash value account, the distributed proceeds will be penalized 10% as an early withdrawal.

Upon the insured's death, a policy classified as a MEC will have no adverse tax consequences when the death benefit is paid to the beneficiary.

Chapter Review

TERMS TO KNOW

Term Insurance

Permanent Insurance

Living Benefits

Level Term

Decreasing Term

Increasing Term

Renewable Term

Convertible Term

Insurability

Attained Age

Level Premium Term

Annually Renewable Term

Attained Age Rate

Original Age Rate

Cash Value

Guaranteed Growth Rate

Cost Basis

Loan

Withdrawal

Beneficiary

Continuous Premium/Straight Life Premium

Limited Pay Whole Life

Single Premium

Adjustable Life Insurance

Variable Whole Life

Separate Account

Universal Life Insurance

- Grace Period
- Rider
- Waiver of Cost of Insurance
- Waiver of Premium Rider
- Universal Life Option A
- Universal Life Option B
- Risk Corridor
- Variable Universal Life
- Interest Sensitive Whole Life
- Equity Indexed Life
- Joint Life
- Joint and Survivor Life
- Family (Protection) Policy
- Units
- Modified Life
- Graded Premium
- Juvenile Life
- Payor Rider or Benefit
- Guaranteed Insurability Rider
- Credit Life
- Modified Endowment Contracts (MEC)
- 7-Pay Test

NUMBERS AND TIME PERIODS

Age 100 - Whole life matures and endows

30 day - Grace period

Age 95 – Minimum maturity date for newer policies

14 day - Waiting period for newborns and adopted children

Age 21 - Jumping Juvenile benefit jumps 5 times its value

7- Pay Test – MEC rules

SAMPLE QUESTIONS

1. Which of the following would be best suited for level term insurance?
   a) John needs protection for life, but wants to keep his premiums as low as possible
   b) Jill owns a thriving business and needs a significant amount of insurance protection
   c) Joe has 3 children and is just beginning a new career with great future possibilities for advancement
   d) Jim just purchased a house and needs insurance to protect the house for his family in the event of early death

2. Which type of life insurance policy provides temporary coverage for a temporary need?
   a) Universal Life
   b) Term
   c) Permanent
   d) Whole Life

3. The primary advantage of renewable term insurance is:
   a) The right to renew the term with no health questions asked
   b) The right to renew the term without an increase in premium
   c) The right to renew the term at original age rates
   d) The right to renew the term

4. All of the following are true concerning convertible term, EXCEPT:
   a) The insured does not have to prove insurability
   b) The insured is able to convert from term to permanent
   c) The insured is able to convert from permanent to term *implies early death anticipated*
   d) This is a good product for those people who develop a health condition after taking out a life policy

5. A level term policy provides a:
   a) Level premium throughout the life of the policy
   b) Increasing death benefit
   c) Level death benefit
   d) Decreasing death benefit

6. Decreasing term is a good product to protect all of the following, EXCEPT:
   a) Debt
   b) Loan
   c) Mortgage
   d) Return of Premium Rider ✓

7. The traditional whole life policy matures and endows:
   a) At age 100 ✓
   b) At age 95
   c) At completion of premium payments
   d) Anytime after a 7 year payment period

8. Which of the following would be accurate concerning the cash value accumulation and the <u>risk assumed by the traditional whole life policy?</u>
   a) Cash value accumulation accelerates the longer the policy is in effect; Risk reduces over time ✓ *to insurer*
   b) Risk increases over time; Cash value is greatest initially
   c) Risk is greater at the end of the policy; Cash value is greatest at the beginning
   d) Risk and cash value both increase over the term of coverage

9. The maximum loan value on a permanent life insurance policy is:
   a) Equal to the cash value within the product
   b) Equal to the face amount of the policy
   c) Is slightly less than the face amount of the policy
   d) Is equal to the cash value less interest for that year ✓

10. Which of the following **would not** be considered a living benefit?
    a) Cash value
    b) Accelerated death benefit
    c) Nonforfeiture option
    d) Payment to the beneficiary ✓

11. A limited pay whole life policy:
    a) Provides a limited death benefit with a limited premium paying period
    b) Provides a limited paying period with lifetime protection ✓
    c) Provides limited protection with a lifetime premium obligation
    d) Limits the payment of the whole life death benefit in the event of early death

client

12. All things being equal, which of the following policies would be the most <u>expensive</u> assuming that death occurred one year after purchase?
    a) Straight whole life
    b) 20 pay whole life ⬅
    c) 20 year level term
    d) 20 year decreasing term

13. All of the following would be characteristics of a variable product, <u>EXCEPT</u>:
    a) A variable product require dual licensing
    b) The investment risk is assumed by the insurer ⬅
    c) The variable product uses a separate account for investing
    d) The specific investment strategy must be decided by the insured

14. Two postings are made to the universal life product cash value account. The insurer will:
    a) Debit premium payment; Credit cash value
    b) Debit the cost of protection; Credit guaranteed interest rate
    c) Credit cost of protection; Debit current interest rate
    d) Debit cost of protection; Credit current interest rate ⬅ ?

15. The difference between a withdrawal and a loan on a <u>universal life</u> policy is that:
    a) They both must be repaid, but withdrawals will not be charged interest
    b) Withdrawals do not have to be repaid and will not be charged interest ⬅
    c) Only one withdrawal may be made per year; Loans can be made an indefinite number of times
    d) Loans will be taxed above their cost basis; Withdrawals will not

16. Which universal life death benefit has a death benefit that automatically increases with the cash value accumulation?
    a) Option A
    b) Option B ⬅
    c) Both Option A and B
    d) Neither Option A or B

17. What protects option A of the universal life policy from early maturity?
    a) Risk corridor
    b) Reduction of the death benefit
    c) Additional payments required by the insurer
    d) Early maturity will not be possible prior to age 100

18. Marlin and Margaret have purchased a policy that covers both of them, but will only pay once (when the last one dies). What did they purchase?
    a) Joint life
    b) Joint and survivor
    c) Family policy
    d) Family maintenance policy

19. The policy that will provide permanent protection, but offer a premium structure that increases for five years and then levels off, would be:
    a) Graded premium policy
    b) Modified life policy
    c) Increasing term
    d) Convertible term

20. One policy that may pay out multiple death benefits would be:
    a) Universal life
    b) Family protection policy
    c) Joint life
    d) Survivorship policy

21. The juvenile policy typically includes:
    a) Payor rider and waiver of premium rider
    b) Guaranteed insurability benefit and waiver of premium
    c) Payor benefit and guaranteed insurability benefit
    d) Accidental indemnity with a term rider

22. A policy that has become a MEC has violated the:
    a) Cash value accumulation test
    b) 5 pay test
    c) LIFO test
    d) 7 pay test

23. Cash value in a permanent life insurance policy is considered:
   a) Tax deferred
   b) Tax free *(circled)*
   c) Tax free above its cost basis
   d) Taxable as withdrawn

24. The death benefit of a life insurance policy will be:
   a) Taxed above its cash value accumulation
   b) Tax free *(circled)*
   c) Taxed as ordinary income
   d) Taxed on a LIFO basis

25. If a policy is a MEC, all of the following would be consequences, EXCEPT:
   a) All loans and withdrawals will be taxed on a LIFO basis
   b) 10% penalty on anything withdrawn above the cost basis, prior to 59 ½
   c) Death benefits will be taxed above the cost basis *(circled)*
   d) Loans will be taxed above their cost basis, regardless of age

Answers: 1.c 2.b 3.a 4.c 5.c 6.d 7.a 8.a 9.d 10.d 11.b 12.b 13.b 14.d 15.b 16.b 17.a 18.b 19.a 20.b 21.c 22.d 23.a 24.b 25.c

Chapter 3

Annuity Contracts

The annuity contract is a product that can be used for many different purposes. This product can be used as an accumulation product, to be used later as an income product. While it is in the accumulation phase, it works much like a savings account with an insurance company. It can also be used to create a retirement income. Since it is a life insurance product, it comes with additional tax advantages.

The annuity is a product that serves multiple purposes. The definition of the annuity is the "**liquidation of an estate**." One of the main purposes of the annuity is to **create a stream of income that one cannot outlive**. The life insurance policy protects the insured against premature death. In contrast, **the annuity protects the annuitant from living too long (or outliving his/her money)**. In order to accomplish this, an estate must first be established. Originally this was done with a life insurance death benefit. After the death of the insured, the insurance company offers a settlement to the beneficiary in the form of an income stream. Another way of establishing an estate would be by accumulating money with the insurance company to be used at a later date for retirement income or other needs.

The annuity then has two sides to the product. On one side, it is being used to accumulate an estate. On the other side, it is used to create a stream of income.

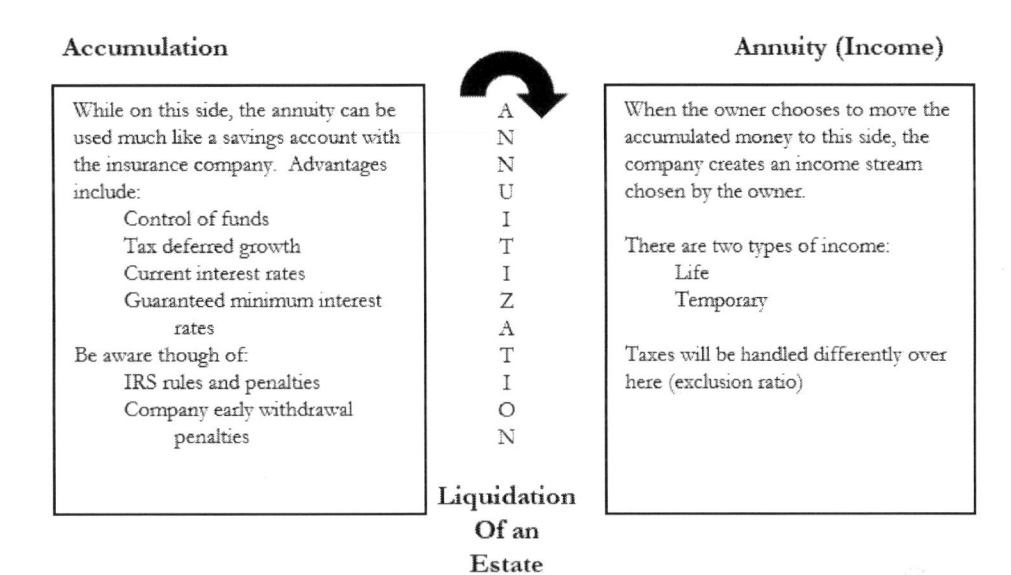

Accumulation		Annuity (Income)
While on this side, the annuity can be used much like a savings account with the insurance company. Advantages include: 　　Control of funds 　　Tax deferred growth 　　Current interest rates 　　Guaranteed minimum interest rates Be aware though of: 　　IRS rules and penalties 　　Company early withdrawal penalties	A N N U I T I Z A T I O N	When the owner chooses to move the accumulated money to this side, the company creates an income stream chosen by the owner. There are two types of income: 　　Life 　　Temporary Taxes will be handled differently over here (exclusion ratio)

Liquidation
Of an
Estate

PARTIES TO THE ANNUITY

There are three parties in the annuity contract:

Owner is the one who **controls the policy**. The **owner has all the rights**. Rights include choosing the beneficiary, choosing when or if to annuitize, choosing the income options or any other choices in the policy.

Annuitant is **who the policy is based upon**. The annuitant and the owner may be the same person or they could be two different parties. When the annuitant dies, the policy ends. When the annuity is annuitized, the income will be based upon the life expectancy of the annuitant.

Beneficiary is the **recipient of the death benefit**. Just like in life insurance when the annuitant dies, if there is a death benefit, it will be paid to the beneficiary.

ACCUMULATION OR PAY IN PERIOD

There are several issues that need to be understood during the accumulation or pay in phase of the annuity. When the annuity is in the accumulation period, it is much like a savings account. Instead of the account being at a bank, it is with the insurance company.

Premium Payment Options

When payments are made into the annuity, they are actually premium payments. If payments are being made into the product, it is on the accumulation side. There are several different methods an owner can use to make payments into the plan.

Single premium products are characterized by one individual payment into the plan. If an owner purchases a single premium product, he/she will have the option to annuitize immediately or defer annuitization to a later date.

An **immediate annuity** is a product where the owner makes a single payment into the plan and requests immediate liquidation or income stream. In this case, the income would begin one payment period interval after **annuitization**.

Hanz is getting ready to retire. He has $500,000 in his 401k. Hanz wants to take his $500,000 out of its present plan and put it into an annuity. He will make one single payment. Hanz then wants to begin receiving income checks one month after annuitization and every month thereafter. He has purchased a single premium immediate annuity (SPIA).

The owner of the annuity may not want to annuitize immediately. In this case the owner buys a **deferred annuity**. In a deferred annuity, annuitization is delayed. The owner will decide at what time, if ever, to cross the line of annuitization.

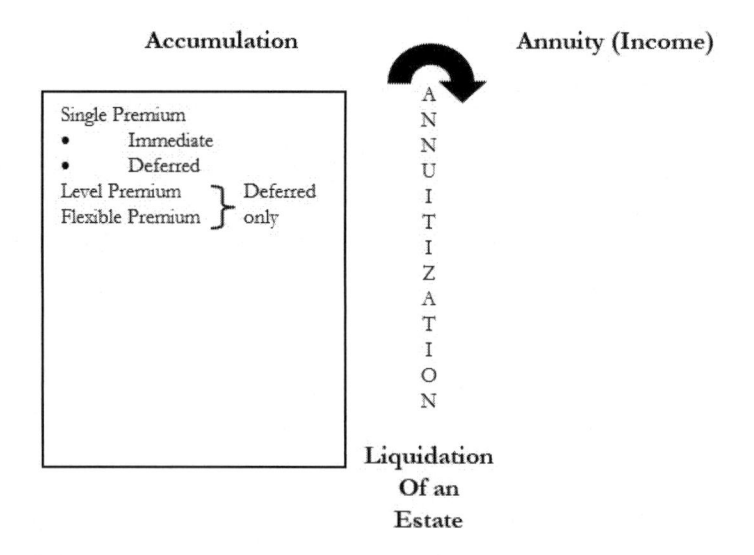

Accumulation | Annuity (Income)

Single Premium
- Immediate
- Deferred

Level Premium ⎱ Deferred
Flexible Premium ⎰ only

ANNUITIZATION

Liquidation
Of an
Estate

Greta has just inherited $200,000 from a long lost relative. Since Greta is only 35, she does not want the money right at this time. Greta has decided to set this money aside for her future retirement. Greta makes a single payment into an annuity and lets it draw interest, tax deferred, for the next 30 years. At 65 she plans on converting her funds into an income stream. Greta has purchased a single premium deferred annuity (SPDA).

In a **Level premium** annuity, payments are made at regular intervals into the product. In addition, the payments are also for a fixed amount. Level premium annuities always have multiple premium payments and cannot be immediate. **Level premium annuities are always deferred annuities**.

Flexible premium annuities **allow for a premium payment of flexible amounts and irregular intervals**. The flexible premium annuities cannot be immediate annuities. **They must also be deferred**.

CASH VALUE GROWTH

As the money is left to accumulate in the annuity, it will accumulate at **current interest rates** with a **guaranteed minimum** rate of return. Since it is an insurance product, it receives favorable tax treatment, even though the principal payments made into the **non-qualified** annuity has already been taxed. The **growth that follows is tax deferred**.

This means that there are now two types of money in the plan. Some of the money has already been taxed (principal). Some of the money is tax deferred and will not be taxed until withdrawn from the plan (growth or interest).

TAX CONSEQUENCES DURING THE PAY-IN OR ACCUMULATION PERIOD OF THE ANNUITY

Since some of the money on the accumulation side of the annuity has received a tax deferral (growth), when the money is withdrawn the tax consequences must be dealt with.

When Greta was 35 years old, she put $200,000 into an annuity for retirement purposes. After ten years, her account value has grown to $275,000. Now at 45, Greta needs $50,000 for a personal need. If she takes the $50,000, what will be her tax consequences?

Greta has two concerns. First, any money withdrawn from the account will be withdrawn on a **last in first out (LIFO)** basis. Since the principal is the first money deposited into the account and interest follows after the fact, interest is considered the last in portion. Last in will be first to come out. This interest has not previously been taxed and will now be taxed as regular income.

Second, when the government gave Greta the incentive to save for her retirement by giving her a tax break, they also gave her a penalty for early withdrawal. Any tax deferred money withdrawn from this plan prior to the age of **59 ½** will incur an additional **10% penalty**.

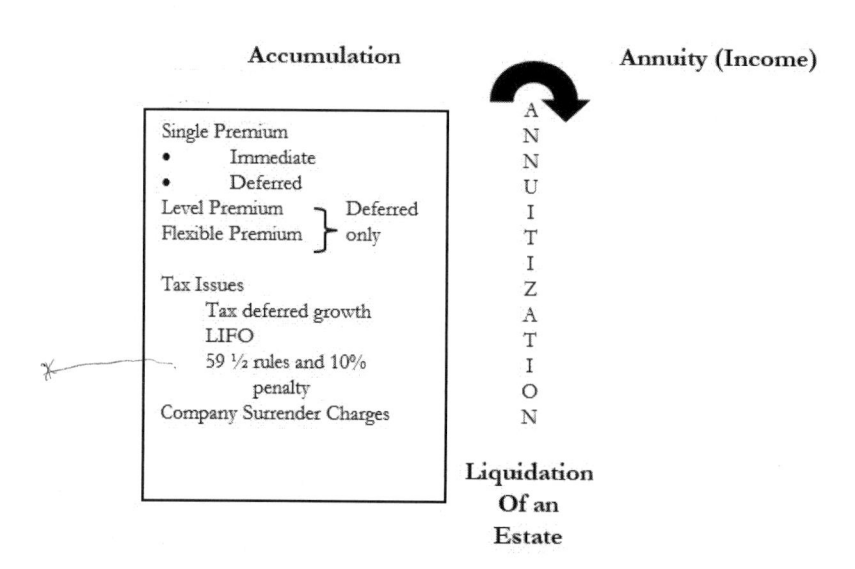

```
                    Accumulation              Annuity (Income)
                                    ↶
                         ┌─────────────────┐  A
                         │ Single Premium  │  N
                         │   • Immediate   │  N
                         │   • Deferred    │  U
                         │ Level Premium  ⎤ │ I
                         │ Flexible Premium⎦Deferred  T
                         │                 only│ I
                         │ Tax Issues      │  Z
                         │   Tax deferred growth │ A
                         │   LIFO          │  T
                         │   59 ½ rules and 10% │ I
                         │     penalty     │  O
                         │ Company Surrender Charges │ N
                         └─────────────────┘
                                              Liquidation
                                                Of an
                                                Estate
```

In addition to the above IRS issues, Greta may also have a penalty for early withdrawal with the insurance company. These penalties differ from company to company. Many of these **surrender charges** are a disappearing penalty. For example, the company may say that if Greta surrenders the policy within the first year the penalty will be 7%. After the first year, the penalty will go down 1% each year until after 7 years there will be no penalty. If this were the case, the penalty has disappeared and Greta is now beyond the time frame that the company charges a surrender charges.

What would happen if Greta would die during the accumulation phase of her annuity? If she died at age 50, her beneficiary would receive the death benefit of the annuity. In most cases, the death benefit equals the accumulation amount. The beneficiaries will be responsible for any tax consequence of the money. Tax deferred means that eventually someone will pay taxes on this money, if not Greta, then her beneficiaries.

SECTION 1035 EXCHANGE RULES

The 1035 allows an individual to move proceeds from one plan to another without tax consequences or penalties. If the insured is moving from like plan to like plan or to a lesser plan, then the transfer qualifies for the 1035 exchange. The following would qualify for the exchange rules:

- Annuity to an Annuity
- Life policy to Life policy
- Life policy to an Annuity

Since going from annuity to the life product would add a death benefit to the contract that did not exist under the annuity, this transaction would not be acceptable.

The Annuity (Pay-out/Liquidation) Period

Once the owner is ready to establish an income, it is time to annuitize the product. When the product is annuitized, the funds are used to purchase an income stream. The owner chooses the type of income stream that best suit his/her needs. At this point, the money that has been accumulated is spent. It is used to purchase an income stream. The owner has several different options to choose from. All of the options fall into two categories: life annuities or temporary annuities. In a life annuity product, the owner cannot outlive the funds. A temporary annuity guarantees a complete payout of principal and interest.

Life Annuities

A life annuity is designed to pay out as long as the annuitant is alive. Any time an individual chooses to take the interest earned and a portion of principal as an income, the funds will last for a limited period of time. But, if the annuitant takes the same money and purchases a life annuity, the insurance company will assume the risk of outliving the funds. The insurance company will determine a payment based upon the amount of money provided, interest on that money, life expectancy, and option chosen. Regardless of how long one lives, payments will continue for life.

The different life annuity options include:

> Straight Life – No minimum guarantees

Straight Life or Life Only Annuity

The straight life annuity pays an income that is derived from both principal and interest until the annuitant dies. At death, the income ends. This option has no minimum guarantee pay out. It is the riskiest choice of all the annuity options; however, the advantage is that out of all the annuity options, it pays the largest amount per payment period. It has the greatest chance of paying out the most overall.

If one chose the straight life option and died one year later, the payments would stop at death. However, if the individual chose the straight life option and lived a long time, you could easily come out ahead. It all depends on how long you live.

Life Annuity with Period Certain

The life annuity with period certain guarantees an income for life with a minimum guarantee, based upon a period of time chosen by the annuitant. Examples would include life with 10 years certain or life with 20 years certain. If an annuitant died before the certain time period is exhausted, the beneficiary would continue receiving payments until the period certain has been paid out. If the annuitant outlived the period certain and then died, the income stream would end. Since this guarantees a minimum payout, it will not provide an income check as large as the straight life. This is the tradeoff for the minimum guarantee. As a general rule, the more you choose to guarantee the less your monthly payment will be.

Life w/ 10 Year Certain – Guarantees a period of time, at least

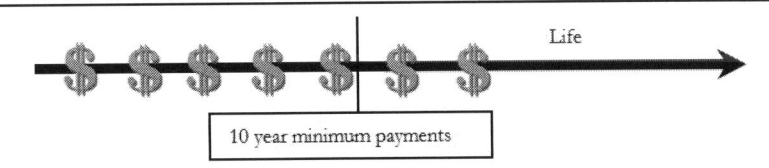

(10 year minimum payments, then Life)

Refund Life Annuity

Refund life annuity pays an income for life with a minimum guarantee based upon the amount that the annuitant annuitized. This is the amount used to purchase the annuity or income.

There are two different types of refund annuities. The **"cash refund"** annuity pays a lump sum balance to the beneficiary after the annuitant dies, if the annuitant did not receive the minimum amount guaranteed. The **"installment refund"** annuity would continue the payments to the beneficiary until the company's obligation has been met.

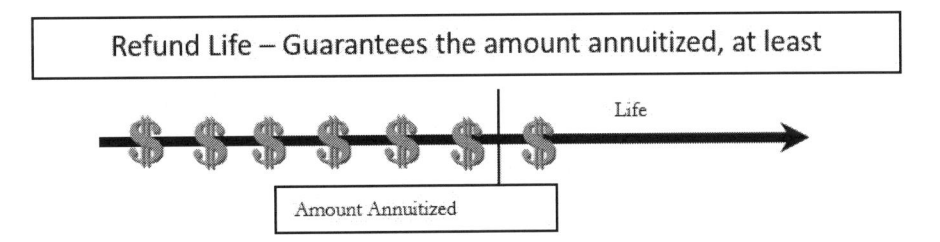

Refund Life – Guarantees the amount annuitized, at least

(Amount Annuitized, then Life)

Joint and Survivor Life Annuity

The joint and survivor life annuity will provide an income based upon the life expectance of multiple people. Payments will be provided until the first death. After the first death, the survivor will continue receiving payments until the survivor dies (last to die). The joint annuities are the only annuities that pay an income to more than one person at the same time.

Joint and survivor annuities do not always pay the same amount for the survivor as they pay initially while both annuitants are alive. Products consist of joint and 100%, 75%, 2/3rds, or 50% to the survivor. Joint and 100% survivor would continue making payments of the same amount even after the first death. Joint and 50% survivor would pay a greater payment while the two are alive and 50% of the joint payment for the survivor.

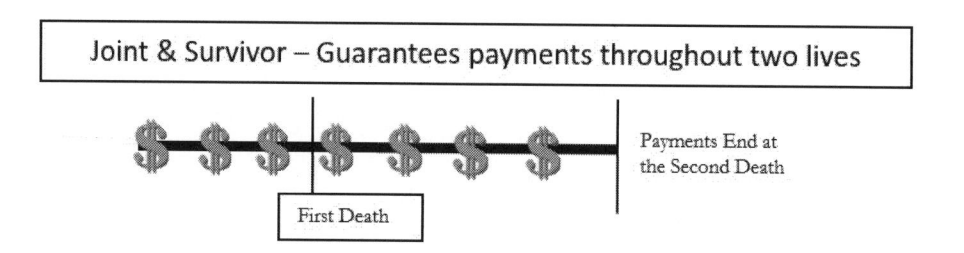

ANNUITY CERTAIN

There are two types of annuity certain products. They are fixed period (period certain) and fixed amount (amount certain). In either case, these annuities do not guarantee an income for life. These annuities could be outlived. They do promise to pay out the total principal and interest earned throughout the liquidation phase. At the end of the certain pay out, there will be nothing left with the company and payments would cease.

Fixed Period

The emphasis on the fixed period annuity is the period of income needed. The owner determines the period of time that payments are needed and the insurer will determine the amount of each income check.

For example, Bob is 55 years old and needs an income stream for 10 years. When he turns 65, his Social Security and pension plans will begin. Bob needs coverage for a fixed period of time. The fixed period annuity is a perfect fit for his needs.

Fixed Amount

The emphasis on the fixed amount annuity is the amount of income needed per month. The owner determines the amount of the payment needed and the insurer will then determine how long the funds will last.

Fixed Amount

Annuitant determines how much they want the insurance company to pay each payment period

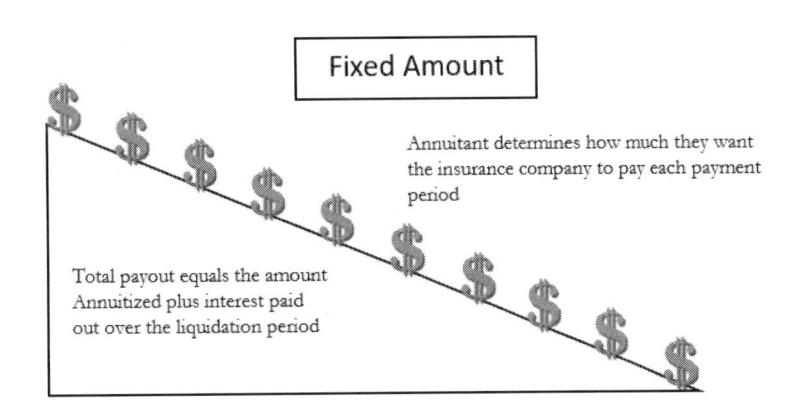

Total payout equals the amount Annuitized plus interest paid out over the liquidation period

Once the annuitant chooses the amount, the insurance company established the term

Jane's husband has just passed away. Jane needs an additional income of $2,000 per month in order to pay her bills. She needs a fixed amount annuity.

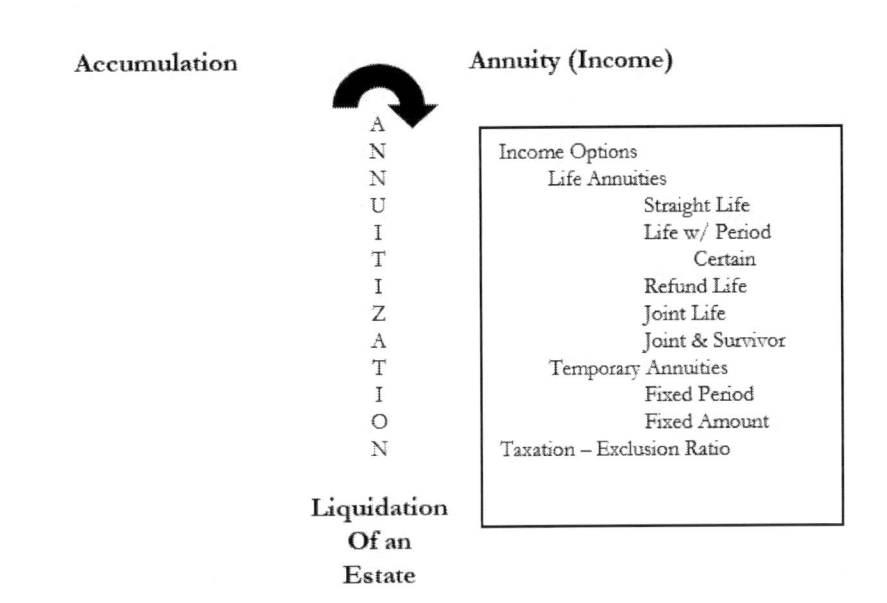

Accumulation   **Annuity (Income)**

A
N
N
U
I
T
I
Z
A
T
I
O
N

Income Options
- Life Annuities
  - Straight Life
  - Life w/ Period Certain
  - Refund Life
  - Joint Life
  - Joint & Survivor
- Temporary Annuities
  - Fixed Period
  - Fixed Amount
- Taxation – Exclusion Ratio

Liquidation Of an Estate

ANNUITY PREMIUM DETERMINATION

When an individual is considering the purchase of an annuity, the question may be asked, **"How much must the owner pay to obtain the income needed?"** The amount submitted by the owner, is the premium that is used to purchase the benefit desired. There are five factors that determine the premium of the annuity:

1. The **income amount** desired and the **minimum guarantees** chosen

2. The annuitant's **age** and life expectancy

3. The annuitant's **sex**

4. The **interest** rate to be used to generate the income amount

5. Company **expenses**

Once the company obtains this information, it can then determine the premium that must be paid into the product, to generate the option chosen.

EXCLUSION RATIO

Since the growth on the annuity has not been income taxed, the government will expect taxes to be paid when withdrawn from the annuity. On the accumulation side, we withdrew growth on a LIFO basis. But, on the annuity side we use the exclusion ratio. Using the exclusion ratio method, a part of each income check consists of growth and a part will consist of principal. This means that the annuitant will have to pay taxes on a portion of each check. The exclusion ratio is used to determine which portion is taxed and which is not. The ratio is:

$$\frac{\text{\textbf{Principal (amount that has been previously taxed)}}}{\textbf{Expected return}}$$

Marcella has put $50,000 into a deferred annuity and over time, it has grown to $75,000. Marcella now chooses to annuitize it. If the company determines that based upon her life expectancy and the income choices that she has made, her lifetime income is expected to be $150,000. Then 1/3 ($50,000/$150,000) of each check will be excluded from taxation.

If the insured does live beyond his/her life expectancy and the company pays out beyond its predicted time, any payments received after the life expectancy age has been reached, will be growth only and taxed accordingly.

Types of Annuities

Fixed Annuities

A fixed (conventional) annuity is a product in which the insurance company pays an interest to the owner for the use of the money. When the owner pays a premium into the product, the company takes that payment and inter mingles it with the other payments that it may collect from other annuity holders in the company's "**general account**." The **company then assumes the investment risk** as it is re-invested by the company. Regardless of the company's investment results, the policyholders are paid for the use of their money.

The insurance company **guarantees a minimum payment of interest**. If the company does well, it hopes to pay better than minimum guarantee by being able to pay a higher **current rate**.

This product is **regulated by the Department of Insurance**; therefore, in order to sell this product, **the agent must hold an insurance license**.

Variable Annuities

A variable product is any product that takes the cash value in the product and invests it in a **separate account** chosen by the insured. **The insured will then assume the investment risk** with the potential for gain or loss on the investment.

In order to sell this product, the representative must be dually licensed. Since it is an insurance product, the representative will be required to have an insurance license and will be regulated by the state Department of Insurance. This product has investment risk in it also, and must be sold by a securities licensed representative licensed through the **Financial Industry Regulatory Authority (FINRA)** and regulated by the **Securities Exchange Commission (SEC)**.

The investment risk differs from the fixed product. In the variable product, the policyholder assumes the investment risk. With the traditional concept, the insurance company pays its policyholders an interest for the use of their money. The funds are then intermingled in the company's **general account** where it will use it with other premium dollars to invest as it chooses. If the investment fails, the insurer pays the interest to the policyholder regardless. It is the insurance company that takes the investment risk.

In a variable product, the consumer maintains control of the funds by choosing to place them in a separate investment account very similar to the mutual fund concept. It is now the policyholder who is making the investment decision and assumes the investment risk.

Equity Indexed Annuities

The equity indexed product takes the cash value in the product and pays an interest based upon the change in a particular equity index. This product also has a flexible interest rate. This interest rate is directly tied to the movement in an equity index fund like the Dow Jones Industrial Average or the Standard and Poor 500. As the index changes throughout the years, the product will reflect an interest rate based upon those changes.

Today there are multiple types of equity index products on the market. They will differ based upon how they determine the insured's growth, which index fund they will be based upon, caps or limited rates credited and the percentage of the change credited to the account. The similarity between all equity indexed products is that the greater the change in the underlying index fund the greater the interest credited.

Also, since the insurance company takes the investment risk and not the owner, if the index drops over the designated period of time, the policy never shows an investment loss.

This policy has an upside potential gain based upon the company's investment experience without the downside risk for the consumer.

Two Tiered Annuities

The two tiered annuity is a product that calculates a different interest rate on the funds if they are cashed in versus annuitized. To encourage annuitization, this product would offer a better interest rate if the owner annuitizes the product. If the owner cashes the annuity in without annuitizing it, the product penalizes the owner by recalculating the interest at a lower rate. This is to discourage the use of this product as a savings vehicle only.

Retirement Income Annuities

A retirement income annuity combines the accumulation of retirement funds within an annuity with a decreasing term to age 65 life insurance policy. Under this plan, if an annuitant lives to age 65, enough time has passed to accumulate the funds desired for retirement; the life insurance is no longer needed and it expires. If the annuitant dies prior to age 65, the term will pay a benefit out in along with the money accumulated in the annuity. The total amount from both the annuity and the term will now be used to provide the appropriate protection for the beneficiary.

Market Value Adjusted Annuity

The market value annuities pay a fixed interest rate similar to the fixed annuity concept. The market value comes into play if the contract is surrendered early. In this case, the contract is recalculated based upon the markets past performance. The end result could lead to a return greater than or less than the fixed rate. Since the risk in this product is assumed by the owner, this is considered a securities product and requires an extra license to sell.

Chapter review

TERMS TO KNOW

Annuity

Owner

Annuitant

Beneficiary

Accumulation

Single Premium

Immediate Annuity

Annuitize

Deferred Annuity

Level Premium

Flexible Premium

Non-Qualified

Qualified

Current Interest Rate

Guaranteed Minimum Rate

Last in first out (LIFO)

Surrender Charge

The Annuity Period (Pay-out/Liquidation)

Life Annuities

Straight Life/ Life Only Annuity

Life Annuity with Period Certain

Refund Life Annuity

Joint and Survivor Life Annuity

Annuity Certain

Fixed Period

Fixed Amount

Exclusion Ratio

Fixed Annuities
Variable Annuities
Equity Indexed Annuity
Two Tiered Annuity
Retirement Income Annuity
Market Value Adjusted Annuity

NUMBERS AND TIME PERIODS

59 ½ and 10% penalty

SAMPLE QUESTIONS

1. An annuity is defined as the:
   a) Liquidation of an estate
   b) Creation of an estate
   c) Accumulation of an estate
   d) Savings account with a life insurance company

2. Hanze has an annuity that allows him to make payments of differing amounts. He does not plan on annuitizing the product until he reaches age 65. At that point, he would like to establish an income that will last as long as he lives. He will probably want to guarantee a minimum amount. Hanze has:
   a) A life with period certain
   b) A deferred annuity
   c) An immediate annuity
   d) A variable annuity

3. Greta is 50 years of age. Several years ago she paid $50,000, which she received as a life insurance settlement, into an annuity. Her account balance is now $75,000. Greta must withdraw $10,000. What will be the IRS consequences of this withdrawal?
   a) Greta will have to pay taxes on the whole $10,000
   b) Greta will pay taxes on a portion of the $10,000
   c) Not only will Greta pay taxes on the $10,000, she will also pay a $1,000 penalty on the withdrawal
   d) Greta will have to pay a 10% penalty on the withdrawal

4. All the following would be allowable 1035 exchanges, EXCEPT:
   a) Annuity to annuity
   b) Life policy to life policy
   c) Life policy to annuity
   d) Annuity to life policy

5. Joey has an income that will pay regardless of how long he lives. If he dies within 20 years the income payments will continue to his wife for the remainder of the 20 year period. Joey has:
   a) A life with period certain annuity
   b) A joint annuity
   c) A joint and survivor annuity
   d) 20 year certain annuity

6. Jack and his wife Jill will receive an income until the first one dies. After which, the survivor will continue to receive an income for half of the original payment. This is:
   a) A straight life with 50% certain
   b) A joint annuity
   c) A joint and 50% survivor
   d) A refund life annuity

7. Taxes prior to annuitization will be paid based upon:
   a) Exclusion ratio
   b) FIFO
   c) LIFO — TGIF shift worker example
   d) LIPO

8. An equity indexed annuity:
   a) Is a fixed annuity with investment returns tied to changes in a specific equity index
   b) Is a variable product with investment returns based upon the performance of the separate account
   c) Is a fixed annuity with investment returns based upon the insured's investment in an equity index account
   d) Is a fixed annuity based upon market value returns

9. Betty is planning for her future retirement. She is trying to figure out, how much it will cost her to create the income needed for retirement. All of the following factors need to be considered, EXCEPT:
   a) The income amount desired and any guarantees that she chooses to include
   b) Her current age, sex and life expectancy
   c) Interest rate that the insurer will use to generate the income amount
   d) Company expenses to establish the plan

10. The exclusion ratio:
    a) Is used prior to annuitization and states that a portion of each payment will be taxed
    b) Is used after annuitization and states that growth is withdrawn first
    c) Is used prior to annuitization and states that withdrawals will be treated on a LIFO basis
    d) Is used after annuitization and states that a portion of each payment will be taxed as received and a portion will not be

11. Jay needs an income over the next ten years. At that point his social security will kick in and he will take his retirement income. The best product for Jay might be:
    a) Life with 10 years certain
    b) Fixed amount annuity
    c) Fixed period annuity
    d) Variable annuity

12. All the following are characteristics of a variable annuity, EXCEPT:
    a) It will use a separate account for investments
    b) It is regulated by the insurance industry and the securities industry
    c) The risk is assumed by the investment company
    d) It requires dual licensing

Answers: 1.a 2.b 3.c 4.d 5.a 6.c 7.c 8.a 9.b 10.d 11.c 12.c

Chapter 4

Life Insurance Policy Provisions

The provisions in the policy are the rules and conditions of the contract. Some provisions are required to be within the insurance contract. Since the insurer is responsible for the writing of the contract, some provisions are required to be in the policy for the benefit of the insured. These provisions are required by the state law in order to protect the insured either directly or indirectly from the insurer. Other provisions are discretionary. These provisions will be placed in the contract at the discretion of the insurer. These provisions are designed to protect the insurer from the insured.

REQUIRED PROVISIONS

The following provisions are required to be written into the insurance contract according to state law.

ENTIRE CONTRACT/CHANGES CLAUSE

This provision states exactly what makes up the total contract. It states **the policy and any attachments (including the application) comprise the entire contract.** By clarifying what consists of the entire contract, this prevents either party from using any outside evidence to modify the existing contract. If there is a disagreement or difference in interpretation, the contract is what a court will look to, in order to establish the final outcome.

The section of the entire contract that deals with making changes to the contract states, **only an executive officer of the company can make a change in the contract**. In particular, **the agent docs not have the authority to change or alter a contract**. As a contract of adhesion, the insurer is responsible for the wording in the agreement. Changes to the policy (riders) are signed by an executive officer of the company.

Keep in mind, that once a contract has been accepted by the policyholder, it can only be altered with consent and acceptance from the policyholder. This could happen if the policyholder requests a change or alteration that would be acceptable to the insurer.

INSURING CLAUSE

The insuring clause is sometimes described as the "**heart**" of the policy. The policy is centered around this statement. **This clause states the promise** that the parties have agreed to. The insuring clause is a **general** statement that lists the **parties** to the contract and states the **promise** made by the insurer, to pay in the event of certain covered **perils** (accident or sickness).

PREMIUM PAYMENT CLAUSE

Premiums are calculated on an annual basis. The insurer assumes that premiums will be paid in advance. This gives the company the opportunity to invest some of the premium funds immediately and use the payment and the interest earned to pay claims as they develop over the year. Because of this, the gross premium paid is reduced by the interest earned.

If a policyowner chooses to make the payments more often than once a year, (semi-annually, quarterly or monthly) the company must re-consider the amount necessary to provide the protection.

If the policyowner does pay the premium more often than annually the **premium will be higher over the course of the year due to two reasons:**

- **Loss of interest** or investment return. The company makes up its lost time to invest and the lost investment dollars by charging the policyholder a higher premium.

- **Extra expenses** The company will be required to mail more statements to the insured. This means more expenses: paper, stamps, processing, calculating and recording expenses.

INCONTESTABLE CLAUSE

The incontestable clause is **the period of time the company has to challenge the information on the application**. After this time period expires, the policy is said to be incontestable (unchallengeable). The company has **2 years** to contest or challenge the application.

Misstatement of Age and Sex Clause

If a misstatement of age or sex occurs on the application, this clause allows the insurance company to correct the situation. The insured is protected by this clause because it does not allow the company to void the policy, but to correct the mistake and maintain coverage. Misstatement of age and sex is not considered **material** information. This protects the policyholder from a voided contract without penalizing the company for a common mistake.

This clause allows the insurer to adjust the death benefit, to reflect the actual age that the contract should have been based upon.

Joey pays $800 per year for a $100,000 life insurance policy. When applying for the policy he told the company on the application that he was age 30 years old, when in fact he was 35. He should have paid a higher rate than $800/year because the $800 rate is based upon age 30. So, Joey should have paid the age 35 rate which is $1,000/year. Five years later after taking out the policy, Joey dies. Upon his death, the mistake is discovered on the death certificate. To correct the mistake, the company pays a death benefit of $80,000. This is what $800 per year would have bought Joey had the company issued the policy at his correct age 35.

Grace Period

The grace period is the period of time the owner has to pay the premium payment after the policy comes due. In life insurance, the policyholder has **30 days** after the premium is due to make the premium payment. If the insured were to die during the grace period, **coverage does apply**. If an insured were to die during the grace period and the company were to pay the claim, **the company would have the right to deduct the late payment from the death benefit.**

Reinstatement Clause

It is possible that the owner of a life insurance policy may decide to drop the coverage by not paying the premium. After the fact, the owner may reconsider and desire to reinstate the policy for one of many reasons. The reinstatement clause establishes the rules for reinstating the policy. These rules are designed to be fair to the company (since the company is not the party who backed out of the agreement), and still allow for a customer to get coverage back in force that may be needed.

There are three reinstatement rules:

- **Reinstatement must be within 3 years**.

- **Back premiums (plus interest) must be paid.** The company will be putting coverage back in place as if the policy had never been dropped. Back premiums are necessary for the company to maintain its policy responsibilities.

- **Proof of insurability must be established.** Since the insured backed out of the contract, this is required to be fair to the company. If the insured discovered a new health condition, the company would not be required to reinstate the policy. If the insured's health has not changed, there is no reason for the company to not accept them back.

OWNERSHIP CLAUSE

The ownership clause states who has the rights within the policy. Since the contract is between the owner and the company, it is the **owner who has the rights**. Ownership rights include the right to name the beneficiary, settlement options, dividend options or any other choices that may be available to the owner.

There are three parties in the life insurance contract: the beneficiary, the insured, and the owner. The beneficiary is the recipient of the death benefit. The insured is who the policy covers. The contract is based on the life of the insured. The **owner is the one who controls the policy**. In many cases the owner and the insured are the same person; however, it is best to think of them as separate entities with separate roles.

ASSIGNMENT CLAUSE

To assign a right means to give that right to another party. The owner has the rights in the policy, so it is the owner who can assign rights to others. There are two types of assignment:

Total or permanent assignment is when **the owner gives all of his/her rights** of ownership over to another person or party. This is **a total relinquishment of rights and ownership. Once this is done, it is permanent**. A father may choose to give a policy purchased on his son to him after the son reaches the age of maturity. Now the son becomes the owner and has the right to change beneficiary designation, cash it in, or exercise any other rights that come with ownership.

Partial or temporary assignment is when the owner gives up some of the ownership rights for a temporary period of time. Since the permanent policy has equity (cash value) in the policy, **the owner could use the equity as collateral for a loan**. In this case, the owner gives up the right to access the cash value (collateral) until the loan is paid off. At that time, all of the rights of the owner are re-instated.

Loan Values and Automatic Premium Loan (APL) Provision

On a permanent policy, the amount available for borrowing is based upon the policy's cash value. The **maximum loan value would be the cash value minus the first year's interest**. If at any time the total loan value equals the total cash value of the policy, the coverage will end. There must be an amount of money left in the cash value in order for coverage to remain in force.

The Automatic Premium Loan Provision is a rider that companies provide at no extra cost. This provision states that when the policy comes due, if the owner does not make the premium payment it allows the insurer to deduct the premium payment obligation from the cash value. This payment will then be considered a loan which will draw interest.

Time Limit on Lawsuits

If the customer is dissatisfied or has an issue with the insurer and chooses to sue the insurer, this provision allows the insurer an adequate amount of time to make payment and requires the insured to act within a stated period of time. The company has 60 days to pay the claim and the insured has 3 years (2 in some states) to sue.

The Practice of Backdating

The application can be backdated up to **6 months in order to save age**. Backdating an application does not change the Incontestability Clause.

Free Look Provision

The free look provision is a **10 day** time period that begins when the policy is **delivered** that allows the insured to review the contract. If for any reason the owner chooses to return the policy, a full refund must be provided.

Discretionary Provisions (Exclusions)

The following provisions may be added at the discretion of the insurance company.

Suicide Clause

When the insurance company prices the risk, they look at the chance of death occurring at each age. This includes suicide. This means that the insurance company has priced the product with suicide considered. This clause states that if suicide **occurs during the first two years of the policy, it will not be covered.** In this event, the **company will refund all premiums** collected.

If suicide occurs after the policy has been in effect over two years, the company will be required to pay the full claim.

Hazardous Occupation (or Hobby/Avocation) Clause

In the underwriting process, the company will ask questions to determine the risk involved. Certain occupations or hobbies may be determined to be extra hazardous, which increases the risk of death. Because of the higher risk, these occupations or hobbies may be excluded from coverage or the insurer may charge extra premium in order to these risks to be covered. Hazardous hobbies could include kayaking, rock climbing, skydiving and other extreme sports.

Another common exclusion could include flying. What is typically covered would be any fare paying passenger on a regularly scheduled airline. If this is an excluded event, then pilots, stewardesses or ultra-lights would not be covered. These situations could be covered if the exclusion is not included. In that event, the company may still ask and rate up the policy to cover the higher risk.

Beneficiary Designations

The beneficiary is the recipient of the death benefit. Even though the beneficiary is the party who receives the death benefit, the owner of the policy (the one who purchased the benefit) will have all the rights of the policy. **The policyowner has the right to name or change a beneficiary designation**. The owner has the right to choose how the benefit will be paid out to the beneficiary, if the owner so desires. Choosing the method that the death benefit will be paid out is referred to as a **settlement option**. The owner has the right to choose a settlement option for the beneficiary. If the owner does not choose a settlement option in advance, the choice will be made by the beneficiary at the time of the death.

When a benefit is claimed, the insurer is required to pay the full amount of the benefit claimed, within a reasonable time period. Occasionally, the insurer will pay less than the face amount of the policy. Reasons why a company may be less than the face amount owed could include:

- Current premium obligation has not been paid.
- A loan is outstanding.
- Misstatement of age or sex.

PRIMARY AND CONTINGENT BENEFICIARIES

The primary beneficiary is the first person designated to receive the death benefit. Anyone listed after the primary is a contingent beneficiary designation. This may include a secondary or a tertiary designation. The contingent beneficiaries are in line for consideration, but them receiving a benefit is **contingent (dependent) upon the ones listed ahead of them (primary) dying prior to the insured**.

Larry names his sister Mary as the primary beneficiary of his life insurance policy. He names his other sister Martha as his secondary beneficiary. In order for Martha to receive the proceeds, Mary must die before Larry. If Larry died first, the proceeds would go to Mary. If Mary then died later, any amount left with the company would then go to Mary's estate, not to Martha.

The owner may list multiple primary or contingent beneficiaries. The owner may also determine what percentage each beneficiary may receive.

REVOCABLE AND IRREVOCABLE DESIGNATIONS

A revocable beneficiary is a beneficiary designation that can be changed by the owner. When the owner names a revocable beneficiary, he/she maintains the right to change designations if so desired.

When the owner names a beneficiary as irrevocable, then the owner limits his/her right to alter the beneficiary. The designation may only be changed if the beneficiary chooses to give up the irrevocable designation. Even though the owner has "tied" up the right to change the designation, if a designation is to be changed it is still the owner that will make the change. At this time, the owner is unable to exercise the right due to the irrevocable designation. The beneficiary still does not have any rights. The beneficiary cannot borrow or use the cash value in the policy. They do not have any rights. The owner has all the rights.

THE ESTATE AS BENEFICIARY

The estate may be the recipient of the death proceeds. This is not considered to be an ideal situation because now the proceeds will go through the probate process. This means that there will be added expense and time delay on the availability of the funds. The life insurance product is designed to avoid probate. When the proceeds go to the estate, it creates a probate situation. There are three scenarios in which the estate would receive the proceeds.

- The estate could be listed as the beneficiary. If the estate is listed as beneficiary, then the insurer will send the proceeds to the estate to be processed.

- All listed beneficiaries have predeceased the insured. If the beneficiary designations are not kept up to date, it is possible that the beneficiaries originally designated have died prior to the insured's death. In this case, the insurance company has not been notified who to send the proceeds to. When the company has not been kept up to date and does not know who to send the proceeds to, it will send them to through the probate process.

- No designation is listed on the application. Most companies will not allow this to happen, but if it does occur, then the company will have no choice but to pay the proceeds to the court.

- If at any time it is not clear who the benefit is owed to, the company will send it to the court for them to determine. Occasionally, the designation is not clear or multiple people claim a right to the benefit. Since the company knows that it owes the claim and it cannot afford to pay it out to the wrong party, when in doubt it will be left to the legal process to make the proper determination.

A TRUST AS BENEFICIARY

A trust may also be named as a beneficiary. Trusts are commonly used to manage the death benefits of a life insurance policy. It would not be unusual for someone to use a trust to manage the proceeds after their death.

A trust could be used to distribute the estate in a pre-arranged manner by the owner. Unlike a will, a trust is a legal contract that avoids the probate process. The owner of the trust spells out in much detail how to transfer the estate to the beneficiaries.

It is common for parents to name their children as beneficiaries. A problem arises with this situation however; minors cannot assume legal ownership of a death benefit. This is why establishing a trust is beneficial; it is an effective way for the funds to be managed for the children. **Trusts are commonly used to manage the funds for a juvenile.**

The owner can list a trustee that will be responsible for overseeing the finances as spelled out under the rules of the trust and for the benefit of the beneficiary.

Minors (Children) as Beneficiaries

Children may be listed as beneficiaries. The primary problem with listing children as a beneficiary is that they cannot legally release the insurance company from their payment responsibility. This is why we would probably need a trust established to manage the funds for the children. This could be done prior to death by the owner or after death by the legal system. Another option would be if the company was requested to hold the funds for the child until the child is old enough to receive the proceeds.

Applicant Control or Ownership Clause

When the proposed insured is a minor, typically the parent is the applicant. This clause allows the applicant to maintain control of the contract until the insured is of a certain age.

Uniform Simultaneous Death Act

This act or legislation deals with the situation where the insured and the primary beneficiary die in a simultaneous accident. In this situation, it may not be possible to determine which person died first. If the primary beneficiary dies first then the proceeds would then go to the contingent beneficiary as designated by the owner. But if the insured were to die first, technically the proceeds would go to the primary beneficiary and then when the primary beneficiary dies the proceeds would go to the insured's estate, not the contingents listed by the owner.

To avoid this situation, the Uniform Simultaneous Death Act makes the assumption that in a simultaneous accident, when order of death cannot be established, **it will be assumed that the insured outlived the primary beneficiary.** This will then see that the money is paid out to the contingent as listed by the owner. It is the goal of the company to meet the wishes of the owner to the best of its knowledge and ability.

Naming Beneficiaries (Per Capita or Per Stirpes)

The owner may be interested in naming multiple designations on the same level. What would happen if one of these individuals died prior to the insured? Where would their portion of the benefit go? Who would receive it?

Barbara has a life insurance policy that names her three children as primary beneficiaries. Each is to receive one third of her death benefit. What would happen if Tom died prior to the Barbara, the insured? Would the money designated to Tom go to his heirs (Little Tommy and Tommy Junior)? Or would the money go to Dick and Harriet?

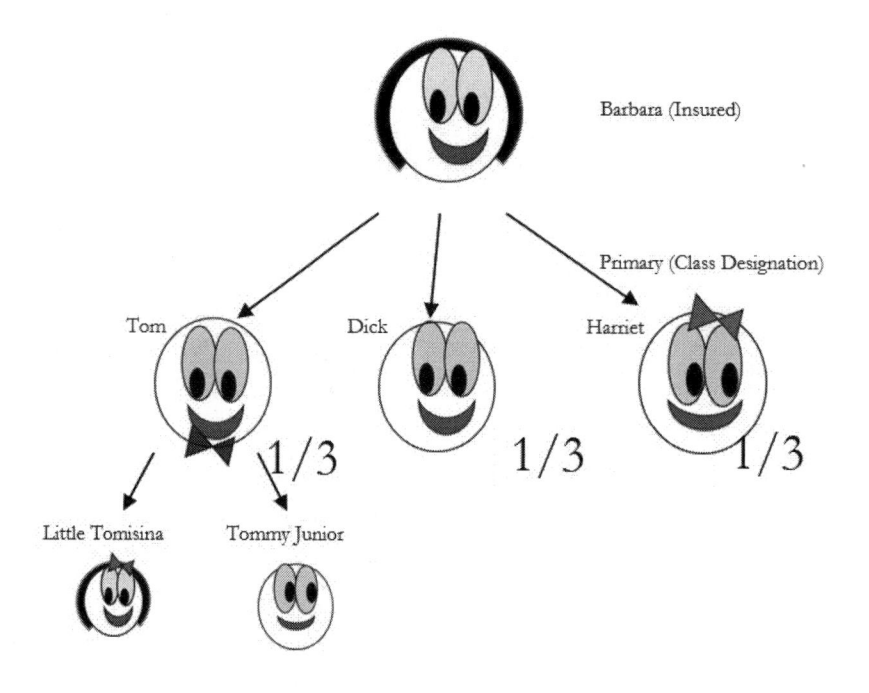

A **Per Capita** beneficiary designation distributes the benefit to the surviving beneficiaries on an **equal basis**. In this situation, the company would be directed to divide the proceeds equally between the surviving primary beneficiaries. Dick and Harriet would each receive one half of the proceeds. Little Tommy and Tommy Junior would receive nothing.

Per Capita

Barbara (Insured)

Primary (Class Designation)

Tom — Dick — Harriet

½ ½

Little Tomisina — Tommy Junior

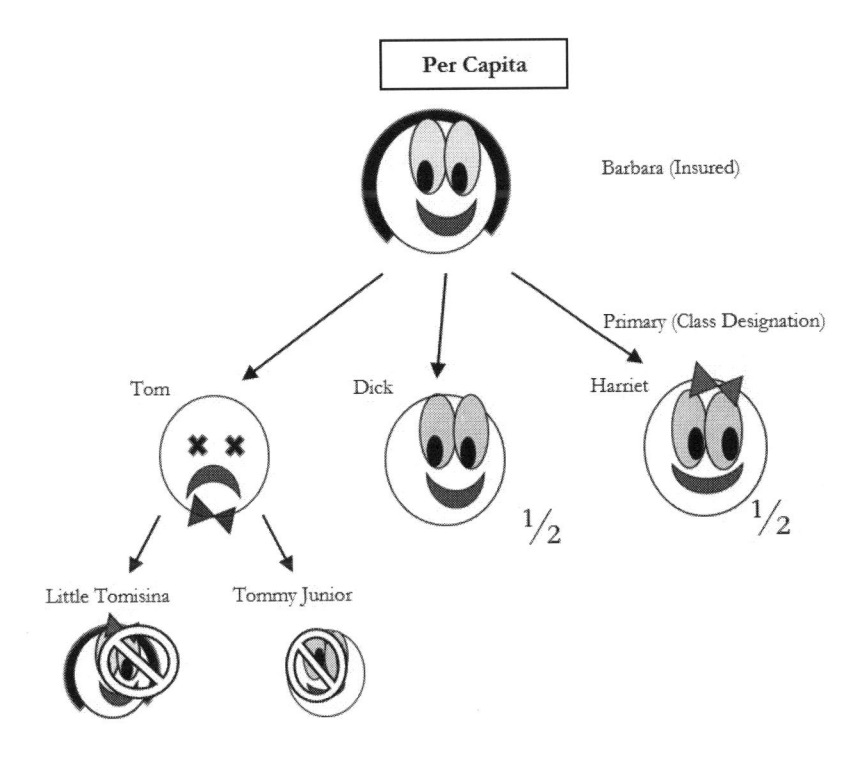

Under a **per stirpes** designation Tom's proceeds would pass to his heirs. The phrase per stirpes comes from the Latin meaning, **through the root**. When this designation is used, the company has been directed to distribute the deceased beneficiary's portion of the proceeds to his/her heirs in a descending order, according to the proximity of each heir's relationship to the deceased.

Per Stirpes

- Barbara (Insured)
- Primary (Class Designation)
- Tom
- Dick — 1/3
- Harriet — 1/3
- Little Tomisina — 1/6
- Tommy Junior — 1/6

THE SPENDTHRIFT CLAUSE

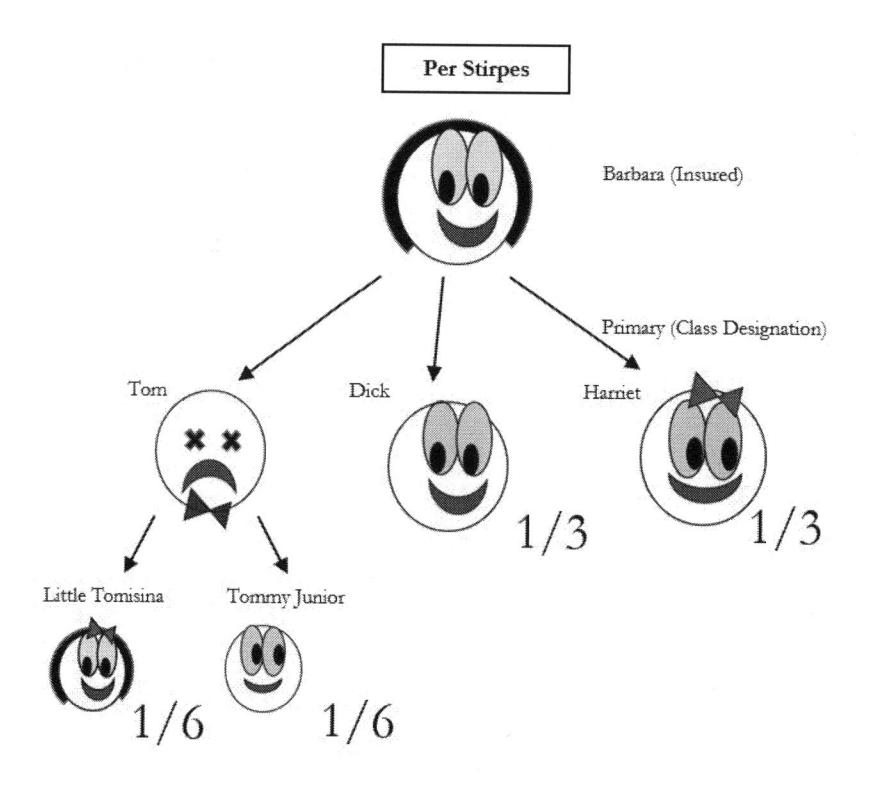

The spendthrift clause is a condition written into the policy that is designed to protect the proceeds from the beneficiary and from the creditors of the beneficiary.

When Barbara purchased her insurance policy, she named Dick as one of her beneficiaries. Dick has had several problems with multiple creditors. When Barbara dies, she has designated that Dick will receive interest only for the first 5 years. Afterwards, he will receive the balance. Dick's creditors cannot get to the principal during that first five years. They cannot attach it. Dick cannot assign it. Dick cannot even use it for collateral. Dick cannot access the principal until the first 5 years are past and neither can the creditors. The money is protected from Dick and his creditors.

PRIVILEGE OF CHANGE CLAUSE

This clause allows the owner to change the policy to another within the company for the same face amount. The general rule is that if the owner chooses to change to a policy with a lower premium, since the face amount is the same and the cost is less, the insured is asking the insurer to assume a greater risk. This would require proof of insurability. If the change went from a low to a higher premium product, the risk is lower and no health questions would be asked.

Chapter Review

Terms to Know

Required Provision

Entire Contract/Changes

Insuring Clause

Premium Mode

Incontestable Clause

Misstatement of Age and Sex

Grace Period

Reinstatement

Ownership

Assignment

Total Assignment

Partial Assignment

Time Limit on Lawsuits

Backdating

Application of State Law

Free Look Provision

Discretionary Provisions

Suicide Clause

Hazardous Occupation Clause

Rate Up

Primary Beneficiary

Contingent Beneficiary

Revocable Beneficiary

Irrevocable Beneficiary

Probate

Uniform Simultaneous Death Act

Per Capita

Per Stirpes

Spendthrift Clause

NUMBERS AND TIME PERIODS

2 years - Incontestable Clause

30 days - Grace Period

3 years - Reinstatement

3 years - Time Limit on Lawsuits

6 months - Backdating

10 days - Free Look Provision

2 years - Suicide Clause

SAMPLE QUESTIONS

1. If an insured commits suicide within the first 2 years of the policy, the insurance company:
   a) Pays the death benefit to the beneficiary
   b) Pays half of the death benefit to the beneficiary
   c) Returns the premiums paid to the insured's heirs
   d) Pays double the death benefit to the beneficiary

2. Once the insured's premium is due, the company gives the insured a ___ day grace period to make a payment.
   a) 30
   b) 31
   c) 20
   d) 10

3. Which of the following premium modes will charge the highest premium per year?
   a) Annually
   b) Monthly
   c) Quarterly
   d) Semi-Annually

4. If an insured lies about age on the application, the insurer will:
   a) Void the policy
   b) Cancel coverage
   c) Reinstate the policy
   d) Adjust the death benefit

5. All of the following are true about reinstatement EXCEPT:
   a) Reinstatement must be within 3 years
   b) Proof of insurability must be established
   c) Reinstatement must be within 5 years
   d) Back premiums must be paid

6. An application can be backdated up to:
    a) 6 months
    b) 12 months
    c) 3 months
    d) 1 month

7. The free look time period on life insurance is:
    a) 5 days
    b) 30 days
    c) 15 days
    d) 10 days

8. The irrevocable beneficiary designation means:
    a) The owner can change the beneficiary at any time
    b) The owner can only change the designation with the beneficiary's permission
    c) The beneficiary can change the designation at any time
    d) The agent can change the designation at any time

9. The estate may be the recipient of the death proceeds in all of the following situations EXCEPT:
    a) The estate could be listed as the beneficiary
    b) No beneficiary is listed on the application
    c) All listed beneficiaries have predeceased the insured
    d) The insured's trust is listed as the beneficiary

10. The per stirpes designation means:
    a) Equally distributing the benefit to surviving beneficiaries
    b) The benefit is paid through the root
    c) The designation cannot be changed
    d) The designation can be changed

Answers: 1.c 2.a 3.b 4.d 5.c 6.a 7.d 8.b 9.d 10.b

Chapter 5

Life Insurance Policy Options

Depending on the type of policy purchased, the policy holder may find themselves with some choices to make. This chapter will define the choices available to the policyholder.

The owner of the policy is the one with all the options. The owner is in control of the product. There are three primary sets of options that the owner of the policy may need to make a decision on. These options include:

- Dividend options
- Nonforfeiture options
- Settlement options

DIVIDEND OPTIONS

The dividend from a participating product is defined as a **return of premium**. The policyholder previously paid a premium to the insurance company in exchange for coverage. If the insurance company has a favorable experience throughout the year, the insurance company will not need as much of that premium as it expected earlier in the year. Thus, the company sends back to the insured a portion of the premium paid at the beginning of the year. The **gross premium** of the insurance contract is determined by three sources; risk, interest and expenses. The formula for the gross premium is:

Gross Premium = Risk − Interest + Expenses

When an insurance company has favorable experience in any of the above areas, then the company may declare a dividend. For example, if fewer people had claims than the company expected in the current year, the company may not need as much as it collected and as a result have a divisible surplus. If its investments are better than expected or its expenses are lower than anticipated a similar result could occur. Since the dividend is actually a return of the policy holders' premium and since this premium was paid with previously taxed money, **any dividend returned to the policy holder will not be taxed**.

Also, keep in mind that since dividends are based upon three areas that cannot be precisely predicted, **the agent cannot guarantee a dividend** will be paid in the future. Dividends can be projected, but never guaranteed.

John has the following participating life insurance policy. He has been receiving a steady dividend check of $100 per year. If John continues to receive this amount, in what ways can he choose to take his dividend?

John's Policy

- *Death Benefit - $100,000*
- *Cash Value - $20,000*
- *Premium - $1,000*
- *Dividend - $100*

What options does John have? In what ways can he take his dividend?

CASH

The first option that John has is to ask the insurance company to send him his dividend each year in the form of a check. **Each year the company declares a dividend, it will send him a check.** Since it is a return of premium, this amount will not be taxed.

REDUCTION OF PREMIUM

John owes the company a premium of $1,000. The company owes John a dividend check of $100. **John could request that the dividend be applied towards his premium**. This would then lower his premium obligation for that year. John would send the company a premium payment of $900.

ACCUMULATE AT INTEREST

If John chooses, he could ask the insurance company to hold the money for him and allow it to draw interest. Over time this could add up to a substantial amount of money.

The amount accumulated is over and above the cash value and the death benefit in the policy. It is a separate account. If John wants to use it in the future, all he needs to do is request it. **Since the interest on this money is newly made, it will be taxed the year it is earned.**

Paid—Up Additions

With this option, John chooses to take the dividend each year and spend it. **The company would then sell him a single premium paid up whole life policy in addition to the underlying policy.** This option would allow him to build up his death benefit over time without paying an additional premium. Building up his protection for the future may be John's primary concern. Each Paid – Up Addition is a separate permanent policy with cash value accumulation. Not only does it increase his death benefit over time, it would also enhance his total cash value.

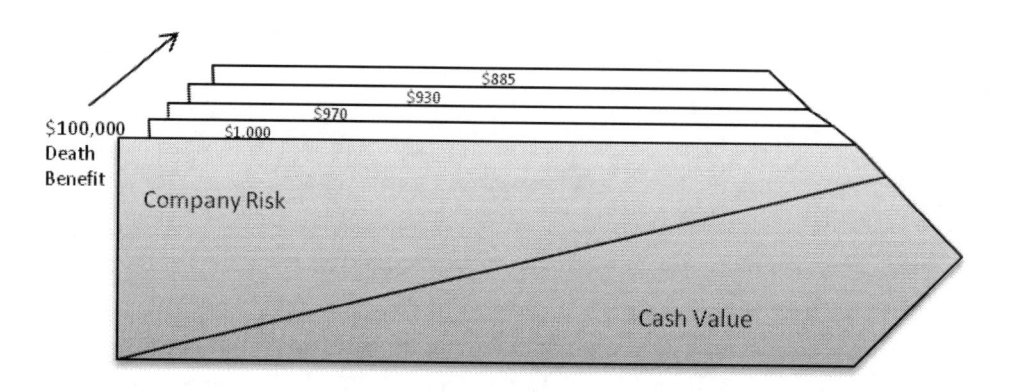

In the above example, John can take his $100 dividend and purchase an additional paid up benefit of $1,000. At this time, if John were to die, his beneficiary would receive $101,000. The second year, if John receives another dividend of $100, he would be able to add another paid up benefit. Notice that this benefit is only $970. Even though his dividend is the same, John is a year older. The risk is a little greater as John gets older. In other words, John purchases his dividend option at **attained age** rates.

ONE—YEAR TERM

Instead of purchasing permanent paid up policies, John could choose to use his dividend to purchase term insurance protection for one year. Each year that John receives a dividend, he will be able to purchase term protection for that year. The term protection will also be purchased at attained age rates. As the years go by, John's dividend will not be able to purchase as much, since he is getting older and the risk is increasing. This will maximize his coverage early.

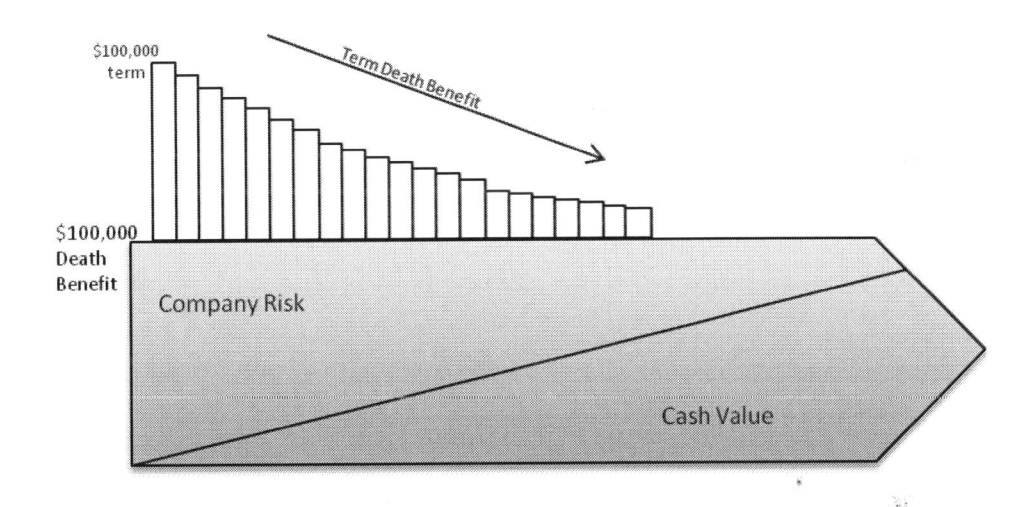

PAID—UP LIFE

If John had a Limited Pay product (20 pay life), he could take the $100 dividend and apply it to the back end of his payments. Instead of paying the policy off in 20 years, John may be able to pay it up earlier with the help of his dividends.

NONFORFEITURE OPTIONS

18 years after buying the policy, John decides his life insurance needs have changed. He no longer believes that he needs the same $100,000 protection that he has originally purchased. He has decided to cancel or forfeit his original policy. John also wishes to forfeit his $1,000 premium responsibilities. But **John does not want to forfeit his**

$20,800 equity that he has built up in his policy. In other words, John wants to choose a non-forfeiture option. The $20,800 cash value that John has built up in his policy is his equity. There are three ways that John could choose to receive his cash value. These are his non-forfeiture options.

John's Policy

- *Death Benefit - $100,000*

- *Cash Value - $20,800*

- *Premium - $1,000*

- *Dividend - $100*

CASH

The first option that John may choose is the cash option. If John chooses this option he is asking the company to end his policy and **send him a check for the full cash value** of the policy. In this example, the company would send him a check for $20,800.

Policy Year	Cash or Loan Value	Reduced Paid-up	Extended Term	
			Years	Days
1	$0	$0	0	0
2	$0	$0	0	0
3	$0	$0	0	0
4	$100	$400	1	
5	$600	$1,900	4	200
6	$1,500	$4,700	6	320
7	$3,000	$9,200	8	122
8	$5,200	$16,000	10	15
9	$7,000	$21,100	11	45
10	$8,200	$24,600	12	123
11	$10,000	$30,000	13	154
12	$12,000	$35,600	15	75
13	$13,400	$40,100	16	86
14	$14,800	$44,200	17	45
15	$16,200	$48,000	18	23
16	$17,300	$51,100	19	12
17	$19,700	$57,000	20	45
18	$20,800	$60,000	20	236
19	$22,400	$64,200	21	221
20	$24,000	$69,500	22	125
		Permanent Protection	Temporary Protection	

If John had an outstanding loan when he made this request, **the company must first settle the loan.** If the loan in the above example had a current balance of $5,000, the company would send John a check for the balance of $15,800.

REDUCED PAID-UP

Since the company is in the business of assuming risk, another option that the insurer would give John is the opportunity to **use his cash value to purchase a new reduced, but paid up life insurance policy.** Obviously, since John has not finished paying for the original death benefit, the accumulated cash value at this point would not be enough to purchase the full amount. The insurer would take the cash value John has accumulated and determine how much death benefit the current amount would be able to purchase. Once the new coverage has been purchased, no further payments need to be made.

John takes his $20,800 cash value and purchases a reduced paid up policy. Based upon his age and the amount of cash value, John can purchase $60,000 worth of death benefit. There will be **no health questions** asked when John chooses this option.

John might choose this option for many reasons. Perhaps his children are fully grown and he has little debt. John might now use the lesser benefit for his final expenses and know that he does not have to make any further payments for the rest of his life.

If there is an outstanding loan, it must first be dealt with before anything else is done. An outstanding loan would give John less money to use when purchasing a paid up policy. This results in a lower death benefit. If John had a $5,000 outstanding loan, he would pay it off first, leaving him only $15,800. Instead of receiving a $60,000 death benefit, he might only be able to purchase a $45,000 paid up policy.

Extended Term Insurance

The third option that John has is that he can take his $20,000 in cash value and use it to purchase term insurance. The insurance company would then take John's $20,800 and **purchase an amount of term equal to the original policy death benefit for as long as the $20,800 would pay for**. Perhaps this would purchase John $100,000 worth of coverage that would last him 20 years 236 days. For this time period, if John were to die, his beneficiaries would receive a full benefit. However, after the 20 years and 236 days, his beneficiaries will receive nothing upon his death; his insurance would expire.

Again, if there is a loan, John must first pay it off prior to purchasing the term. In this case, **the loan will affect John's coverage in two ways**. First, if the outstanding loan was $5,000, he will only be able to purchase a total amount of the original death benefit minus the outstanding loan. In this case, he would purchase a $95,000 death benefit. Secondly, the money used to purchase the death benefit would be a lesser amount ($15,800) that would pay for a shorter period of time.

The nonforfeiture option is **the choice of the owner**. If the owner refuses to make this choice and lets the policy lapse by not paying the premium, the choice will then pass to the company. In this case, **the company's automatic choice will be the third option, extended term**.

Reinstatement

It is possible that after an insured has dropped their coverage they may have second thoughts. It may be their desire to reinstate a policy that they have previously dropped. In order to qualify for a reinstatement, the company can require three things:

- Reinstatement must be within **3 years** of dropping the policy.

- The company can require the insured to pay all **past due premium paid plus interest**.

- The company can require that the insured **proof of insurability**.

If the three above points are satisfied, then the company will reinstate. One of the primary advantages of reinstating a policy versus buying a new one is that the reinstated policy will continue at the original age rate, as if it had never been dropped.

When reinstating the policy, the cash value that was taken out of the policy when it was cancelled will have to be paid back.

Settlement Options

When the insured dies, the policy matures. Upon maturity, the death benefit is owed to the insured's beneficiaries. How the benefits will be paid out will first be the choice of the owner. If the owner does not designate the option, prior to death, then the choice will pass to the beneficiary. Insurance companies offer several options in how the proceeds may be paid to the beneficiary.

Cash

The first and simplest option is cash. Under this option, upon maturity, the beneficiary would receive **one lump sum payment**. This death benefit is paid out income tax free. If there is an outstanding loan, it will be deducted from the death benefit.

Interest

The beneficiary could ask the insurance company to hold onto the principal amount and pay him or her interest only. This would provide a payment of indeterminate years since interest never reduces principal. The **interest paid is new money and thus will need**

to be taxed. Even though the principal is income tax fee, the interest will be taxed the year it is earned.

ANNUITY OPTIONS

The beneficiary could choose to use the proceeds of the policy to purchase a stream of income. The annuity options discussed in an earlier unit are now available as a settlement option.

Temporary Annuities

- Fixed Period or a Period Certain option would allow the beneficiary to receive an income based upon a fixed period of time. This option is temporary and could be outlived. If the primary concern is to cover a period of time, then this may be ideal.

- Fixed Amount or Amount Certain option would allow the beneficiary to receive an income based upon a fixed amount of money. If the primary concern is to provide a certain amount of income, then this may be ideal. This is also a temporary annuity and may be outlived.

Life Annuities

- Straight Life or Life only provides an income that cannot be outlived. This option has no minimum guarantee. It provides the highest monthly income, but assumes the greatest risk for the beneficiary.

- Life Annuity with Period Certain provides an income that cannot be outlived with a guarantee based upon a period of time. This monthly check will not be as large, but it will provide a minimum number of checks based upon the period of time that the beneficiary chooses.

- Refund Annuities also provide an income that an insured cannot outlive, but the minimum guarantee is based upon the amount that the insured purchased the annuity with.

- Joint and survivor Life Annuities pay a benefit based upon two or more life expectancies.

Living Benefit Options

The primary purpose of the life insurance product is the death benefit. But, the life insurance policy may have some benefits that can be taken advantage of while the insured is alive. A living benefit is any benefit that an owner can utilize while alive.

Cash Value

The cash value is a living benefit option the insured can utilize through the use of loans and nonforfeiture options.

Viatical Settlements

Since the life insurance policy is a contract, it is possible that it could be sold or exchanged. Since the owner of the policy has all the rights of the contract, the owner then could choose to sell the policy. Earlier it was stated that insurable interest only had to exist at the time of the sale. After the policy has been issued, the owner could sell the policy to an outside investor. An investor would purchase the policy in anticipation of collecting the death benefit upon the death of the insured. As the new owner, the investor could now change the beneficiary designation to themselves.

Once this is done, the product now becomes an investment. Since the owner no longer has an insurable interest and the primary motivation is a return on the invested funds, this becomes an income taxable product for the investor.

The question may be, why anyone would sell a death benefit to someone who does not have an insurable interest in seeing the insured live. If done properly, this could be a means of collecting a portion of the death benefit without having to die first. This would allow the insured to use the money in a way that could be beneficial to the situation.

Obviously, this is a situation that if not properly regulated could pose a danger to society or those in a position to be taken advantage of due to financial circumstances or limited life expectancies. Today, these transactions are highly regulated.

Accelerated Death Benefit

This benefit **allows the insured to collect all or part of the death benefit prior to death,** under certain defined circumstances. The benefit is an advance on the death benefit, not the cash value. As such, the government does **not consider it taxable income,** nor is it a loan. Any amount paid out to the insured will reduce the overall death benefit paid to the beneficiaries upon the insured's death.

Accelerated death benefits may be paid out as a result of:

- **Confinement in a nursing facility**

- **Diagnosis of a terminal condition**
- **Diagnosis of a dread disease**
- **Any reason approved by the state insurance commissioner**

Specific details concerning limitations and qualification rules would be spelled out in the contract. This option could be included in the policy or some companies may allow the agent to add it as a rider.

Chapter Review

Terms to Know

Dividend Options

Cash

Reduction of Premium

Accumulate at Interest

Paid-Up Additions

One-year Term

Paid-Up Life

Nonforfeiture Options

Cash

Reduced Paid-Up

Extended Term

Reinstatement

Settlement Options

Cash

Interest

Annuity Options

Temporary Annuities

Life Annuities

Living Benefit Options

Cash Value

Viatical Settlements

Accelerated Death Benefit

Numbers and Time Periods

3 years - Reinstatement

SAMPLE QUESTIONS

1. Which of the following dividend options allows the dividend to accumulate in a separate account?

    a) Cash
    b) Reduction of Premium
    c) Accumulate at Interest
    d) One-Year Term

2. Which dividend option allows the insured to purchase smaller whole life policies over and above the original?

    a) Reduction of Premium
    b) Paid-Up Additions
    c) Paid-Up Life
    d) Reduced Paid Up

3. John would like to maximize his death benefit, without increasing his annual premium. He is more interested in receiving the death benefit early, while his children are home, than later. Which option would you recommend?

    a) Reduced paid up
    b) Extended term
    c) Paid up additions
    d) One year term

4. Which nonforfeiture option allows the insured to purchase a permanent policy with the cash value, but with a lesser death benefit amount?

    a) Reduction of Premium
    b) Extended Term
    c) Paid Up Insurance
    d) Reduced Paid-Up

5. Which nonforfeiture option allows the insured to use the cash value to purchase a death benefit of the same value as the original policy?

    a) Extended Term
    b) One-Year Term
    c) Paid-Up Life
    d) Term

6. John has a whole life policy. He did not pay his premium when it came due. What will happen to John's policy?

   a) It will lapse

   b) The premium obligation will be paid out of the cash value and coverage will continue

   c) After 30 days if the premium has still not been paid, it will go on extended term

   d) It will go through a 30 day grace period, and then lapse

7. Which of the following is NOT a settlement option?

   a) Cash

   b) Interest

   c) Annuities

   d) Reduction of Premium

8. Which of the following is NOT a reason accelerated death benefits may be paid out?

   a) Confinement in a nursing facility

   b) Diagnosis of a terminal condition

   c) The insured needs the money to buy a new car

   d) Diagnosis of a dread disease

Answers: 1.c 2.b 3.d 4.d 5.a 6.c 7.d 8.c

Chapter 6

Life Insurance Policy Riders

*A rider or an endorsement is simply defined as a **change** in a policy. Sometimes a change increases coverage, sometimes the change decreases coverage and sometimes the change is neutral.*

When the agent discusses coverage with an applicant, the applicant may desire to change or enhance coverage by including one or several optional riders on the policy. These riders are typically included in the policy at the time of the sale and most will require an additional cost to the insured. This unit will explain some of the more common riders available to the insured and how they will benefit the insured.

MULTIPLE INDEMNITY/ACCIDENTAL DEATH RIDER

The multiple indemnity rider increases the death benefit, if the insured dies as a result of an accident. The most common multiple indemnity rider is **double indemnity**. Double indemnity states that if the insured died as a result of an accident, the policy would double its death benefit. If the death is not a result of an accident, the policy would only pay the face amount.

Joe bought a $100,000 life insurance policy with a double indemnity rider attached and had a $20,000 loan on the policy prior to death. If Joe died due to an accident, how much would the policy pay? It would pay a benefit of $180,000. The $20,000 loan comes off the base death benefit only. The extra $100,000 paid for the accident is paid in full and has nothing to do with the loan.

Since Joe has enhanced his coverage, he is paying an extra amount above his base premium amount. **This additional premium amount does not enhance his cash value** growth. The premium paid for the rider is applied only toward the extra protection provided by this rider.

In order to qualify for this benefit, the definition of an accident could be very important. The term "accident" could be defined differently by different companies. Some companies are more restrictive than others when it comes to defining an accident. An insured may be involved in an accident and die days later due to complications from the accident. The insured does not have to die immediately. Many companies will allow the death to occur within a specified period of time of the accident. A common time period is three to six months, but varies by company.

GUARANTEED INSURABILITY RIDER

The guaranteed insurability rider **allows the insured to purchase additional amounts of insurance at predetermined times without proving insurability**. As the purchase options become available (typically every 3 or 5 years), the insured has a limited amount of time to take advantage of the option. The time frame varies from company to company, but usually is around 30 or 60 days. Once the time period ends, that option is no longer available, the insured has to wait another 3 to 5 years for the next option. When an option is chosen, the insured purchases the additional protection based upon **attained age rates**.

This rider is commonly included in a juvenile policy. As children get older and go through life changes (marriage, homeownership, children, etc.), their insurance needs change. This rider guarantees that regardless of future health issues, this person will be able to purchase additional insurance protection without having to worry about insurability.

For reasons such as marriage and the birth of a child, some companies allow the insured to exercise an option early. In this scenario, the company does not give the insured an additional option, only the opportunity to exercise an upcoming option early.

Chet has a $20,000 policy with a guaranteed insurability rider of $20,000. Chet will get the option to increase his coverage every 3 years beginning at age 25. At age 25 he chooses to take full advantage of his option, increasing his total death benefit to $40,000. At age 26, Chet meets and marries his perfect match. Because his policy has a marriage provision, he will be allowed to take his next option early. Chet decides to increase his coverage another $10,000. His benefit is now up to $50,000. The extra $10,000 that he chooses not to take will not be available to him in the future. At age 31, Chet does not feel the need to increase his benefit, so he waives his option to increase his death benefit. But when Chet turns 32, he finds out that he is going to be a father. He also finds that he has a serious heart condition. Since his policy has a stork provision, he chooses to exercise his coming option early. He also knows that the company will not ask or charge him for his heart condition. At this point, Chet has $70,000 worth of death benefit.

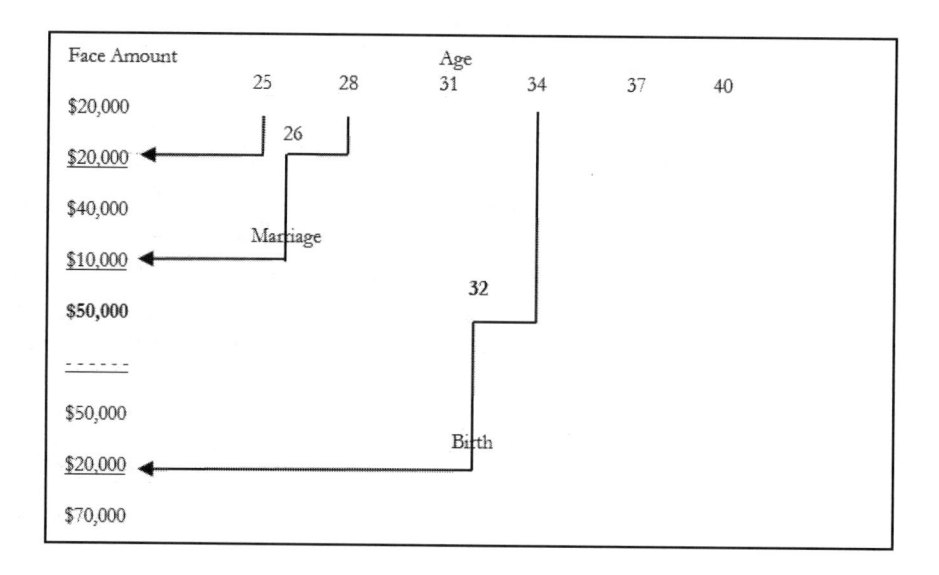

```
Face Amount                    Age
                 25      28    31      34      37      40
$20,000
                         26
$20,000 ◄────────┐ │
                 │ │
$40,000          │ │
              Marriage
$10,000 ◄────────┘
$50,000
- - - - -
                                32
$50,000
                              Birth
$20,000 ◄──────────────────────┘
$70,000
```

Cost of Living Rider

This rider is designed to keep the coverage or protection relevant to the ever changing cost of living. With this rider the death benefit will increase each year based upon a pre determined percentage. It is intended to keep pace with inflation, the changing cost of final expenses and needs of the insured.

Term Riders

Term insurance can be sold as a rider to a permanent policy. This allows an insured to meet both temporary and permanent needs in one policy. Riders can be level, decreasing or increasing term.

The increasing term rider can be used to provide for a return of premium. In this case, the rider's death benefit is designed to match the amount of premium paid into the policy.

Waiver of Premium Rider

To waive means to voluntarily give up or to relinquish a right. Waiver of premium is when **the insurance company voluntarily waives its right to collect the insured's premiums due to the insured's disability**. The policy may have a period of time that the insured must be disabled before the waiver of premium benefit takes over. This period may be 30, 60, or 90 days. Once the insured has met the policy definition of disability for the stated number of days, the company will take over the premium obligation as it comes due for as long as the insured is disabled. Qualification for this benefit may be limited by age.

Under the Universal Life policy, instead of waiving the premium (which is the amount paid into the policy), the company would waive the cost of protection. This is the cost that is deducted from the cash value account to cover the risk assumed by the company. This would protect the policy from lapsing. It would not contribute to the buildup of additional cash value.

Disability Income Rider

Disability is sometimes referred to as a living death. Like life insurance, the family has lost the income producing ability of the breadwinner. Because disability addresses a similar need of the breadwinner, the disability benefit could be offered as a rider to the life insurance policy. This rider would replace an income if the insured became disabled.

Payor Benefit Rider

The payor benefit rider is a **waiver of premium on the payor** instead of the insured. This is typically included on a juvenile policy. On a juvenile policy the insured is the child. But, it is the parent who is responsible for the payment of the premium. If the payor becomes **disabled** or **dies**, the policy could be in jeopardy. The payor rider would maintain the premium obligation until the child reaches a certain age (typically 21 or 25). At this time the insured would be responsible for future payment obligations.

Accelerated Death Benefit Rider

This benefit **allows the insured to collect all or part of the death benefit prior to death** under certain defined circumstances. The benefit is an advance on the death benefit, not the cash value. As such, the government does **not consider it taxable**

income nor is it a loan. Any amount paid to the insured will reduce the overall death benefit paid out at death.

Accelerated death benefits may be paid out as a result of;

- **Confinement in a nursing facility**
- **Diagnosis of a terminal condition**
- **Diagnosis of a dread disease**
- **Any other reason approved by the Commissioner or Director**

Specific details concerning limitations and qualification rules would be spelled out in the contract. This option could be included in the policy or some companies may allow the agent to add it as a rider.

Automatic Premium Loan Rider

This rider is designed to maintain the policy by making the premium payment out of the cash value account. If the insured chooses this option, usually without an extra premium obligation, when the policy comes due and the grace period expires without payment, the **company will deduct the premium payment from the cash value account**. This deduction then becomes a loan on the policy and as such **will charge interest** as any other loan on the policy would.

Chapter Review

Terms to know

Rider

Multiple Indemnity/Accidental Death Rider

Guaranteed Insurability Rider

Cost of Living Rider

Term Rider

Waiver of Premium Rider

Disability Income Rider

Payor Benefit Rider

Accelerated Death Benefit Rider

Automatic Premium Loan Rider

SAMPLE QUESTIONS

1. Which of the following riders pays double indemnity if the insured dies due to an accident?
   a) Payor Rider
   b) Accelerated Death Benefit Rider
   c) Multiple Indemnity   make whole (x)
   d) Viatical Settlement

2. The guaranteed insurability rider allows the insured:
   a) To purchase additional amounts of insurance at certain times without proving insurability
   b) To convert from term to permanent
   c) To convert from permanent to term
   d) To increase the death benefit as cost of living increases

3. If an insured becomes disabled, which rider allows the premium to be waived?
   a) Guaranteed Insurability Rider
   b) Waiver of Premium Rider
   c) Cost of Living Rider
   d) Term Rider

4. Which rider would typically be included on a juvenile policy?
   a) Accelerated Death Benefit Rider
   b) Term Rider
   c) Waiver of Premium Rider
   d) Payor Benefit Rider

5. Which rider allows the premium to be paid out of the cash value account if the premium is past due?
   a) Automatic Premium Loan Rider
   b) Payor Benefit Rider
   c) Accelerated Death Benefit Rider
   d) Guaranteed Insurability Rider

6. Joe has a $100,000 policy with double indemnity. Prior to an accidental death, Joey had borrowed $10,000. How much will Joey's beneficiaries receive?

   a) $90,000

   b) $180,000

   c) $190,000

   d) $200,000

Answers: 1.c 2.a 3.b 4.d 5.a 6.c

Chapter 7

Business Uses of Life Insurance

A life insurance policy can be used to protect the interest of a business. When a business loses a key employee, the businesses suffers. As a result, businesses have an insurable interest in certain employees and can purchase and own insurance on those employees to protect their interest.

There are several different ways in which a business can use a life insurance policy to protect its interest. The following are a few situations where life insurance could be appropriate.

KEY EMPLOYEE LIFE POLICIES

A key employee is any employee that would impact the business in a financial way if this individual died prematurely. This person could be an owner, partner, sales person or any number of positions of importance to the business. This means that the business has an insurable interest in the key person. The purpose of the key employee insurance is to protect the business from the financial loss that results from the key employee's death. This means that the business is the owner and beneficiary of the plan, while the employee is the insured. Since the employee is the insured and the business is the owner, the employee would first have to give consent in order for the business to purchase coverage on the employee's life.

BUY SELL AGREEMENT

Another situation that may arise in a business environment is the death of an owner. When an owner dies, their ownership share of the business comes into question. Without a pre-arranged agreement, his/her ownership would pass to the heirs of the deceased owner. This may not be an ideal situation for the business or other owners within the business. The business could now find itself being operated by someone with little experience, knowledge or motivation. The buy-sell agreement helps deal with this situation.

The buy-sell agreement is a contract that defines how this problem will be dealt with at the owner's death. The buy-sell agreement establishes two different issues. **First, it states that if an owner dies prematurely their portion of the business will be bought out for a pre-arranged price.** This price is usually established in advance, based upon a formula that reflects the ever changing value of a business. **Second it states that the deceased owners heirs will sell their ownership for the agreed upon value.** The end result is that the heirs receive the financial value of the business and the business can continue without dealing with an inexperienced owner.

Life insurance is used to fund the agreement. At the time of death, money must be immediately available to buy out the heirs. This is best done by having a life insurance policy on the owner, equal to the value of their share of the business.

There are two different buy-sell arrangements that can be established by the owners.

- Stock purchase or entity plan
- Cross purchase plan

The stock purchase plan allows the corporation to buy out the shares of the deceased owner. Once the shares are bought out, they can then be retired. The remaining stock holders would then have control of the company according to the percentage of outstanding shares owned. In this case, **the company (entity) would own the life insurance on the owner.** The entity would then use the proceeds to fund this purchase.

Stock Redemption or Entity Plan

Outstanding Shares Owned **Prior to Death**
1/3   1/3   1/3

Outstanding Shares **after Death**

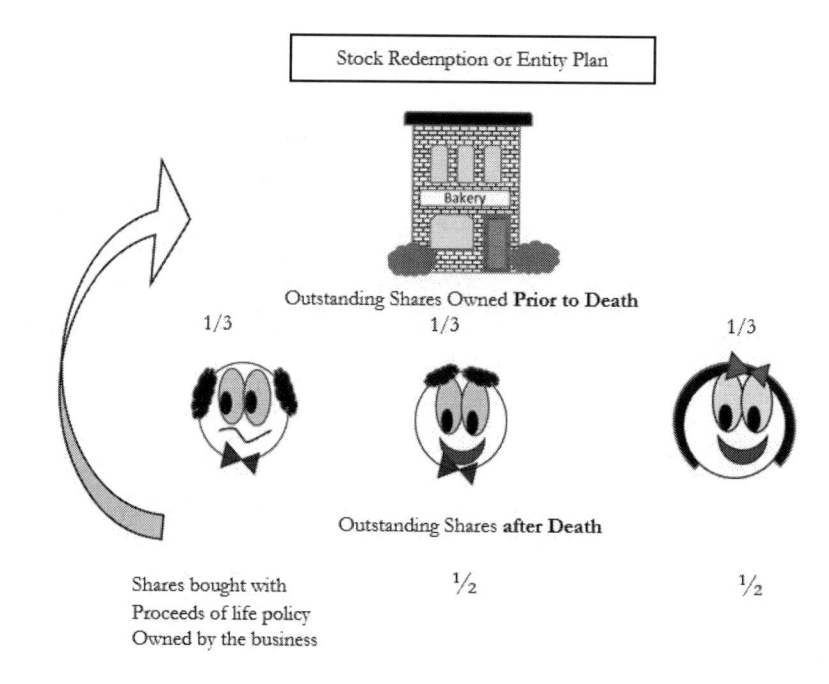

Shares bought with
Proceeds of life policy
Owned by the business

½   ½

In the cross purchase plan the owners **each own a life insurance on each of the other owners.** At the time of death, the surviving owners use the proceeds from the life insurance policy to buy out the heirs of the deceased owner.

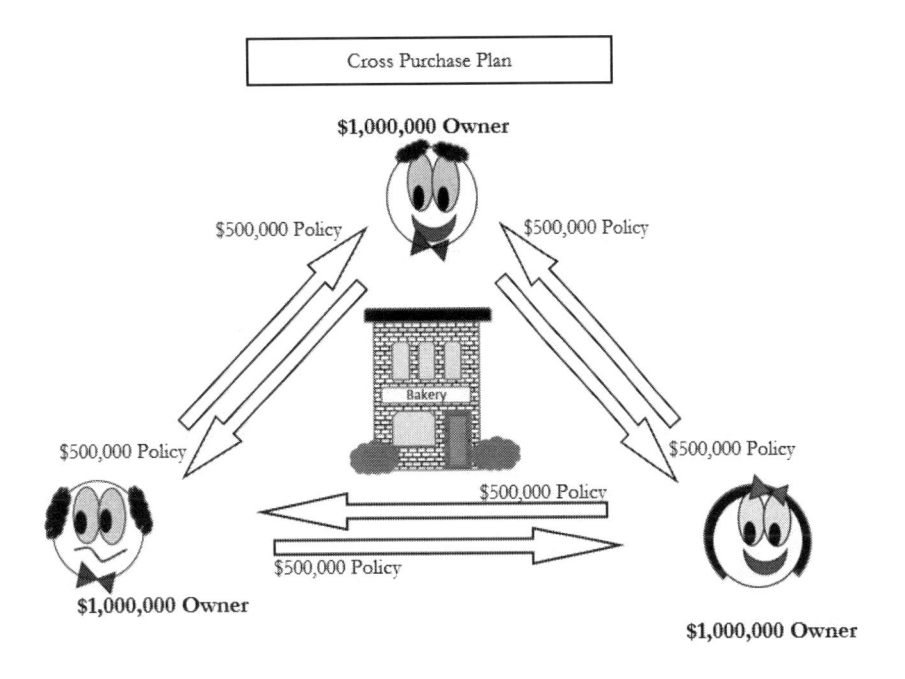

The face amount of each policy will be equal to the amount that the surviving owner would need to fund their obligation in buying out the heir. If there are three partners, each partner would need a policy on each of the other partners. This means that with three partners, six policies would need to be provided. If there were four partners, then each partner (four) would buy one policy on each of the other owners (three) for a total of twelve policies.

SPLIT DOLLAR PLANS

A split dollar plan is a method used to purchase permanent insurance by an employer and employee. The permanent policy is a policy purchased on the life of the employee. It is funded by both the employer and the employee. The employer usually pays an amount equal to the cash value growth within the policy. This means that the employee will pay a higher amount in the early years but as the years pass, the cash value becomes a larger portion of the premium. The death benefit is usually based on the proportion of the premium paid by each party.

Usually the employer is the owner of the policy and has control of the cash value. This creates an inexpensive way for the employee to purchase insurance while giving the employer protection against the premature death of a key employee.

Chapter Review

TERMS TO KNOW

Business Uses of Life Insurance

Key Employee Life Policy

Buy Sell Agreement

Stock Purchase Plan

Cross Purchase Plan

Split Dollar Plan

Sample Questions

1. If a business has 4 owners, how many policies will be sold in a cross purchase plan?
   a) 8
   b) 4
   c) 16
   d) 12

2. The policy owner of the stock purchase plan is:
   a) The business entity
   b) The key employee
   c) The employer
   d) The individual owners

3. Which of the following is false concerning a key employee life policy?
   a) The key employee must give consent
   b) The business has insurable interest in the key employee
   c) The key employee does not give consent
   d) The policy protects the business in the event the key employee dies.

4. A split dollar plan is:
   a) A buy sell agreement
   b) A policy funded by both the employer and employee
   c) A policy used to purchase a deceased owner's interest
   d) Both a & b

Answers: 1.d 2.a 3.c 4.b

Chapter 8

Qualified Retirement Plans

Saving for the future can be a real challenge when people are overwhelmed with current financial obligation. The government feels that saving for our future is important to our society. For this reason, several different retirement plans have been established that encourage saving, assist with discipline and discourage the misuse of retirement money.

Retirement plans come in many different types with a variety of characteristics. In this chapter we will answer; what is a qualified retirement plan? How will each product differ from one another?

QUALIFIED VERSUS NONQUALIFIED PLANS

A qualified plan is **defined by the Internal Revenue Service**. The IRS establishes funding limitations, participation requirements and tax advantages for each plan. Whereas a qualified plan is typically established through an employer and qualifies for specific tax advantages, a nonqualified plan does not enjoy the same tax advantages.

CHARACTERISTICS OF QUALIFIED PLANS

The qualified plan is a plan that is established through an employer. One reason that an employer may be interested in establishing a plan is for personal benefit. In order for an employer to establish a qualified plan, the employer will be required to maintain certain non-discrimination, vesting, and participation rules. Most of these rules are designed to protect the rank and file employee.

Non-discrimination rules require the employer to include all eligible employees in the plan on a fair and equal basis. The opportunity to participate and who can participate will be defined for each plan by the IRS.

The word **vesting means ownership**. Vesting rules define when the employee owns the money that has been set aside in the retirement account. Any money contributed by the employee into the account is always 100% vested from the moment it is deposited into the account. Money that the employer contributes may be vested immediately or after a set period of time, based upon a set schedule approved by the IRS.

Participation rules define who can participate. Each plan will define when the employee will be able to participate and who can participate.

Tax Treatment

One of the primary advantages of the qualified plan is the tax treatment of the contributions made. Some of these advantages of include:

- **Tax deductible business** expense

- **Tax deferred contributions** for the employee

- Typically **tax deferred growth** for the employee

Tax advantages are provided to encourage people to save for retirement. The IRS will also discourage people from using the money for reasons other than retirement by setting penalties for early withdrawal. **If funds are withdrawn prior to age 59 ½, the amount withdrawn will typically be penalized by 10%.** Not only will the amount withdrawn be penalized, **it will also be taxed the year it is withdrawn**. There are a few exceptions to the 59 ½ rule. **Typical exceptions for early withdrawal include death, disability, divorce, etc.**

The IRS allows the individual to delay paying taxes, in order to encourage them to save for retirement. But, the IRS does want the money withdrawn at some point. **Most plans require that the individual begin making minimum distributions the year after the individual turns 70 ½.** At this point, the money will be taxed as it is withdrawn.

Defined Contribution Plans versus Defined Benefit Plans

Two common types of qualified plans would include the defined contribution plan and the defined benefit plan. Each of the plans has distinct advantages and disadvantages.

Defined Benefit Plans

Defined benefit plans define the benefit the employee will receive upon retirement. The amount that an employee qualifies for is typically based upon a formula established by the employer based upon factors like years of employment, position achieved, and salary status prior to retirement.

This plan is a more expensive option for the employer. The employer must review the status of the employees year by year. A determination must be made to determine if the employer is prepared to meet their financial obligation of retiring employees. The advantage of the plan is to reward loyalty and good performance.

Defined Contribution Plans

The defined contribution plan establishes (defines) the amount that is being contributed into the plan. The end result will not be known until it is time to use the plan. Contributions are made each year prior to retirement for each employee. When the employee retires, the lump sum accumulated will be available to the employee to be used for their retirement. After retirement, the employer has no further or ongoing responsibility to the employee. The employee would then be responsible for determining how the lump sum should be used for their retirement.

This plan is easier and less expensive to maintain for the employer. The employee has full control over the use of the retirement fund.

Common Types of Qualified Retirement Plans

401k Plans

401k plans are referred to as **deferred compensation plans**. This plan allows employees to defer a portion of their paychecks into the retirement account. This is sometimes referred to as a **CODA**, cash or deferred arrangement. The employee has the option to take a full pay check each week (cash), or defer a portion of each check into a retirement account. It is common, although not required, for an employer to match the employee's contribution. The employer determines how much the match will be. Examples of a match could be dollar for dollar or fifty cents for each dollar contributed.

Money from the employee is 100% immediately vested and does not have to be included as income. Any money in the account will grow tax deferred. Employer contributions may be subject to a vesting schedule.

403b Plans

A 403b plan is very similar to the 401k. Both plans are **deferred compensation plans** or **CODA's**. Both may have an employer match. They are each subject to the same contribution rules. The main difference between the two plans is who they were established for. The 403b plan was established for the **nonprofit organizations (501C corporations)** and people who work for them. These are commonly used by teachers, churches, hospitals and other nonprofit organizations.

Keogh (HR-10)

What makes the Keogh plan unique, is that it is a retirement plan specifically for the **self-employed** individual and those who work for the self-employed. This plan is used by farmers, doctors, lawyers, and other professionals. The Keogh plan is fully funded by the self-employed individual. Unlike the previous plans, it is not a deferred compensation plan. The Keogh can be sold as a defined contribution plan or a defined benefit plan.

The funds in the Keogh accumulate tax deferred and the amount contributed is deductible. The Keogh is subject to IRS penalties for early withdrawal at 59 ½. Vesting schedules and discrimination rules apply.

Simplified Employee Pension (SEP) Plans

The SEP is designed for the **small business owner** and for the self-employed. It is a simplified plan because **it establishes separate individual retirement accounts (IRA's)** for each employee, under the employee's name and ownership. By setting up separate accounts this gave the control of the funds to the employee in the plan. This means that the **funds are immediately vested** and that the employee will have the full responsibility of choosing investment strategy and tracking the results. This takes much time and responsibility away from the employer, making this plan simpler to create and track.

The SEP is designed specifically for the small business. It is funded by the employer and must meet nondiscriminatory rules. The funds are not included as income and grow tax deferred. It is 100% vested from day one and is not subject to a vesting schedule.

SIMPLE Retirement Plans

The SIMPLE plans are also designed for small employers. The IRS defines the small employer to be a business of less than 100 employees. Like the SEP, this plan establishes separate IRA accounts for the retirement money to be deposited into. This plan is a simplified CODA. An employer match is included with certain limits.

Individual Retirement Accounts (IRA's)

The IRAs are qualified retirement accounts set up independently of an employer. These accounts are **maintained and established by the individual**. **Anyone with an earned income can establish an IRA.** The tax advantages may be limited due to income. There are two different types of IRA's, the traditional IRA and the Roth IRA.

Traditional IRA

This IRA is very similar to the previously discussed retirement plans. The funds going into the plan may be deductible, the plan grows tax deferred, it is subject to early withdrawal penalties and withdrawals must begin the year after the owner turns 70 ½. The primary difference is that it is set up by the individual and is maintained by the individual.

The deductibility of the contribution is dependent on a few factors. First, if the individual does not have a qualified retirement plan through their employer they will be allowed to deduct the amount contributed into the plan the year it is contributed. But, if the individual does have a qualified plan through their employer, then they may or may not be able to deduct the contribution. The deduction depends upon the adjusted earned income of the participant. There are three scenarios that the participant could fall in:

- If their adjusted gross income is **less** than the IRA designated amount for that year and they are eligible for an employer sponsored retirement plan, then they may contribute the full amount for that year and deduct the whole contribution.

- If their adjusted gross income is **more** than the IRA designated amount for that year and they are eligible for an employer sponsored retirement plan, then they may contribute the full amount for that year but they will not be able to deduct the contribution. It will still grow tax deferred.

- If their adjusted gross income falls **in between** the minimum IRA designated amount and the maximum designated amount then the participant will be eligible for a partial deduction on the amount contributed. Earnings always grow tax deferred.

ROTH IRA

The tax advantages of the Roth IRA are considerably different than the other qualified retirement plans. Under this plan the **contributions to the plan will be taxed**. The Roth participant does not get a tax advantage on the money contributed into the plan. The real advantage to this plan is the growth. Instead of being tax deferred, **the growth of the Roth is tax free.** When the money is withdrawn under the other traditional concepts, the funds will be taxed. But the Roth will not tax any of the growth. So, when this money is withdrawn, the participant can receive their funds tax free.

To make tax free withdrawals the owner must be at least 59 ½ and have owned the account for at least 5 years. The contribution limits for the Roth will be the same as the traditional. The Roth will also penalize you for early withdrawal except for certain exceptions.

2017 PLAN LIMITATIONS

Most of the limits regulated by the IRS are indexed based upon inflation. As a result, many of these numbers and amounts will change from year to year. The following are some of the 2016 numbers.

401k	• Contribution Limit - $18,000 • CODA • Catch up over 50 - $6,000
403b	• Contribution Limit - $18,000 • CODA • Catch up over 50 - $6,000
Keogh	• Self employed and employees • Employer funded
SEP	• Small Business plan • Individual retirement account
SIMPLE	Contribution limit - $12,500 Catch up over 50 - $3,000
Traditional & Roth IRA	Contribution limit - $5,500 Catch up over 50 - $1,000 Tax deferred on traditional, tax free growth for Roth

Plan Roll-Overs

A tax free rollover allows an employee to move money from an employer sponsored retirement fund into an IRA. This may be important to an employee who may be leaving a current employer. By rolling the money over to an IRA, the employee is taking control of their retirement funds. When rolling the money over properly, the employee should be able to avoid all tax penalties.

The IRS allows an employee to transfer funds from one account to another without penalty or consequence, as long as the transfer is made within **60** days. If the employee requests the funds from the qualified retirement account, the employee must move the full amount into an IRA within the 60 day time period or the funds will be taxed. The 10% penalty could also apply if under age 59 ½.

If the funds are requested from an employer sponsored plan, **the company would be required to send 20% to the IRS** and then sending the balance to the individual. Regardless, the individual is still responsible for depositing 100% of the requested funds into the IRA or be subject to the tax consequences on any amount not deposited in the IRA.

Joe leaves his place of employment and decides to move his $100,000 retirement fund to an IRA. He requests that the funds be sent to him. He intends to deposit the whole amount into an IRA he has just opened for this reason. The company sends $20,000 to the IRS. Joe receives a check for $80,000. Joe must deposit $100,000 into the IRA. If not, he will pay taxes on the $20,000. Since he is under age 59 ½, he will also be penalized 10%.

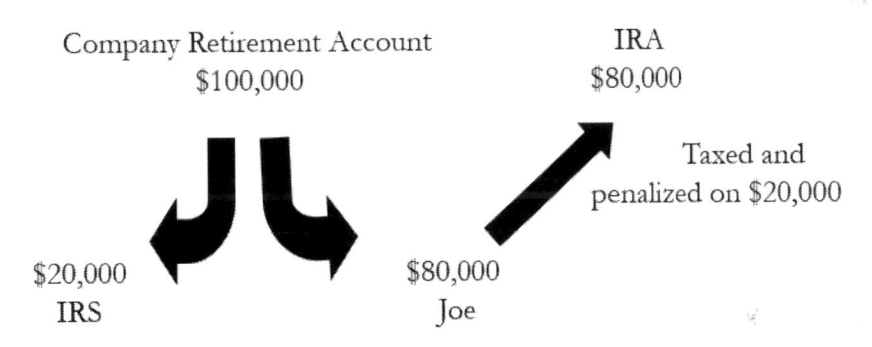

```
    Company Retirement Account              IRA
           $100,000                        $80,000
                                              ↑
              ↙  ↘                    Taxed and
                                  penalized on $20,000
      $20,000        $80,000
        IRS            Joe
```

The above situation could be avoided if Joe makes a **direct transfer**. In this case Joe requests the first company to send the requested funds directly to the IRA. If Joe is not sent the money directly, then the IRS will allow the company to send the whole $100,000 to the IRA.

Chapter Review

TERMS TO KNOW

Qualified

Nonqualified

Vesting

Tax Deductible

Tax Deferred Contributions

Tax Deferred Growth

Defined Benefit Plan

Defined Contribution Plan

401k

CODA

403b

Keogh

Simplified Employee Pension Plan

SIMPLE Retirement Plan

Individual Retirement Account (IRA)

Traditional IRA

Roth IRA

Plan Roll Over

Direct Transfer

NUMBERS AND TIME PERIODS

59 ½ - IRS age for retirement

10% - IRS penalty

70 ½ - Required Minimum Distributions

100% vested - Employee contributions

403b established for non-profits (501C)

100 employees - SIMPLE

60 days - Transfer

20% - Deleted for rollovers

SAMPLE QUESTIONS

1. Which of the following is NOT an advantage of a qualified plan?
    a) Tax deductible business expense
    b) Tax deferred contributions for the employee
    c) Tax deferred growth for the employee
    d) Qualified plans have no tax advantages

2. Which type of retirement plan is specifically for the self-employed?
    a) Keogh
    b) SIMPLE
    c) 403b
    d) 401k

3. Which type of retirement plan was established for nonprofit organizations?
    a) Keogh
    b) 401k
    c) 403b
    d) SEP

4. Which type of retirement plan is designed for small business owners?
    a) 403b
    b) SEP
    c) Roth IRA
    d) 401k

5. Which type of retirement plan allows for tax free growth?
    a) Roth IRA
    b) Traditional IRA
    c) SEP
    d) 403b

6. The IRS allows an employee to transfer funds from one account to another without penalty if the transfer is made within how many days?

   a) 45
   b) 60
   c) 90
   d) 30

Answers: 1.d 2.a 3.c 4.b 5.a 6.b

Chapter 9

Group Life Insurance

In addition to being sold as an individual product, life insurance can also be sold on a group basis. Purchasing life insurance through a group has many advantages. Group life insurance makes coverage available to those individuals who may not qualify otherwise. In group insurance, employers participate in the funding of the plan which makes the insurance easy to obtain and more affordable for employees.

Group insurance has many unique characteristics. It is defined as one policy written on several individuals. The following chapter will look at the concepts and characteristics unique to the group concept. These include the policy itself, underwriting, eligible groups and conversion privileges.

GROUP LIFE CONCEPTS

The most common type of group insurance sold is the employer/employee group. In this situation, the employer chooses the product that will be available to its employees. The most common product used in group insurance is annually renewable term. Annually renewable term makes the most sense to the employer since it provides adequate coverage while the employee is employed, at the most reasonable cost to the employer.

ELIGIBLE GROUPS

In order for a group to be eligible to purchase group insurance, it must be formed for a reason other than with the intent to buy insurance. Insurance must be incidental to the group. This concept helps protect the insurer from adverse selection. The insurance company is looking for a natural group. Natural groups can be formed for many reasons.

Single Employers – Single employer groups are one of the most common groups purchasing insurance.

Labor Union – Under certain circumstances, members of labor unions may be able to purchase group life insurance through the union.

Associations – For an association to offer group coverage it must have a minimum of 100 members and be established for a purpose other than to buy insurance.

Credit Unions – Credit unions can offer credit insurance to their members as a group product.

Creditors (Credit Life Insurance) – Credit life is a form of group used to cover loans. The creditor is the owner and beneficiary. The debtor pays the premium. The death benefit is used to pay off the loan in the event of the debtor's death. The creditor can only collect up to its insurable interest, the amount owed on the loan.

Multiple Employer Trusts (METs) – A MET is a group of **small employers** from a common industry, coming together and **purchasing insurance** through a trust. Earlier we said that purchasing insurance must be an incidental reason for the formation of the group. In this case, the group's common bond is being a part of the same industry. This allows small employers to come together and to create a group large enough to negotiate a better policy.

Multiple Employer Welfare Arrangement (MEWA) – A MEWA is similar to a MET. The main difference is that after a MEWA is formed, the group **self-insures** instead of purchase insurance. By coming together, the employers are able to form a group large enough to have the capability of insuring themselves.

THE GROUP CONTRACT

In group insurance there is only one policy issued. The contract is an agreement between the insurer and the employer. The employer holds the policy; the policy is referred to as the **master policy**.

Since the policy is issued to the employer, each employee receives a document stating proof of coverage. The employee's proof of coverage comes in the form of an **individual certificate of insurance**.

GROUP UNDERWRITING

Underwriting is the process of gathering information to evaluate the risk to be assumed, processing and categorizing that risk, and then placing a price on the risk if it is to be assumed. One of the primary responsibilities of the underwriter is to avoid adverse selection. Adverse selection is an unhealthy mix of risk. In group, health questions are not asked. The insurance company must use other tools to avoid adverse selection.

The **group risk selection** process is different than that of the individual product. In group, the insurer is looking at the group as one complete unit. This means that the group underwriting process will take into consideration average age of the group, the mix of male and female in the group, the geographical area and the occupation of those that make up the group.

EXPERIENCE VS. COMMUNITY RATING

With the experience rating method, **the future rates of the group are based directly on the group's claim experience**. The more claims the group experiences, the greater the impact will be on the group's renewal rate. If the group experiences few claims, rate increases will be limited. This method works best for the larger groups. The larger the group, the more control and influence the employer may have on the health issues and lifestyle issues. Many companies will install a wellness program, stop smoking drives, or exercise programs in order to promote healthy lifestyles. Healthy employees mean manageable rates.

For the smaller group, it may be more costly and difficult to provide these extra wellness programs. If one person experiences a significant claim in a small group, it would be a significant portion of the group. Experience rating may not be ideal for the smaller group. For the smaller group, the community rating is a better fit. **Community rating bundles the group with others of their size and in their location.** By creating a larger pool of participants in the group, the insurer can provide a more stable, less volatile, premium scenario.

CONTRIBUTORY VS. NON-CONTRIBUTORY

It is essential that a majority of the employees participate in the plan. If not, the insurer could find itself in an adverse selection situation. The participation requirements depend on how the employer chooses to fund the plan.

In a **contributory plan, the employee makes a partial contribution** to the cost of the coverage and the employer pays part. If the plan is a contributory plan, at **least 75% of the eligible employees must participate** in the coverage. This allows for some employees to reject coverage. Some employees may not want to pay even a small part for their coverage.

In a **non-contributory plan, the employer pays the full cost of the plan** and the employee will not pay anything. Since it is fully funded by the employer, the insurer will require **100% participation** from the eligible employees.

Reduced Adverse Selection

Adverse selection occurs when the insurance company has too many poor risks. In order to protect the insurer from an adverse situation, the insurer:

- Requires that purchasing insurance for the group is **incidental to the formation of the group.** This group cannot formulate for the purpose of buying insurance. If insurance was the primary purpose of the group's formation, then an adverse group could be created to avoid the asking of health questions.

- The insurer will require **a percentage of participation of its employees**. The insurer is interested in getting the majority of the group **(contributory 75% or non-contributory 100%)**. The insurer knows that there will be some high risk participants, but by requiring the majority of the group's participation they also know that they will be able to offset this risk with healthy participants.

- By limiting enrollment to a specified **enrollment period**, this restricts the employee from last minute participation based upon a new health situation. New employees may be required to meet a probationary period before being eligible for enrollment. The **probationary period is the period of time, chosen by the employer, prior to eligibility for enrollment**. Once the probationary period is met, the employee will typically be given one month to enroll with little or no health questions. This period of time is referred to as the **enrollment period**.

- The **nature of the group itself** is a protection against adverse selection.

    - Groups typically enroll younger healthier individuals and older individuals retire and leave the group. This **turnover** becomes a natural protection against adverse selection.

    - In an employer group, the employees exhibit a certain level of health simply by being able to get up, get out, and work a full day.

Reduced Administrative Costs

One of the advantages of the group concept is lower overall administrative costs. Administrative costs will be lower for several reasons.

- Since the underwriting process looks at the group as a whole, as opposed to evaluating each individual, the cost of underwriting is significantly reduced.

- In order to keep overall costs down, one contract is issued, as opposed to multiple policies. By working through the employer, persistency of the business is more stable.

- The commission structure on a group sale is typically lower than that of an individual sale.

LIFE CONVERSION PRIVILEGES

In today's business environment, employees commonly find themselves leaving their employer for one reason or another. When an employee leaves his/her employer and group coverage, he/she will have the right to continue coverage with an individual policy under the following conditions:

- The insurer may require the group term to be **converted to an individual whole life policy**.

- It must be converted and paid for within **31** days of leaving the group. If the employee dies within this time period, the employee is covered whether the conversion was applied for or not.

- It will be converted at **attained age**.

The primary advantage to converting the group to an individual policy is **guaranteed insurability**. The insurer will ask no health questions. Regardless of the health status of the individual, coverage will continue through an individual policy.

Chapter Review

Terms to know

Group life

Eligible Groups

MET

MEWA

Master Policy

Group Underwriting

Experience Rating

Community Rating

Contributory Plan

Non-Contributory Plan

Reduced Adverse Selection

Life Conversion Privileges

Numbers and Time periods

100 - Association minimum to offer group coverage

75% participation - Contributory Plan

100% participation - Non-Contributory Plan

31 days – Life conversion period

SAMPLE QUESTIONS

1. Which of the following is NOT an eligible group?

    a) MET

    b) MEWA

    c) An association with 50 members

    d) An associations with 200 members

2. What is a MEWA?

    a) A labor union purchasing group insurance

    b) A group of small employers in the same industry coming together to purchase group insurance

    c) A credit union offering benefits to its members

    d) A group of small employers coming together to self-insure

3. In group insurance, who holds the master policy?

    a) The employer

    b) The employee

    c) The insurer

    d) The agent

4. With a contributory plan, how much participation is required?

    a) 100%

    b) 50%

    c) 75%

    d) 25%

5. Which of the following is not a way a group reduces adverse selection?

    a) The formation of the group must be incidental

    b) A certain percentage of employees must participate

    c) Each employee must answer health questions

    d) Enrollment is limited to a specified enrollment period

Answers: 1.c 2.d 3.a 4.c 5.c

Chapter 10

Government Insurance – Social Security

Social Security provides limited benefits for qualifying survivors. It is important for the life agent to understand these benefits and the qualifying rules. The benefits provided can be considered in the client's protection plan. Any gaps or limitations in these benefits would also be an important consideration.

In 1935, federal legislation enacted the **Old Age, Survivors, and Disability Insurance (OASDI)** act. This is what is most commonly referred to as Social Security. **It is funded by both employers and employees through payroll taxes**. The program pays a retirement income benefit, early disability income benefit and a survivor benefit for those with dependent children.

ELIGIBILITY OF BENEFITS

Social Security provides benefits in three main areas.

- **Retirement income** - This benefit provides a monthly check to a retiree after reaching the retirement age, as defined by Social Security. Retirement income can be taken as early as age 62, if the retiree is willing to take a reduced amount. Otherwise, it will pay a full benefit from the designated retirement age.

- **Disability income** – If an individual meets the early disability requirements of Social Security, it is possible to qualify for an income earlier than retirement age.

- **Survivor benefits** – Survivors who have lost their spouses may qualify for a temporary income and/or death benefit.

In order to qualify for the above benefits, the recipient must first meet several guidelines. First, in order to be insured, Social Security requires that the individual has participated in the program for a designated period of time. Since Social Security is funded through payroll taxes, eligibility is based upon the amount of time workers have worked and had the tax deducted from their paychecks.

Most employees will qualify for Social Security benefits at some time in their lives. But, there are a few industries that will not be eligible for benefits since they do not participate in the program. For example, railroad workers contribute to their own retirement system. Other examples of those who do not participate include some clergy and very low income self-employed individuals.

For those who will be eligible for benefits, the specific benefits they qualify for will depend on their status with Social Security. If the individual has worked **40 quarters** or one quarter of coverage since age 21 with a minimum of 6, then they are classified as **fully insured**. If workers are classified as fully insured, then they are eligible for all Social Security benefits.

If workers earn at least **6 quarters within the last 13**, they will qualify as **currently** insured. A currently insured person is only eligible for the child's survivor benefit and the lump sum death benefit.

If workers are fully insured and have earned at least **20 quarters** of credit in the last 40 calendar quarter periods, then they will be eligible for early **disability income** benefits.

Benefits	Insured Status		
Retirement	Fully		
Disability	Fully	Disability	
Lump Sum Death Bft	Fully		Currently
Spousal Survivor Income	Fully		
Child's Survivor Income	Fully		Currently
Parent's Survivor Bft	Fully		
Other Benefits	Fully		

PRIMARY INSURANCE AMOUNT

Once qualified for an income benefit from Social Security, **the amount a person will receive is based upon the individual's primary insurance amount.** The primary insurance amount is determined by how much the employee has paid into the system. The more workers earn, the more that is taken out of their paycheck. The results are a higher primary insurance amount. The specific benefit amount received is then based upon this amount.

BLACKOUT PERIOD

The blackout period is the period of time in which a survivor no longer qualifies for the survivor benefit and is not old enough to receive the retirement benefit.

Jack is fully insured when he dies. Jack's survivors include his wife Jackie and his daughter Jacqueline. At the time of Jack's death, Jackie is 40 years old and Jacqueline is 10 years old. Jackie and Jacqueline will qualify for the following income benefits from Social Security:

- Jackie will qualify for a monthly check until her youngest (Jacqueline) is 16. This means that Social Security will provide her an income for the next 6 years.

- Jackie will be eligible for her survivor retirement income at age 60.

- Jacqueline will qualify as a dependent for an income up to age 18.

When Jackie reaches age 46, her assistance from Social Security will end. She will not be eligible for another income until she is 60. This period of time between age 46 and age 60 (14 years) is Jackie's blackout period.

This is important for the agent to understand. If you are selling a life insurance policy to replace lost income for the family, you must understand what assistance is available and when assistance is no longer available to adequately recommend the proper coverage.

Chapter Review

Terms to know

OASDI

Retirement Income

Disability Income

Survivor Benefits

Primary Insurance Amount

Blackout Period

Numbers and Time periods

40 quarters - Fully Insured

SAMPLE QUESTIONS

1. Which of the following is not a Social Security benefit?

    a) Retirement Income

    b) Disability Income

    c) Survivor Benefits

    d) Life Insurance

2. The benefit amount received from social security is referred to as:

    a) OASDI

    b) APB

    c) PIA — *PRIMARY Insurance Amount*

    d) PTI

3. A fully insured individual has worked:

    a) 40 quarters — *10 years*

    b) 21 quarters

    c) 20 quarters

    d) 13 quarters

4. With regards to the <u>blackout</u> rule, the surviving spouse does not receive a benefit after the youngest child turns __16__ and until the surviving spouse turns __60__.

    a) 18, 60

    b) 16, 60

    c) 16, 65

    d) 15, 55

of Age

Answers: 1.d 2.c 3.a 4.b

PROFESSIONAL TRAINING INSTITUTION

Chapter 11

Health Insurance Basics

The better you know and understand the basics, the better prepared you will be for the exam.

A substantial portion of the questions on the exam will be over the basic terms and definitions. For that reason, you need to be familiar with these concepts. But, it is not just memorizing definitions; it is the comprehending of these terms and concepts and being able to understand them in the context of the questions. For a student new to the insurance industry, learning the terms and how to use them properly is much like learning a new language.

DEFINITIONS OF KEY TERMS

The understanding of the insurance industry begins with understanding basic terms and concepts that help define this industry.

INSURING CLAUSE

The insuring clause is the statement in the policy that states the promise the insurer makes to the insured. It is the **promise to pay** under the conditions stated within the policy. It is a general statement that includes the **general** scope of coverage and sets forth the conditions under which benefits will be paid.

CONSIDERATION CLAUSE

The **consideration is defined as the something of value** the parties exchange, according to the terms of the contract. The consideration clause specifies what each party to the contract has exchanged in order to validate the contract. **The insured provides a premium and statements on the application as consideration.** In exchange, **the insurer gives the promises** (the promise to pay) within the contract.

Free Look Provision

When the agent delivers the policy, this is the first time the insured will have to see the actual contract. The free look provision states that the insurance company must give the insured some time to review the contract when it is first received. This allows the insured time to review the terms of the contract and to verify the policy covers what it was expected to cover. The free look time period lasts **10 days** and **begins the date the policy is delivered.** If for any reason the owner chooses to return the policy, **a full refund must be provided.**

Probationary (Waiting) Period

A probationary period is **a period of time in which the insured must wait, before coverage is available for sickness**. The probationary period begins on the effective date of the policy. The primary purpose of the probationary period is to provide a waiting period for health conditions that existed prior to the application. These conditions are referred to as **pre-existing conditions**. Even though there is a waiting period before sickness is covered, accidents will be covered immediately.

Elimination Period

Elimination periods are common on disability and long term care policies. An elimination period is **a period of time in which the insured must wait, before coverage is available for sickness or accidents.** The elimination period begins each time a benefit period begins. This period is sometimes referred to as a **deductible of time.** An insured could have multiple elimination periods.

Elimination Period 30 days → **Benefit Period $2,000 per month**

On a disability policy, for example, the date of the disability is the beginning of the elimination period. In our example, the insured must wait 30 days before receiving disability income payments. This is a different type of deductible; the insured must wait 30 days before the policy pays a benefit. The longer the elimination period on the policy the lower the premium charged to the insured.

Probationary Period	Elimination Period
• Begins at the policy effective date • Affects sickness only • One time only	• Begins with the benefit period • Accident & Sickness • Could occur multiple times

PERILS

A peril is an event that **causes the loss** to the insured. Perils are the events an insured needs protection from. In health insurance, the perils that the insurer protects the insured from are financial loss as a result of **accident** or **sickness**.

An accident is defined as a **sudden and unexpected event**, not under the control of the insured, resulting in injury or damage. Some policies cover accidents only. Some may cover both accidents and sickness.

DEDUCTIBLES

A deductible is **the amount of the risk that the insured retains** full responsibility for. **The primary purpose of the deductible is to control over utilization.** The insured is less likely to run to the doctor if there is a personal responsibility for the doctor bill generated. The deductible is designed to encourage the insured to think twice about using the health insurance policy for every little thing. **The larger the deductible is, the lower the premium will be.**

There are several different types of deductibles that companies may use in their products.

- Calendar year deductibles begin anew at the beginning of each year.

- Policy year deductibles begin anew on the policy anniversary date based on the effective date.

- Per person deductibles apply a separate deductible for each person on the policy. These deductibles may limit the number of total deductibles applied per year. An example would be a $500 deductible per person with a maximum of 2 deductibles per family.

- Family deductibles apply one deductible for everyone on the policy. This deductible could be met by one person, or it could be met by combining bills from several people on the policy.

Policies will sometimes include a **carryover provision**. The carryover provision states that if the insured uses the policy at the end of the year (usually the last 3 months), the insured can carry over those expenses to apply toward the next year's deductible. This means the insured will not have to pay the deductible twice just because a new year has begun.

Policy Renewal Provisions

When the contract is written, the insurer will include the renewability rights of the contract. The renewability rights are listed on the **front of the policy, and properly labeled,** where the insured will most likely see it. Some policies provide better rights than others. Listed below are the renewability right options. The list is from the renewability provision that gives the customer the least rights to the ones that give the most rights.

Term – The term policy **does not give the insured the right to renew** the contract. This policy is good for a specified period of time, after which the policy will end. These policies are typically used when insureds finds themselves in between coverage. Term policies may last anywhere from 3 months to 2 years. Some companies may allow the agent to re-write the coverage once for a new term, but this is not considered a renewal.

Cancellable – A cancellable policy gives the insurer the right to cancel the contract in the middle of the term, as well as when it is due for renewal. The insurer must give the insured at least 5 days notice prior to cancellation. If an insurer cancels during the middle of the term, the company will be responsible for the refund of any unearned premium.

If a claim is in process when coverage is being ended, the insurer must fulfill the obligation towards the current claim according to the contract obligation. A company could not cancel coverage during a hospital stay without meeting the obligation for that stay.

Optionally renewable – This provision states that the company will have the option to renew the insured or not, when the policy comes due for renewal. The right to renew is at the option of the company.

Conditionally renewable – This type of policy is renewable except under certain conditions that have been spelled out in the original contract. For example: a policy may state that the contract can only be cancelled if the company cancels everyone within the class. This protects the insured from being singled out due to health conditions.

Guaranteed renewable – This provision also **guarantees the insured the right to renew and maintain the coverage.** The insurer guarantees the insured the right to renew the coverage. The difference between guaranteed renewable and noncancellable is that the company does not make the same premium obligation in a guaranteed renewable policy as it does in a noncancellable product.

Premiums can be increased on a class basis; therefore, if there is a premium increase, it affects the insured's entire class. The insured cannot be singled out solely based upon his or her own health conditions. The insured's premium can only be changed if everyone in their class is changed also. The insured is protected by numbers.

This renewability provision could also be limited by age.

Noncancellable – A noncancellable policy gives the best protection for the insured. This provision states that when the policy comes due, **the insured has the right to renew and maintain the protection.** The insurer cannot cancel the insured. As long as the insured meets the premium obligation, coverage will be maintained. What makes this renewability option better than all the others is that, not only does the insured have the right to renew coverage; the **premium is locked in and cannot be altered.** The insurer has committed to the amount of the premium.

The noncancellable provision may be limited to a certain age. The provision may be noncancellable up to age 60 or 65. This would mean that up until the given age the policy is noncancellable. But, at the age listed, the policy would be cancelled.

Preexisting Conditions

A preexisting condition is **a health condition that existed prior to the purchase of the insurance policy.** Preexisting conditions includes anything the applicant has had a medical history of or a condition that a normal or prudent person would have sought medical advice for.

A preexisting condition may or may not be covered by the policy. A company has several options when dealing with a preexisting condition. The company could exclude coverage on that condition permanently, the condition could be covered, or a waiting period may be placed on the policy before the condition will be covered (probationary period). A preexisting waiting period is designed to keep a person from buying the insurance prior to receiving treatment for a condition that they were previously aware of.

Coinsurance

Coinsurance is a way for the insured and insurer to share the cost of a medical bill. Coinsurance coverage usually follows a deductible. When the bill exceeds the deductible, the insurer will begin paying a **percentage** of the bills up to a stop loss specified in the policy. The percentage participation may be anywhere from 90/10 to 50/50, with the insurer paying the larger percentage. The purpose of the coinsurance coverage is to first assist the insured financially as the medical expenses increase. At the same time, the insurer knows that as long as the insured has a financial responsibility, the insured is more likely to monitor the expenses.

Stop Loss

Once the medical bills reach a certain amount, as specified in the policy, **the insurance company begins to pay 100% of covered services.** This stop loss could be defined by the total bills accumulated or it could be based upon an out of pocket maximum. Regardless, once this amount is reached, the insurer pays 100% of the covered services and the loss stops for the insured.

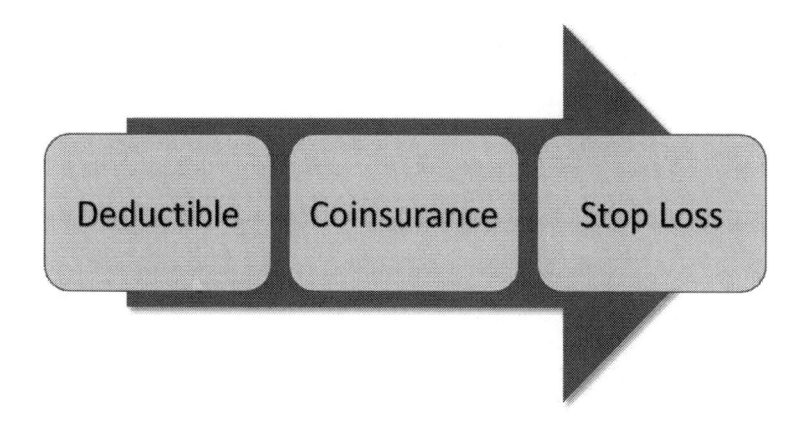

Deductible → Coinsurance → Stop Loss

COMMON EXCLUSIONS

The health insurance policy is designed to assume the risks that are most detrimental to the individual. These are the risks that are more common and have potentially devastating financial consequences to the average person. Even though the policies are designed to cover some of the most extreme concerns, every policy will have areas of protection that will not be covered. These areas are typically excluded from the policy for several reasons. Some of these excluded areas are simply uninsurable and do not fit into the concept of insurance. The following is a list of areas that may be excluded in a health insurance policy.

- War
- Active military duty
- Intentionally self-inflicted injuries
- Participation in a felony
- Preexisting conditions
- Uncomplicated pregnancy and childbirth
- Alcoholism or drug addiction

- Mental illness
- Elective cosmetic surgery
- Routine physical examinations
- Convalescent, custodial or rest care
- Workers compensation claims

COMMON HEALTH INSURANCE RIDERS

A **rider or an endorsement** is simply a change in the original policy. A rider can be used to make any change in the agreement. Some riders will increase coverage, while others may limit coverage. A rider could make a neutral change in the protection. Riders may be included in the original agreement by the company. Or, a rider might be requested by the applicant, when making an offer to the company, to enhance the coverage being applied for. There are numerous types of riders that companies may use. The following are three common riders used in health insurance:

- **Impairment rider** – The impairment rider is a rider that **excludes coverage on a specific impairment**. Six months ago, Jerry had his gallbladder removed. There were no complications and Jerry is feeling very healthy at this time. Jerry has now applied for a health insurance policy. The underwriter will give Jerry a choice, after finding out about the surgery. Jerry can pay a higher premium and the company will cover the gallbladder or any complications that might result from the recent surgery. Or, an impairment rider can be added that would exclude any coverage for the gallbladder or complications from the past surgery. If the impairment rider is added, Jerry will not be charged any additional premium. Jerry feels confident that his gallbladder problems are over and chooses the impairment rider.

- **Guaranteed insurability rider** - The guaranteed insurability rider **allows the insured to purchase additional amounts of insurance at predetermined times without proving insurability**. As the purchase options become available (typically every 3 or 5 years), the insured may have a limited amount of time to take advantage of the option. This time could be 30 or 60 days, it varies from company to company. Once the time period ends, that particular option is no longer available. When an option is chosen, the insured would purchase the additional protection based upon **attained age rates**.

    This rider is commonly included in a disability or long term care policy. This guarantees that regardless of future health issues, this person will be able to purchase additional insurance protection without having to worry about insurability.

Chet's long term care policy pays $3,000 per month. He has a guaranteed insurability rider that allows him to add an extra $300 monthly benefit to his coverage every 3 years. He chooses to take full advantage of his first option, increasing his total monthly benefit to $3,300. When his next option becomes available, Chet decides to take advantage of it also. Chet now has a benefit of $3,600 per month. When the third option becomes available, Chet does not take advantage of the opportunity. Once this option has passed, he will lose his opportunity to increase coverage. As Chet chooses to take advantage of the option to increase coverage, his premium does increase. Premium will increase due to his attained age. It will not increase due to health issues.

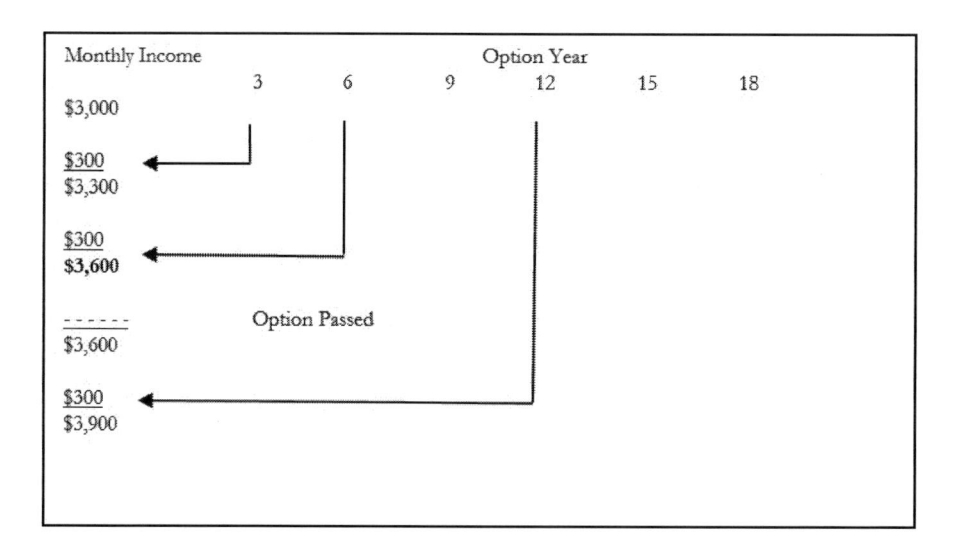

```
Monthly Income              Option Year
                  3     6      9    12    15    18
$3,000

$300      ←──────┘
$3,300

$300      ←─────────────┘
$3,600

- - - - -        Option Passed
$3,600

$300      ←────────────────────────┘
$3,900
```

- Multiple indemnity riders (AD & D) – A multiple indemnity rider pays a multiple of the original benefit (usually double) due to specific qualifying events. The accidental death and disability (AD & D) policy will sometimes pay an extra death benefit due to certain types of accidents. For instance, the policy may double the death benefit if the accident was a transportation accident (trains, planes and automobiles).

Major Health Insurance Providers

There are several different types of health care providers addressing the public's need for protection. These providers have evolved over time and differ for a variety of reasons. The following section looks at the different providers and how they differ from each other.

Stock and Mutual Companies

The primary difference between stock and mutual companies is how the companies were formulated. Both companies may sell similar products. These companies are known for their traditional products, the basic plans and the major medical policies.

Stock companies are insurance companies owned by stock or shareholders. When a stock company makes a profit, the company may pay out that profit in the form of a dividend to the stockholders, who are the owners. The policyholder does not normally participate in receiving any divisible surplus that the company may have earned. Because the policyholder does not usually receive a dividend, both the product and company are referred to as **nonparticipating**. Stock companies do not generally pay dividends to the policyholder.

Mutual companies are companies owned by its policyholders. Since each policyholder has an ownership interest in the company, when the company makes a profit, it pays it out to the policyholder as a divisible surplus. When the divisible surplus is paid out, it is paid out as a dividend to the policyowner. Since the policyowner is receiving the dividend, this is referred to as a **participating** product or company.

PROFESSIONAL TRAINING INSTITUTION

Chapter Review

TERMS TO KNOW

Insuring clause

Consideration clause

Free look provision

Probationary period

Elimination period

Peril

Deductible

Carryover provision

Noncancellable

Guaranteed renewable

Conditionally renewable

Term

Preexisting conditions

Coinsurance

Stop loss

Impairment rider

Guaranteed insurability rider

Stock company

Mutual company

NUMBERS AND TIME PERIODS

10 Free Look

PROFESSIONAL TRAINING INSTITUTION

SAMPLE QUESTIONS

1. What is the purpose of an "impairment rider?"
    a. Exclude coverage on a specific impairment
    b. Add coverage for a specific impairment
    c. Temporarily exclude coverage on a specific impairment
    d. Cover an impairment for an additional premium

2. The "elimination period:"
    a. Begins on the policy effective date
    b. Is the period of time in which preexisting conditions are not covered
    c. Are common on major medical policies
    d. Is defined as a deductible of time

3. If Jay has a $1,000 calendar year deductible with 80/20 coinsurance. His policy has a stop loss at $10,000. If Jay has a medical bill for $8,000, how much will Jay have to pay?
    a. $1,000
    b. $1,400
    c. $1,600
    d. $2,400

4. What is the standard "free look" period for health insurance?
    a. 10 days from the date of the application
    b. 10 days from the date of policy delivery
    c. 20 days from application date
    d. 20 days from delivery date

5. All of the following are true about the guaranteed insurability rider, EXCEPT:
    a. It can be used to help the policyholder keep pace with inflation
    b. The rider will cause premiums to increase, based upon attained age rates, as options are utilized
    c. The insured will be allowed to increase their coverage at certain times without having to prove insurability
    d. A limited number of options are available to choose from, the insured will be able to choose an option based upon their timing needs

6. Guaranteed renewable policies:
    a. Guarantee the right to renew, but may limit renewability up to a designated age
    b. Lock in the premium and guarantee the renewability of the policy
    c. Are sometimes referred to as "guaranteed renewable and noncancellable"
    d. May raise the individuals rate based upon claims experienced

7. Which of the following would be the full consideration of the insured?
    a. The promises in the contract.
    b. The premium paid
    c. The statements made in the application
    d. Both b & c

8. All of the following are true concerning a "mutual" company EXCEPT:
    a. Mutual companies are owned by the policyholders
    b. Mutual companies sell nonparticipating products
    c. Mutual company profits are paid out in the form of a policyholder dividend
    d. A mutual company is sometimes referred to as a participating company

9. The primary purpose of a deductible is to:
    a. Avoid larger claims
    b. Create easier access to healthcare
    c. Control against over utilization
    d. Encourage physician participation

10. A noncancellable policy:
    a. Guarantees the right to renew a policy when it comes due
    b. Does not allow the insured to cancel the policy, midterm
    c. Does not allow the insurer to cancel coverage, midterm and at renewal, and locks in the premium
    d. Guarantees issue of the policy and locks in the premium

11. Coinsurance is:
    a. The portion the insured must pay prior to the insurer paying
    b. A minimum payment designed to encourage preventive care
    c. Coverage that typically follows the stop loss in the policy
    d. A way of sharing the cost of a medical bill between the insured and insurer

Answers: 1.a 2.d 3.d 4.b 5.d 6.a 7.d 8.b 9.c 10.c 11.d

Medical Expense Policies

As medical expenses have continued to increase, protection from the high cost has become an imperative. The medical expense policies are designed to pay hospital and physician expenses, as well as other expenses associated with the high cost of healthcare in society today.

As our healthcare and the delivery of our healthcare has changed, so has the product that the insurance industry offers to protect the insured. Originally, the insurance industry offered policies with low limits; these were described as basic plans. Over time, a better product was needed to meet the needs of the insured. Today, the insured can purchase major medical products that are designed to handle catastrophic expenses.

CHARACTERISTICS OF MEDICAL EXPENSE POLICIES

The medical expense policies pay based upon the medical expenses incurred as a result of an accident of sickness. Some of the common characteristics in a medical expense policy include:

PAYMENT OF MEDICAL EXPENSES

The medical expense policy is designed to be a **reimbursement** policy that pays on a **fee-for-service** basis. At one time, it was not unreasonable for individuals to pay their own medical bills. The insurance contract was set up to reimburse the policyholder for the bills incurred. As healthcare expenses increased, it became unreasonable for the insured to pay a bill first and then wait to be reimbursed. Today, through the right to **assign**, insurers can pay directly to the providers.

Assignment

Assignment is to give up a right to another person. In health insurance, the insured has the right to collect benefits from the policy. Since the health care expense has become as expensive as it is, the insured may give the right to collect the benefit from the policy to the health care provider. This allows the provider to bill the insurer directly. Ultimately, assignment speeds up collections for the provider and simplifies the responsibility of the insured.

Insureds

In a service plan like an HMO or Blue Cross, the participants in the plan are referred to as members or subscribers. A subscriber participates in the benefits available to the participants for the period of membership. The medical expense policies are insurance contracts. The participant is a policy (contract) holder. An agreement between the insurer and the insured has been established. The terms of the contract cannot be altered and must be adhered to by the insurer.

Deductibles

Deductibles are common in a medical expense policy. The deductible is the part of the expense the insured is responsible for before the policy benefits provides coverage. **The primary purpose of a deductible is to control against over utilization** of the policy benefits. When individuals are responsible for the initial expense of their healthcare, they will avoid frivolous and unnecessary medical expenses. **The deductible also reduces the cost of the policy.** The higher the deductible the lower the premium will be.

Coinsurance

Some policies will have a coinsurance within the benefit design. During the coinsurance period, the **cost is shared between the insurer and the insured**. Coinsurance percentages may differ between companies. Examples include: 90/10, 80/20, or 70/30, with the insurer typically paying the higher percentage. While the insured is paying a part of the expense, the insured has a reason to help avoid excess charges or unnecessary expenses.

Stop Loss

Once the insured has reached the stop loss, the insurer will then pay 100% of the covered expenses. Some companies base their stop loss on an "out of pocket" limit. An out of pocket limit is based upon the deductible and the percentage the insured pays after the deductible. Once the insured has paid out an amount equal to the out of pocket limit for the policy, the insured no longer participates in the payment of further expenses.

Policies may include all three of the above elements: the deductible, coinsurance and a stop loss. Arlo has a policy with a $500 calendar year deductible, 80/20 coinsurance with an out of pocket limit of $2500. He has a series of medical bills as follows:

- January $400

- February $1,100

- July $2,000

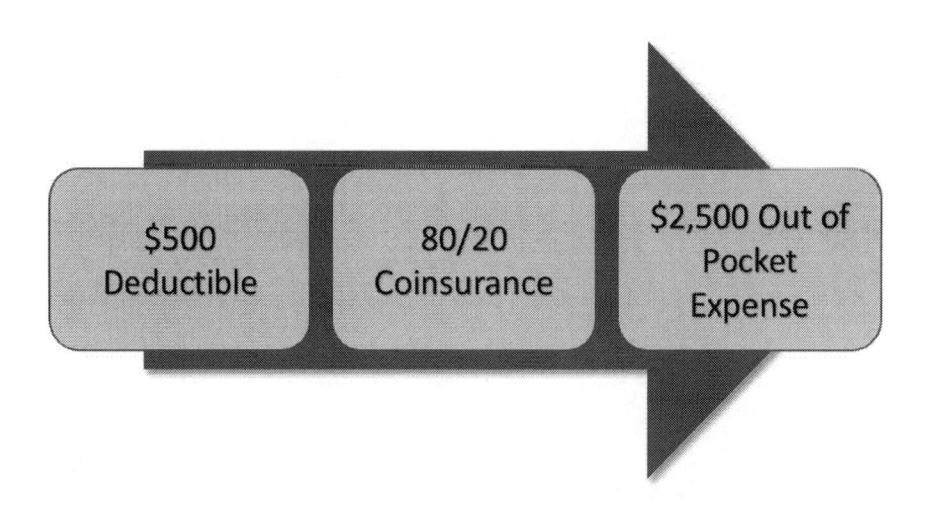

Arlo's first bill is less than the amount of the deductible. Arlo will be responsible for the full $400. Arlo's February bill is $1,100. Since he has met $400 of his $500 calendar year deductible, only $100 of the bill needs to be applied to the deductible. The remaining $1,000 will fall under the 80/20 coinsurance coverage. This means that the insurer will pay $800 of the $1,100 bill. By July, Arlo has met his deductible. The insurer will pay 80% of the $2,000 July bill, or $1,600.

Arlo had a total of $3,500 worth of expenses. He paid a total of $1,100. The insurer paid a total of $2,400.

TAXATION

Benefits from a medical expense policy are designed to reimburse the insured for medical bills. The payment received is not considered an investment return or an income. **Medical expense benefits are not taxable.** The premium may be tax deductible if the insured chooses to itemize when filing a tax return. Along with itemizing, if the premium and other medical expenses exceed 7.5% of the insured's adjusted gross income, then the amount of premium is deductible.

MANAGED CARE

A managed health care system makes an attempt to manage and oversee the care being provided, while controlling expenses at the same time. Managing care is a balancing act, on one hand the program is involved in the care that is provided. Is it necessary care? Is it the best form of treatment? On the other hand, it is an attempt to control cost. Managed care done properly results in appropriate healthcare without financial waste.

Examples of managed care concepts include: case management, second surgical opinions, preventive care, preadmission testing and outpatient utilization. Case managers are used by insurance companies to review large and ongoing claims. Case managers evaluate the appropriateness and necessity of the care.

TYPES OF MEDICAL EXPENSE PLANS

Medical expense plans are designed to reimburse the insured for medical bills incurred. Medical expense plans fall into two different categories: the basic plans or the major medical plans.

BASIC PLANS

Basic plans have been around a long time. They were created during a time when medical expenses were much more manageable and limited. Basic plans have several common characteristics. The following is a list of some of the more common characteristics:

- **Low limits** – Unlike the plans sold today, basic plans were usually limited in how much the policy would pay. These policies were not designed to cover the extreme expenses that insureds face today.

- **Specific benefits** – When the basic plan did pay, the policy was usually limited to very specific coverages.

- **First dollar coverage** – Even though the limit of protection was low, the basic plan typically paid with little to no deductible.

There are a variety of plans that will fall into the category of a basic plan. There are three basic plans that stand out as more common than others:

Basic hospital or hospital expense – This plan was designed to help reimburse the insured for the hospital bills incurred. The policy typically had two areas of coverage:

- Room and board – The policy might pay a daily benefit ($100, $200, or maybe $300) for each day in the hospital.

- Miscellaneous medical expenses – This would cover certain medical expenses, charged by the hospital, while confined to the hospital. It would probably be limited to a multiple of the daily room rate or benefit.

Basic surgical or surgical expense benefit – The surgical expense policy was designed to cover the specific expenses of surgery. Plans may provide scheduled benefits or nonscheduled benefits. A policy that pays on a scheduled basis would provide a schedule of surgeries listed within the policy. The schedule lists the amount to be paid for each particular procedure. This policy is typically sold in **units**. A unit lists the amount paid for each procedure. The insured could buy multiple units of coverage. Ten units pay a benefit of 10 times the amount listed in the schedule.

A nonscheduled benefit would not list specific amounts to be paid. Instead, it pays on a percentage basis. A nonscheduled benefit could pay 80% of the surgical expense.

Basic medical – This policy was designed to cover the doctor visits in the office or hospital.

Major Medical

Whereas the basic policy was limited and coverage was very specific, the major medical is catastrophic and comprehensive. As medical expenses began to increase at an ever alarming rate, the basic plans were becoming less and less effective. The major medical was created to more effectively cover the extreme expenses associated with health care. Characteristics of the major medical include:

- **Catastrophic coverage** – The major medical is designed to cover today's high cost of health care. The policy will typically come with very high limits or be unlimited in the amount that could be paid. The higher the expense, the better the policy pays. As of September 2010 the Affordable Care Act prohibits lifetime limits on major medical policies.

- **Inside limits** – An inside limit is a smaller limit, on a specific benefit, within a catastrophic policy. Examples of coverages that could have an inside limit include: a limit on second surgical opinions, prescription drugs, or mental health care.

- **Comprehensive coverage** – This policy pays in or out patient hospital expenses, surgeries, anesthetist, lab tests, x-rays, and most needs of the typical insured. Compared to the limited benefits of the basic plans, this plan is designed to cover most health care expenses.

- **Deductibles** – Deductibles could be as low as a few hundred dollars or as high as several thousand. Major medical plans will include a deductible.

- **Eligible expenses (usual, necessary and customary)** – Eligible expenses are based upon the usual, necessary and customary expense of the local geographical area. As long as the expense is within a reasonable range of what other providers are charging in that particular area, the expense will be covered.

- **Coinsurance or cost sharing** – Once the deductible has been met, the policy will then pay on a coinsurance basis.

- **Stop loss or out of pocket maximum** – Once the insured has reached the stop loss or out of pocket maximum, the policy will pay 100% of the covered expenses.

Supplemental Major Medical

The supplemental major medical plan is a policy that combines the basic plan with the major medical. The initial benefit is provided through basic coverage. As the claim progresses beyond the basic coverage, the insured is responsible for a deductible (corridor deductible). After which, the major medical benefits kick in with percentage participation up until the stop loss is reached. The following is an example:

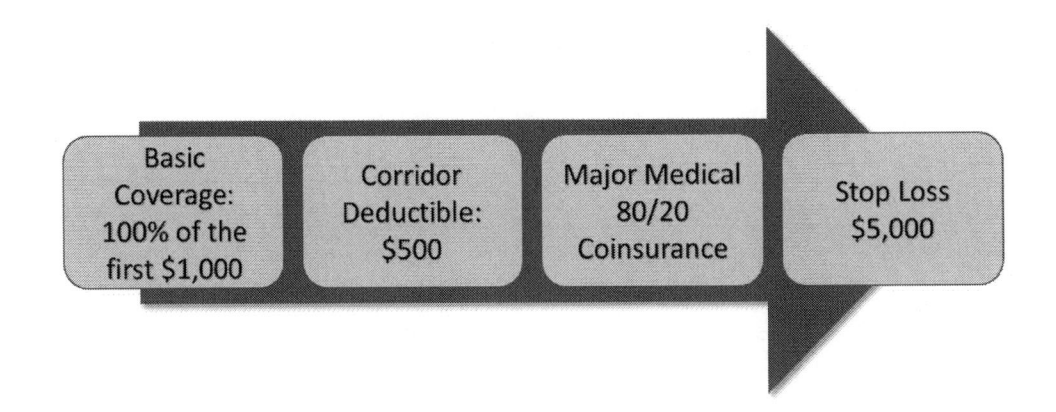

[Basic Coverage: 100% of the first $1,000] → [Corridor Deductible: $500] → [Major Medical 80/20 Coinsurance] → [Stop Loss $5,000]

Miscellaneous Issues

The following are some of the other issues that are applicable to the medical expense policies.

Other Medical Expense Benefits

Maternity benefits – Maternity may or may not be covered in an individual medical expense policy. This is a benefit that is designed to help pay the cost of pregnancy. When maternity is covered, it is usually covered on a limited basis. On a family policy, whether or not maternity is covered, newborn children will be covered from moment of birth. Complications from child birth are also covered under the medical expense policy.

Emergency first aid coverage – Emergency care is always provided in or outside any network within the plan. If there is a network, care must be transferred to the network as soon as reasonably possible to qualify for the network benefits.

Mental infirmity – If mental infirmity is covered, then it will be covered on a limited basis. A policy will typically limit the number of days covered within a mental institution and limit the maximum amount paid for mental infirmity.

Common Exclusions and Limitations

Not everything is covered in a major medical policy. As comprehensive as it is, there will always be some areas in which coverage is limited or excluded. Areas typically excluded include:

- Anything covered by workers compensation

- Care in government facilities
- Well baby care
- Cosmetic surgery
- Dental
- Eyeglasses
- Custodial care

OTHER MAJOR MEDICAL CONCEPTS

Assignment of benefits – Assignment is defined as a **transfer of a legal right or interest in a contract to another.** In health insurance, the insured can assign benefits directly to the medical provider. The insurer then pays the benefit owed to the provider directly.

Rights of conversion – Health insurance policies may provide coverage for the whole family. If a family member comes off of the policy, **the conversion rights allow the individual to convert to his or her own coverage to an individual policy.** This allows the individual to maintain coverage. Conversion might be applicable for a child that comes of age or for a divorce between a husband and wife.

Rights of newborn or adopted children – A family policy is designed to provide coverage for the whole family. When a new child is born or adopted into the family, the child is covered immediately. **Children are covered from moment of birth. Adopted children are covered by date of legal placement.** If the insurer requires the payment of an additional premium, **payment must be made within 31 days** after date of birth or placement in order to continue coverage beyond the 31 day time period.

Rights of dependent children – At some point, children will be required to come off of their parents' policy. Circumstances will determine when this point is. A child who is physically or mentally handicapped and financially dependent on parents will be able to stay on the plan beyond normal circumstances. As of September 2010 federal law allows children to be covered under their parents plan up to age 26. This is regardless of their dependence or student status.

Chapter Review

TERMS TO KNOW

Reimbursement

Fee for service

Assignment

Stop loss

Managed care

Basic plans

Basic hospital

Surgical expense

Units

Surgery schedule

Major medical

Inside limits

Catastrophic coverage

Comprehensive coverage

Usual, necessary and customary

Supplemental major medical

NUMBERS AND TIME PERIODS

Moment of birth coverage for newborns

31 days to pay for newborns

Up to age 26 may stay on parents

Co-insurance math problem

PROFESSIONAL TRAINING INSTITUTION

SAMPLE QUESTIONS

1. Arlo has a policy with a $500 calendar year deductible, 80/20 coinsurance with an out of pocket limit of $2500. Arlo experiences the following medical bills. How much will his insurance policy pay?

    - **February $300**
    - **May $1,400**
    - **October $200**
        a. $720
        b. $1,020
        c. $1,120
        d. $1,520

2. Benefits from a medical expense policy:
    a. Will be taxable as income
    b. Will not be taxable as income
    c. Will only be taxable if it exceeds 7.5% of your adjusted gross income
    d. Is tax deductible

3. Usual, necessary and customary charge is defined as:
    a. The usual cost for care in that geographical area
    b. The medical providers actual charge
    c. What an individual provider charges
    d. The usual cost for care for the insurer

4. Managed care could include all of the following EXCEPT:
    a. Case management
    b. Second surgical opinion
    c. First dollar coverage
    d. Pre-admission testing

5. Basic plans differ from major medical plans, in that:
    a. Basic plans are low limit policies with first dollar coverage
    b. Basic plans usually have high deductibles
    c. Basic plans are designed to cover catastrophic needs
    d. Basic plans are comprehensive in nature unlike the major medical policy

PROFESSIONAL TRAINING INSTITUTION

6. Tim purchased a basic surgical policy with a $1,000 surgery schedule. The schedule states that it will pay $200 for a gallbladder surgery. Tim has 10 units. How much will his policy pay?
    a. $200
    b. $1,000
    c. $1,200
    d. $2,000

7. Children may stay on their parents policy up till age:
    a. 19
    b. 21 if a full time student
    c. 26 if dependent
    d. 26

8. Newborns or adopted children must be included on a family policy:
    a. From moment of birth at no extra cost
    b. From moment of birth with additional payments due immediately
    c. From moment of birth with payment made within 31 days
    d. At the option of the insurer

9. An inside limit is:
    a. A limit within a catastrophic policy
    b. A limit for hospital confinement
    c. A limit within a basic policy
    d. An out of pocket limit for the insured

10. All the following are characteristics of major medical coverage EXCEPT:
    a. Comprehensive coverage
    b. Catastrophic coverage
    c. Collision coverage
    d. Coinsurance or cost sharing

Answers: 1.c 2.b 3.a 4.c 5.a 6.d 7.d 8.c 9.a 10.c

PROFESSIONAL TRAINING INSTITUTION

Chapter 13

Other Healthcare Providers

Traditional insurance plans have not provided all the solutions for the public. Competition has brought new ideas and concepts to the table. As new ideas are tested and proven, our healthcare protection grows and matures.

As our healthcare and the delivery of our healthcare has changed, so has the product that the insurance industry offers to protect the insured. Today's healthcare system has developed and continues to develop to address the needs of the American public.

Blue Cross Blue Shield Companies

Blue Cross Blue Shield came into existence as an alternative to the traditional concept. As healthcare expenses increased, the public found it more difficult to pay the medical bill in advance. As a result, doctors found it more difficult to collect for their services.

Blue Cross Blue Shield is a **nonprofit membership** based **service** organization established primarily for the purpose of providing hospital and medical expense **payments directly to the provider** rather than the individual. A service organization is an organization that provides a service to its members. The service that Blue Cross Blue Shield provides is direct payment to the provider. Traditional insurance is a **reimbursement plan**. Under a reimbursement plan, the insurer pays the bill out of pocket, files a claim, and is reimbursed by the insurer. To avoid this cumbersome approach and to compete with Blue Cross Blue Shield, insurers can pay directly to the provider through **assignment**.

Blue Cross was the original coverage provided, it is the hospital coverage. Blue Shield was added later and covers the medical expenses.

Health Maintenance Organizations (HMO)

A Health Maintenance Organization is a **prepaid service** organization that **provides both the protection against healthcare expenses as well as the healthcare providers themselves.** HMO's specialize in **prevention** and **managed care**. Some of the primary characteristics of the HMO include:

Service organization – The HMO is a service organization that is **membership** based. The healthcare is the service provided. With traditional insurance, healthcare is provided by independent practitioners. The HMO owns and controls the healthcare provider. Traditional insurance provides a policy, which is a contract between the policyholder and the insurer. In a service organization, payment of benefits is not based upon a contract, but the benefits provided to member participants for that year.

Prepaid – The HMO is a prepaid healthcare program. The premium payment made by the member is used to pay the providers in advance. The physician is an employee of the HMO and works under the oversight of the HMO. One method used by HMO's to pay their providers is the **capitation system**. Under the capitation system the doctor is paid a certain amount each month in advance to provide the care for the members under this doctor's care. Whether a doctor sees a member often or rarely, the doctor is paid the same fee.

Primary care physician – After joining a HMO, the member is required to choose a primary care physician (PCP). This is the general practitioner responsible for the oversight of the member's care. This doctor is prepaid to oversee the care for this member.

Gatekeeper system – Obviously, the HMO will have many doctors and specialists accessible to provide the care that will be needed by different members. Typically these specialists tend to cost much more than the use of a general practitioner. The primary care physician will serve as a gatekeeper to these specialists and services provided by the healthcare system. Access to these specialists can be gained through the recommendation of the gatekeeper. The gatekeeper's responsibility is to limit access to these more expensive services to the actual need.

Network – HMO's will have their own network of physicians. **The network consists of the physicians that are employed by the HMO.** These are the physicians that have been prepaid to provide care for the members. As long as a member seeks services within the network, the care has been paid for in advance and protection will be available. If the member receives care outside of the network, protection is not provided. The HMO does not typically provide protection outside of its network, unless it is emergency care. If the member voluntarily receives care outside of the network, then protection is not provided.

Preventive care – The HMO philosophy of providing protection included a new way of thinking. Traditionally, insurance discouraged over usage with deductibles and co insurance. The HMO encourages preventive care. Providing preventive care is encouraged with the hope of reducing or avoiding more extensive and expensive treatment. Early diagnosis along with early treatment may allow the physician to treat a condition while it is still manageable and cost effective.

Co-payments – The co-pay is used by the HMO to make it affordable for the insured to seek treatment. When treatment is expensive, people tend to delay seeking medical treatment from a doctor. The co-pay charges the insured a minimal fee (perhaps $30 or $50) for a visit with the HMO covering the balance. A minimal fee makes it easy to see a doctor, with the hope of early diagnosis. The co-pay encourages the doctor visit.

Managed care – A managed health care system makes the attempt to manage or oversee the care that is being provided and control expenses at the same time. Managing care is a balancing act, on one hand the program is involved in the care that is provided. Is it necessary care? Is it the best form of treatment? On the other hand, it is an attempt to control cost. Managed care done properly results in appropriate healthcare without financial waste.

Emergency care – The Federal government does place some requirements that any HMO must abide by in order operate as an HMO. One of the primary requirements is that all **HMO's must provide for emergency services outside as well as inside the network.** If a member finds themselves with an emergency need outside of the network of physicians provided by their HMO, the HMO must provide coverage until they can reasonably return to the network. Other requirements include making care available to members 24 hour a day 7 days a week.

Open and closed panel systems –Since HMO's owned the physicians, HMO's were limited by two important factors. First, the HMO's were limited by the number of doctors available in the network. Not every doctor wanted to be an employee of the HMO; therefore, the HMO's network of doctors contained a limited number of physicians. Secondly, the HMO had restrictions by physical location. We already know that not every doctor wanted to become an employee of the HMO. If a small town only had one doctor practicing in town, and he chose not to become part of the HMO network, the townspeople insured with HMO's would not be able to see the town's doctor. The member may have had to drive to the closest big city in order to receive treatment from an HMO in network doctor.

In order to provide services to a broader area, HMO's began changing to an open panel concept. In a closed panel, the only physicians available to the member would be those employed solely by the HMO. The open panel system allowed the physicians to maintain their individual practices, as well as represent the HMO. This gives the member more access to more physicians.

Preferred Provider Organization (PPO)

In order to compete with the HMO, the traditional insurance company needed a way to reduce the premiums charged to its customers. By **negotiating** the health care expense with the provider, the insurance company was able to obtain a **prearranged discount** on the services provided. Once the discount was obtained from the provider, the insurer was able to pass this savings on to the insured through a lower premium and better coverage.

Since the PPO is a traditional plan, it allows insureds to choose their physicians. Yet some physicians have agreed to a discount, while others have not. The physicians that have agreed to a discount are the preferred providers within that company's **network** of **preferred providers**. When health care is obtained within the network, the insurer will provide a higher percentage of protection (usually 90/10). When the insured chooses to obtain health care outside of network, coverage is still available but at a lower rate (maybe 70/30). Ultimately, the insured has the **choice** to use either physician, in network or out of network. If the insured stays within the network, the insurer will pass its advantage on to the insured in the form of better protection.

The PPO was created in response to the HMO and has utilized many of the features of the HMO. PPO's may have networks, primary care physicians, gatekeeper systems, copayments and will include different forms of preventive care. The primary difference is that the HMO provides the protection and providers. With the PPO, the protection is provided and the provider (an independent practitioner) gives a discounted service.

Point of Service (POS)

As the PPO's became more popular, competition encouraged the HMO to consider additional concepts. The POS allows the member to leave the HMO for treatment outside of the network. By **providing in and out of network coverage**, the POS can provide competitive choices for the member. To encourage the member to utilize the prepaid network of providers, coverage will be more complete within the network. A POS might provide full coverage within the network and 60% coverage outside of the network.

Traditional Major Medical	PPO	POS	HMO

• Catastrophic coverage
• Comprehensive protection
• Providers are independent practitioners
• Fee for service
• Usual, customary and reasonable
• Benefits may be assigned
• Deductible
• Coinsurance
• Stop Loss
• Inside Limits
• Policy (contact) hoders
	• Traditional major medical and its characteristics
	• Pre arranged provider discounts
	• Network of providers
	• Primary care physician
	• Gatekeeper
	• Managed care
	• May also include:
	  • Preventive care
	  • Co-pays
	  • Open or closed panel system
		• HMO with its characteristics
		• Provides out of network coverage at a lower percentage
		• Less restricted
			• Provides the healthcare services as well as the protection
			• Preventive care
			• Co-pays
			• Network of providers
			• Limited geographically and by network
			• Managed care
			• Gatekeeper
			• Primary care physician
			• Prepaid service
			• Capitation system
			• Service organization
			• Members
			• Open vs closed

AFFORDABLE CARE ACT

The Affordable Care Act, which passed in 2010, has created recent changes in the health insurance industry. This **federal government program** created new health insurance requirements for individuals, employers, and the insurer. It has also created the **Federal Marketplace** that will offer individuals and small businesses a new location to purchase health insurance. All insurance companies must provide the **Essential Health Benefits (EHB)** within the policies that are offered to individuals and small groups.

THE INDIVIDUAL

Since the beginning of the Affordable Care Act health insurance has become a requirement for the individual. This is called the **individual mandate**. If the individual does not maintain the **Minimum Essential Coverage (MEC)** for themselves and their dependents they will receive an IRS tax penalty. MEC is defined by the federal government.

Qualified Health Plans (QHP), which is a health plan that has been certified by the Affordable Care Act, offer plans that meet Minimum Essential Coverage. These plans can be purchased through the Marketplace by the individual during **open enrollment**. Open enrollment is November 15th to December 15th of each calendar year. When an individual applies for a Qualified Health Plan, they will not be denied based on pre-existing conditions. **The only pre-existing condition that can effect an individual's premiums is smoking status.** Age and location will also effect premium.

Eligibility for a Qualified Health Plan in the Marketplace for individuals has the following requirements. Individuals must be **United State citizens and reside in the state** that the insurance was purchased. They must **not be currently incarcerated**. There must be **no other MEC available**. *If a MEC is available through an employer, but the premium exceeds 9.5% of the individual's household income, the individual will be able to purchase a Qualified Health Plan.* An individual will also be eligible for a Premium Tax Credit (Subsidy) if the household income is between **100% - 400%** of the Federal Poverty Level. **The Premium Tax Credit provides assistance with premium payments on plans purchased through the Marketplace.**

The Metal Plans represent the standardized Qualified Health Plans sold through the Marketplace:

- Bronze Plan – 60%
- Silver Plan* – 70%
- Gold Plan – 80%
- Platinum – 90%

Cost-Sharing Reduction is eligible for those who buy through the Marketplace, choose a Sliver Plan, and earn less than 250% of the Federal Poverty Level. If these qualifications are met the individual will receive a lower percentage participation and stop loss. The amount lowered varies with household income between 100% - 250%.

EMPLOYERS

An **Employer Mandate** has also been imposed with the Affordable Care Act. If an employer has over **50 Full Time Equivalent Employees**, health insurance must be provided or the employer will receive an IRS tax penalty. A full time employee is one that works on the average of 30 hours per week. Full Time Equivalent Employees are made up of full time and part time employees. Those part time employee hours are combined together, every combined 30 hours per week represents 1 full time employee. For example, two part time employees that work 15 hours per week has 30 hours per week between them. Those 30 combined hours would create 1 Full Time Equivalent Employee. This is used to determines whether an employer has a large group or small group.

Small Group Employers

A small group employer is not bound to the Employer Mandate and does not have to provide health insurance. However, if desired the small group will be able to provide group insurance that meets the Minimum Essential Coverages or that will be granted access to the **SHOP (Small Business Health Options Program)**. The SHOP gives the opportunity for small employers to allow their employees to choose their own plan in the Marketplace while the employer pays a portion of the premium.

Large Group Employers

Large group employers are bound to the Employer Mandate. If over 50 Full Time Equivalent Employees, the employer must provide health insurance benefits to the employees who work over 30 hours per week on average. Group insurance provided by employers must uphold Minimum Essential Coverage. A large group with no more than 100 employees will also have access to the SHOP like small group employers.

GENERAL TERMS

Guaranteed Availability – Everyone has the opportunity to have health insurance. The Marketplace, group insurance, Medicare, and Medicaid provide that possibility.

Guaranteed Renewable – All Qualified Health Plans must be guaranteed renewable.

Dependent Coverage – Available at the option of the insured up to age 26

Open Enrollment – From November 15th to December 15th each year individuals can enroll in the Marketplace or switch plans.

Special Enrollment Period – A time when the individual may enroll into the Marketplace or switch plans outside the open enrollment time frame. Must be due to a life change

Life Change – Loss of employer plans, marriage, divorce, birth or adoption.

Pre-Existing Condition – Only smoking may be considered and effect premium as a pre-existing condition.

Catastrophic Plan – Available if individual is under the age of 30. Individual is responsible for most health care costs until deductible and out of pocket has been met.

Federal Marketplace – www.healthcare.gov

MULTIPLE EMPLOYER TRUSTS (MET)

A multiple employer trust is several small employers, of like industry, coming together for the purpose of buying insurance. Typically, the insurer will not allow individuals to come together for the purpose of buying insurance. This is to avoid adverse selection. The MET allows employers to come together, of like industry. By limiting the membership to employers of the same industry, the insurer is less likely to obtain a majority or disproportionate mix of unhealthy risks. This "coming together" gives the employers more purchasing power.

MULTIPLE EMPLOYER WELFARE ASSOCIATION (MEWA)

Whereas a MET comes together for the purpose of obtaining an insurance policy, the MEWA comes together for the purpose of **self-insuring**. Many employers like the concept of self-insuring. If there are enough participants in the plan, premiums normally sent to an insurance company can be maintained and used to provide the protection needed. This gives the participants a vested interest in the stability of the plan. Small employers do not have the number of participants needed to take advantage of this concept. By "coming together" small employers can develop a large enough group to insure themselves.

HEALTH SAVINGS ACCOUNTS (HSA)

An HSA is an account established for the purpose of paying health care expenses with tax free money. In order to qualify for a HSA account an individual must first have a high deductible health plan as established by the IRS. For the year 2016, if an individual has a health plan with a minimum deductible of $1,300 and a maximum out-of-pocket expense of $6,550, or a family plan with a minimum of $2,600 and a maximum of $13,100, the insured would then be eligible to establish a health savings account. Another advantage of the HSA besides the taxation, is that unlike other plans it is not a "use it or lose it," plan. Any money paid into the account that is not used by the end of the year will roll over to the next year. Any money withdrawn for reasons other than medical, as of 2012, may be penalized 20%. At age 65, funds can be withdrawn for any reason without penalty. If an individual withdraws funds from an HSA for reasons other than for medical purposes, the funds are then taxed.

Workers Compensation Plans

Workers compensation came to the U.S. in the early 1900's. Prior to workers compensation, employees injured on the job had to establish negligence on the part of the employer, if they expected to be compensated for their time and injuries. This would mean suing the employer for damages. The employer had several common law defenses available that made winning highly unlikely for the employee. Some of these defenses included:

- Fellow servant defense - Basically, the employer would redirect negligence to the fellow employee.

- Contributory negligence – The employer's defense stated that the injured employee damaged themselves through their own negligence.

- Assumption of risk – The employer would argue that the employee knew and assumed the risk of the job when hired.

Due to the unlikelihood of the employee being able to collect from the employer, the workers compensation system was implemented. The basic concept of workers compensation includes:

No fault system – Workers compensation is considered "no fault." If an employee is injured in the course of and out of employment, the employer will be responsible. **Fault does not have to be established.** Each state has established benefits available if injury occurs on the job.

Exclusive remedy – Workers compensation is said to be the exclusive remedy for the employee. This means that if an employee is injured on the job and qualifies for workers compensation benefits, **the benefits established by state law are the exclusive remedy for recovery.** The purpose of this is to reduce or eliminate the need and expense of a law suit in order to recover. Benefits have already been pre-established, suing to recover will not be necessary.

Benefits – The details of the workers compensation benefits are established state by state. All state benefits fall into four common categories.

- **Medical benefits** – medical benefits are **unlimited** in how much could be paid out in benefit. In most cases all medical expenses will be covered, as long as it is a work related injury.

- **Disability benefits** – Workers compensation will replace lost income for job related injuries. Benefits are typically **66 2/3 of the employee's average weekly wages.**

- **Survivor (death) benefits** – Survivor benefits could consist of two different benefits, burial and survivor income.

- **Rehabilitation benefits** – Rehabilitation benefits are designed to get the injured worker back into the work force. This is accomplished through either physical or vocational rehabilitation.

In order for any benefits to be compensable, the injuries must be accidental, arise out of employment, and arise in the course of employment.

Compulsory or elective laws – States are either compulsory or elective. Most states are compulsory, which means if an employer hires **one or more employees, the employer must provide workers compensation protection**. An elective state gives the employer the option to carry workers compensation.

There are a few employee classifications that may be excluded from workers compensation coverage. Two of the more common situations include: farm workers and domestic servants.

Occupational diseases – Workers compensation may also cover an occupational disease. An occupational disease is a disease that is a direct result of the occupation and is inherent to that occupation. For example, black lung is a disease that is associated with coal miners.

Second injury fund – The second injury fund is a fund established through the workers compensation system that is designed to assist the employer in hiring a previously injured individual. Since a second injury could result in a greater financial loss to an employee than another employee who did not have a previous injury, an employer could be hesitant to hire this employee. With the use of the second injury fund, if an employee has a second injury, the employer will only be responsible up to the amount of a first injury. Any additional compensation paid to the employee, will be paid from the second injury fund. The second injury fund is financed by assessing insurance companies writing workers compensation in the state.

Tax Treatment of Health Benefits

The two primary categories of health benefit are medical and disability income. Medical benefits are designed to reimburse or cover the insured for a medical expense; therefore, new money is not generated. Since there is no earned income, **medical benefits are not taxed as income**.

Disability policies are designed to replace lost income. The tax treatment of the disability product is based upon how the premium is paid. If the premium is being paid by the individual, then it is being paid for with money that has been previously earned and taxed. **If the premium dollars have been taxed, then the benefit will not be taxed when it is received.**

If the disability policy is provided through an employer, the benefit may be taxed. In this case, if the employer is paying the premium with pre-taxed dollars, then the employee will receive the benefit as an extension of income. In this case, the benefit would be taxed.

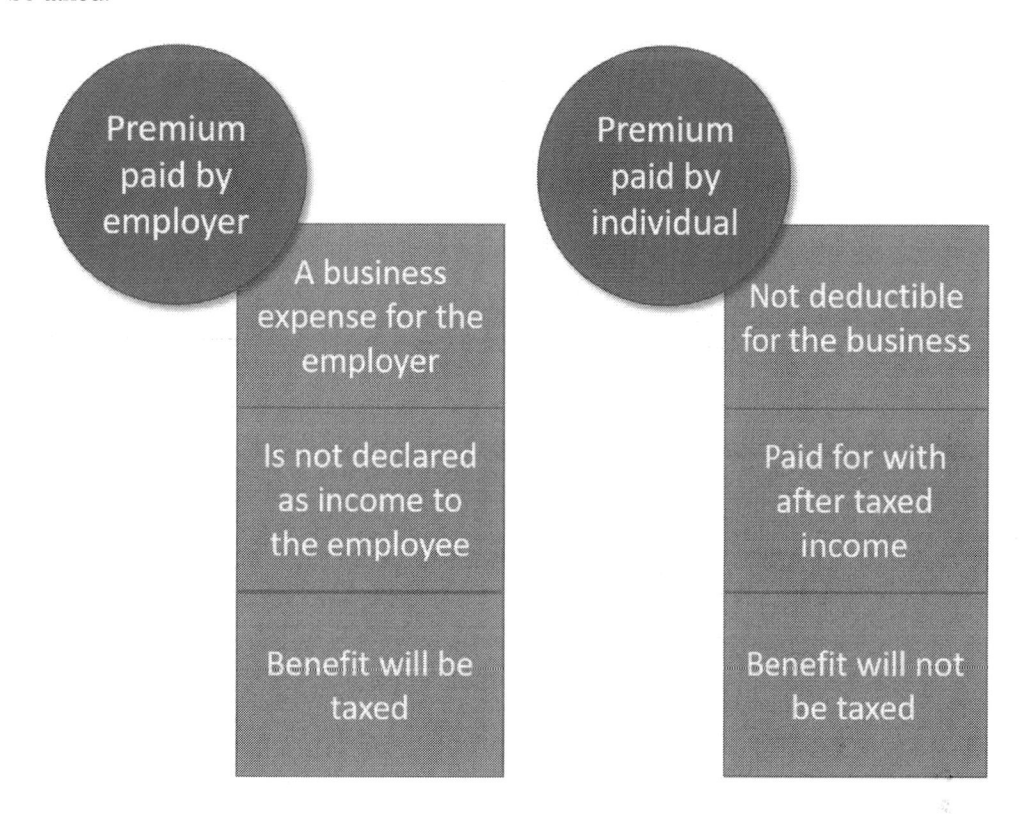

Premium paid by employer
- A business expense for the employer
- Is not declared as income to the employee
- Benefit will be taxed

Premium paid by individual
- Not deductible for the business
- Paid for with after taxed income
- Benefit will not be taxed

If the premium obligation was shared between the employer and the employee, then the tax advantage would be proportionate to the premium.

Occupational vs. Nonoccupational Coverage

A nonoccupational policy is designed to cover accidents and sickness that occur outside of the workplace. Accidents that occur at the workplace are assumed to be covered by the workers compensation policy. A nonoccupational policy would avoid the overlap of protection and only provide coverage away from the job.

PROFESSIONAL TRAINING INSTITUTION

Chapter Review

TERMS TO KNOW

Blue Cross Blue Shield

Service organization

Members

Provider

Health Maintenance Organization

Prepaid healthcare

Primary Care Physician

Gatekeeper

Network

Co Pay

Open and Closed Panel System

Preferred Provider Organization

Prearranged discount

Point of Service

Federal Marketplace

Essential Health Coverage

Individual Mandate

Minimum Essential Coverage (MEC)

Qualified Health Plan (QHP)

Premium Tax Credit (Subsidy)

Cost-Sharing Reduction

Employer Mandate

Full Time Equivalent Employees

SHOP

Multiple Employer Trust (MET)

Multiple Employer Welfare Association (MEWA)

Health Savings Account (HSA)

High deductible health plan (HDHP)

Workers compensation

No fault system

Exclusive remedy

Compulsory laws

Occupational disease

Second injury fund

Nonoccupational coverage

NUMBERS AND TIME PERIODS

Over 50 Full Time Equivalent Employees make a large group

66 2/3 of AWW, Workers Compensation disability benefit

1, minimum employees required for Workers Comp coverage

PROFESSIONAL TRAINING INSTITUTION

SAMPLE QUESTIONS

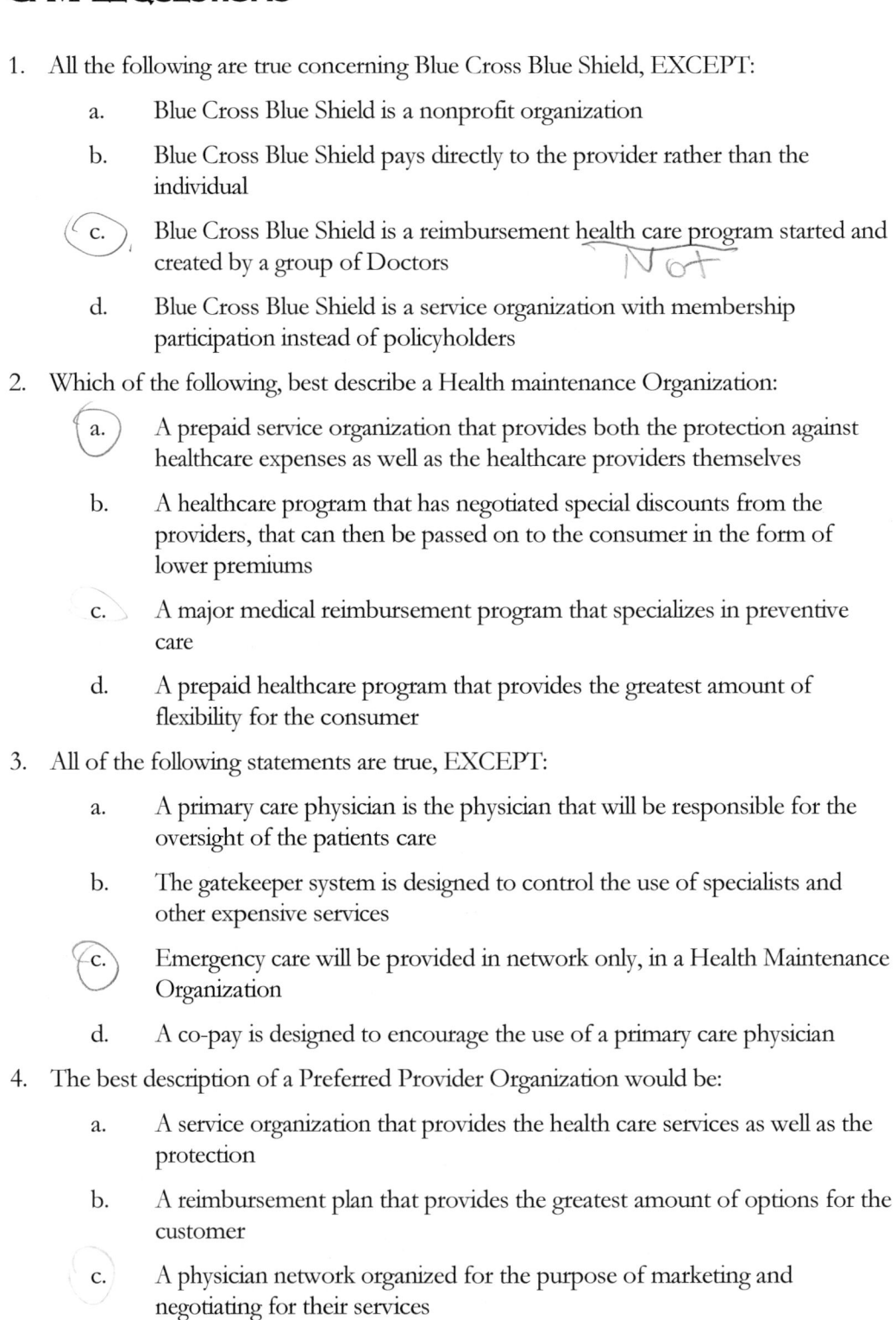

1. All the following are true concerning Blue Cross Blue Shield, EXCEPT:
    a. Blue Cross Blue Shield is a nonprofit organization
    b. Blue Cross Blue Shield pays directly to the provider rather than the individual
    c. Blue Cross Blue Shield is a reimbursement health care program started and created by a group of Doctors
    d. Blue Cross Blue Shield is a service organization with membership participation instead of policyholders

2. Which of the following, best describe a Health maintenance Organization:
    a. A prepaid service organization that provides both the protection against healthcare expenses as well as the healthcare providers themselves
    b. A healthcare program that has negotiated special discounts from the providers, that can then be passed on to the consumer in the form of lower premiums
    c. A major medical reimbursement program that specializes in preventive care
    d. A prepaid healthcare program that provides the greatest amount of flexibility for the consumer

3. All of the following statements are true, EXCEPT:
    a. A primary care physician is the physician that will be responsible for the oversight of the patients care
    b. The gatekeeper system is designed to control the use of specialists and other expensive services
    c. Emergency care will be provided in network only, in a Health Maintenance Organization
    d. A co-pay is designed to encourage the use of a primary care physician

4. The best description of a Preferred Provider Organization would be:
    a. A service organization that provides the health care services as well as the protection
    b. A reimbursement plan that provides the greatest amount of options for the customer
    c. A physician network organized for the purpose of marketing and negotiating for their services
    d. A reimbursement plan that has negotiated a prearranged discount with physicians and can offer better protection within their network

5. A Point of Service (POS) plan:
   - a. Offers both in and out of network coverage ✓
   - b. Offers in network coverage only
   - c. Does not use a network
   - d. Pays best out of network

6. Several employers coming together for the purpose of buying insurance, would be a:
   - a. MEWA
   - b. MET ✓
   - c. MMA
   - d. HSA — Health Savings Accounts

7. A Health Savings Account is an account:
   - a. That is primarily used for retirement purposes
   - b. Is a "use it or lose it" account
   - c. Is used in conjunction with a "high deductible health plan" ✓
   - d. Does not receive special tax advantages

8. Workers Compensation was designed to be:
   - a. A "no fault" system
   - b. Exclusive remedy
   - c. Both a and b ✓
   - d. Neither a nor b

9. The second injury fund is designed to:
   - a. Pay for pain and suffering in gross negligence cases
   - b. Discourage discriminatory hiring practices of the previously disabled ✓
   - c. Penalize the employer for repetitive injuries in the workplace
   - d. Help the employer meet their financial obligation for work related injuries that affect multiple employees

10. Medical benefits:
    - a. Are taxed as ordinary income
    - b. Are tax deductible
    - c. Will not be taxed as income ✓
    - d. Taxed over 7.5% of AGI

11. Under the Affordable Care Act everyone should have health insurance available to them. Which term describes this idea?

    a. Cost-Sharing Reduction

    b. Guaranteed Renewable

    c. Catastrophic Coverage

    d. Guaranteed Available

12. The Premium Tax Credit is available if an individual has a household income between what percentage of the Federal Poverty Level?

    a. 0% - 100%

    b. 100% - 400%

    c. 50% - 100%

    d. 100% - 250%

13. What standardized percentage is given in the Gold Metal Plan?

    a. 60%

    b. 70%

    c. 80%

    d. 90%

14. What pre-existing condition may be considered in underwriting and effect premium?

    a. Smoking

    b. AIDS/HIV

    c. Age

    d. Occupation

15. What term describes the minimum benefits required by the federal government that an individual must carry?

    a. Individual Mandate

    b. Essential Health Benefits

    c. Minimum Essential Coverage

    d. Qualified Health Plan

Answers: 1.c 2.a 3.c 4.d 5.a 6.b 7.c 8.c 9.b 10.c 11.d 12.b 13.c 14.a 15. c

PROFESSIONAL TRAINING INSTITUTION

Chapter 14

Disability Income Insurance

The disability policy is designed to replace lost income due to accident or sickness. It is sometimes referred to as a "loss of income" or "income replacement" policy.

The medical expense policy is designed to pay the medical bills generated due accidents and sicknesses. But when accident and sickness occur, the insured may be left without the ability to earn an income. The disability policy is designed to replace lost income due to the insured becoming disabled and unable to work.

Responsible financial planning always considers the possibility of losing one's ability to earn an income. Some practical considerations include:

- Protecting a minimum amount of income, in the event of disability.

- Protecting accumulated retirement funds and the ability to accumulate funds for retirement in the future.

- Protect against long term, as well as short term disability.

The main advantage of using insurance to protect the above financial risk is the fact that the insurance policy provides an immediate benefit, when needed the most. Other ways of protecting yourself from loss of income include: using savings or investments, depending on spousal income or liquidating accumulated assets. All of these methods include personal risk and uncertainty. The disability insurance policy is there when you need it and in the amount that you need, without liquidating that which has taken years to accumulate.

Characteristics of Disability Income Policies

Qualifying for the disability income benefits is based upon meeting the definition of disability and is limited to a percentage of income. Benefits are typically paid monthly for the length of disability or the term purchased, whichever occurs first. The definitions play a key role in the effectiveness of this policy.

Disability Definitions

Probationary period - A probationary period is **a period of time in which the insured must wait, before coverage is available for sickness**. The probationary period begins on the effective date of the policy. The primary purpose of the probationary period is to provide a waiting period for health conditions that existed prior to the application. These conditions are referred to as **pre-existing conditions**. Accidents are covered immediately.

Elimination period - An elimination period is **a period of time in which the insured must wait, before coverage is available for sickness or accidents.** The elimination period begins each time a benefit period begins. This period is sometimes referred to as a **deductible of time.** Since the elimination begins with each qualifying event, an insured could have multiple elimination periods. Elimination periods are common on disability policies as well as long term care policies.

Benefit period – The benefit period is the length of time in which the policy will pay for any one disability period. Policies are sometimes characterized as short term or long term disability. **A short term disability product has a term of two years or less. A long term would provide a benefit period of over two years.**

Recurrent disability – A new disability period is established by the recurrent disability definition. A recurrent disability is established by a period of time in between disabilities. Jill has a short term disability policy with 12 months worth of benefits after a 30 day elimination period. Her recurrent disability time period is based on a 60 day time period. Jill has a back injury and becomes disabled. After 4 months, she returns to work. After 46 days back to work, Jill re-injures her back and is disabled. If Jill had re-injured her back after 92 days, the injury would not be considered recurrent; it would have been considered a new injury. Because, she has not been free from care for 60 days or longer, this is considered a recurrent disability. The good news is that Jill is covered immediately without a new elimination period. The bad news is that she has used up 4 of her 12 months in her benefit period.

Definitions of total disability – One of the most important definitions within the disability policy are the definitions of the disability itself. Different products may use different definitions.

- **Own occupation** – The own occupation definition defines the disability as the **inability to perform the duties of the insured's own occupation**. Jill is a welder and can no longer handle the material needed to do the job as a result of her back injury. With the own occupation definition, if Jill is unable to do the duties of her current occupation, even if she might be able to do something else, she will be classified as disabled. Jill is disabled and eligible for benefits after she meets her elimination period.

- **Any occupation** – Any occupation definition is considered to be a **more restrictive** definition than the own occupation definition. Any occupation means **the inability to perform the duties of any occupation for which the insured has had past experience, training, or education**. Jill cannot weld. But, she has been trained to teach. Even though Jill has not taught in years, because she's been educated in another occupation, she is not considered disabled. Even if a teaching job isn't readily available, Jill is still considered able to work. She would not collect a disability benefit.

- Sometimes, a policy may begin with an own occupation definition for one or two years and then switch to an any occupation after the designated period of time. This gives the insured time to prepare for the change in definition.

- **Presumptive disability** – A presumptive disability is a disability that is so serious the insurer is not going to challenge the status. It is an automatic qualifying event, regardless of the insured's ability to work. It is typically defined as:

    o Loss of use of any two limbs

    o Total and permanent blindness

    o Loss of speech or hearing

Definitions of Partial Disability – Partial disability is the inability to perform every duty of one's occupation, but the ability to perform one or more important duties of the occupation.

- **Partial disability** – One of the original purposes of the partial disability definition is to allow and encourage the insured to return to work as soon as possible. The typical partial disability benefit would pay 50% of the total disability benefit for a limited period of time. Because this definition was as rigid as it was, it did not always accomplish its original intent. If Jill finds that she is able to return to work, but can only earn 30% of her original wage, the partial disability benefit of 50% would not fully compensate her.

- **Residual disability** – The residual disability benefit recompenses Jill a proportion of her benefit, based on the proportion that she is able to earn. If Jill can earn 30% of her total pay, the policy will pay 70% of her total disability benefit.

Jill is eligible for $4,000 per month in benefits. But, when Jill purchased the policy she chose to purchase a benefit of $3,000 per month. After Jill's disability, she finds that she is able to work part time. If she can earn 30% of her pay, prior to disability, the insurer will pay 70% of her benefit.

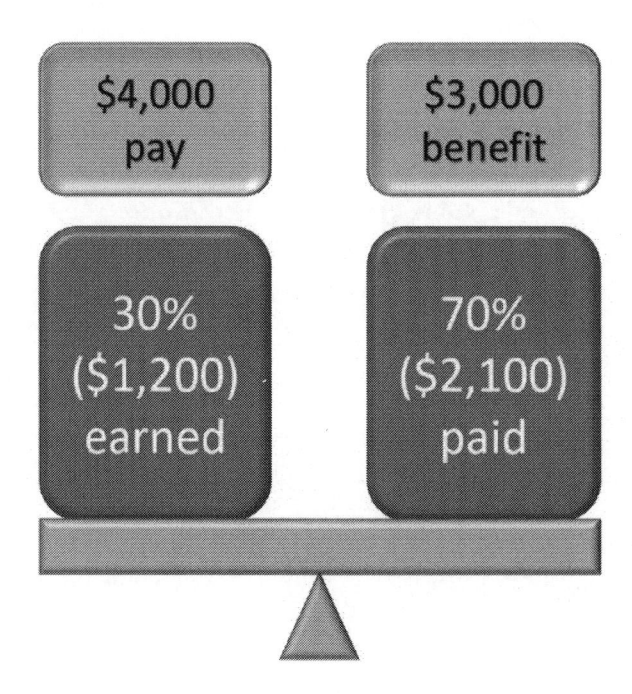

$4,000 pay | $3,000 benefit

30% ($1,200) earned | 70% ($2,100) paid

UNDERWRITING

When underwriting the disability policy, occupation is of special importance. Occupation is a critical element in the pricing of the policy. The more hazardous the occupation, the more the insurer will charge to accept the risk.

BENEFIT LIMITS

The amount of protection available will be based upon a percentage of the insured's average earnings. Typically an insurer will limit the amount of protection available to 66 2/3% or 75%. Based upon the principal of indemnity, the objective is to make the insured whole in the event of a loss, but not to profit. If the insured is more valuable disabled, this would create an incentive for fraud.

Other Disability Benefits

Other benefits may be found on some disability policies. These benefits could be built in or added as a rider.

Waiver of Premium

The waiver of premium benefit **waives the premium in the event of disability**. While you are disabled and the insurer is paying your benefits, the company will not ask you to pay the premium on your policy. There is usually a waiting period (30, 60, or 90 days would be typical) prior to this benefit going into effect. This benefit may be limited to a certain age. If the disability ends, then the insured resumes making premium payments on the policy. The insured would not be responsible for the past waived premiums.

Return of Premium

Some policies may have a return of premium benefit. This allows the insured to receive a return of all premiums paid based upon the qualifying events written in the policy.

Rehabilitation Benefits

This benefit helps pay for the cost of rehabilitation. Rehabilitation can be an expensive process. Rehabilitation can come in two different forms; it could be vocational or physical. Vocational is designed to retrain the disabled person for a new occupation. Physical rehabilitation's goal is to get the insured up, moving and back to working condition.

Taxation of Disability Income Benefits

Disability policies are designed to replace lost income. The tax treatment of the disability product is based upon how the premium is paid. If the premium is being paid by the individual, then it is being paid for with money that has been previously earned and taxed. **If the premium dollars have been taxed, then the benefit will not be taxed when it is received**.

If the disability policy is provided through an employer, the benefit may be taxed. In this case, if the employer is paying the premium with pre-taxed dollars, then the employee will receive the benefit as an extension of income. In this case, the benefit would be taxed.

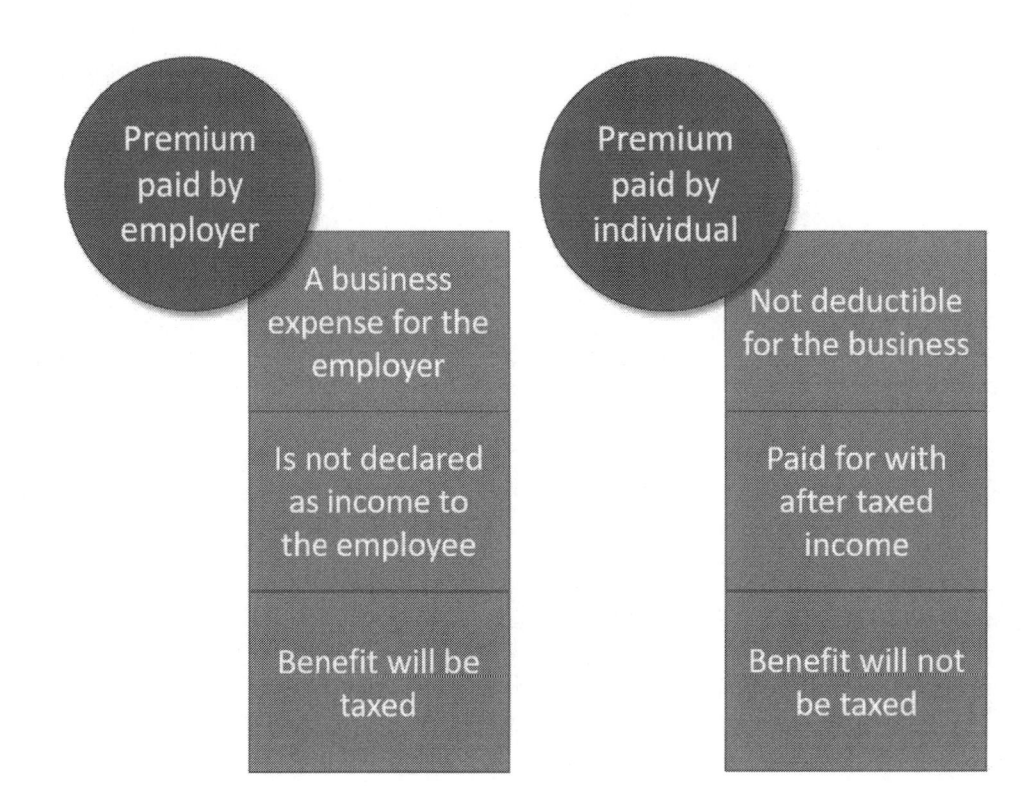

Premium paid by employer
- A business expense for the employer
- Is not declared as income to the employee
- Benefit will be taxed

Premium paid by individual
- Not deductible for the business
- Paid for with after taxed income
- Benefit will not be taxed

If the premium obligation was shared between the employer and the employee, then the tax advantage would be proportionate to the premium.

BUSINESS APPLICATIONS OF DISABILITY INCOME POLICIES

The disability policy may also be used to protect the business. There are several practical uses of the disability policy within a business.

Business Overhead Expense Policy

The business overhead expense policy is designed to **pay the overhead expense to keep the business operating** when the business owner is disabled. Overhead includes expenses like rent, utilities, and employee salaries. The benefit amount is generally not a fixed amount, but pays the amount of expenses actually incurred. The premium paid by the business is tax deductible as a business expense and the benefit will be taxed to the business as received.

Key Employee Disability Income Policy

Key employee disability insurance is designed to protect the business, in the event a key employee becomes disabled. The disability of a key employee could have a financial impact on the income of the business. This policy pays a benefit that replaces profits the business lost due to the disability of the key employee. Since it is a replacement of lost income, the benefit is not considered new money or income. This means that the **premium will be deducted as a business expense and the benefit paid will be tax free**. This policy will be:

- Owned by the business

- Paid for by the business, and

- The benefit will be received by the business as a beneficiary

In order for the business to purchase insurance on the life of the key employee, the employee must grant permission before coverage can be purchased.

Disability Buy-Sell Policy

The buy-sell policy is designed to fund a buy-sell agreement within a business. The agreement is a contract prepared by an attorney. The agreement determines that if an owner of the business becomes disabled and cannot meet the responsibilities to the business, the remaining owners will be allowed to buy out the disabled owner. In the event of disability, the buy-sell policy provides the funds needed for the remaining owners to buy out the disabled owner's share.

Since an owner would not want to be forced to sell his or her ownership position prematurely, **this policy typically has an exceptionally long elimination period**. The elimination period may be one to two years. The policy will typically pay out the benefit in a lump sum amount, instead of a monthly benefit, so that the transaction can be completed.

REDUCING TERM DISABILITY

Reducing term disability is a form of credit insurance. It is a policy designed to pay off the loan if the owner becomes disabled. As the loan is paid down, the amount needed to pay off the loan is reduced. The benefit of the policy is designed to match the loan as it is being paid down.

GROUP DISABILITY INCOME POLICIES

Businesses may purchase a policy that is made available to the employees on a group basis. A variety of benefits may be made available on a group basis. Benefits could be short term or long term. Employers may pay all or part of the premiums. The group may have a probationary period that must be met prior to applying for coverage.

Chapter Review

TERMS TO KNOW

Probationary period

Elimination period

Recurrent disability

Own occupation

Any occupation

Presumptive disability

Partial disability

Residual disability

Waiver of premium

Business Overhead policy

Key Employee Disability policy

Disability buy sell arrangement

Sample Questions

1. Jay has a disability policy. After his accident he had to wait 30 days before benefits began. Jay probably has:

    a. 30 day probationary period

    b. 30 day grace period

    c. 30 day elimination period

    d. Recurrent disability

2. Presumptive disability is:

    a. A type of partial disability

    b. The inability to sustain employment

    c. Typically defined as a disability caused by and occupational disease

    d. Typically defined as loss of two limbs, permanent blindness or loss of speech or hearing

3. Jay's disability policy defines recurrent disability based upon a 60 day time period. After 6 months of disability, Jay returns to work for 45 days and reinjures his back. As a result, this second disability:

    a. Will require a new elimination period, but will begin a new benefit period

    b. Will begin where benefits left off without a new elimination period

    c. Will begin where benefits left off without a new elimination period, but will receive a new benefit period

    d. Will require a new elimination period, and will not begin a new benefit period

4. An "own occupation" definition:

    a. Is more restrictive than the any occupation definition

    b. Is less restrictive than the any occupation definition

    c. Is not any more or less restrictive than the any occupation definition

    d. Is less advantageous to the policyholder

5. John earns $4,000 per month. He chose to purchase $2,000 in disability benefits. After John's disability, his employer is willing to bring him back on a part time basis. He will be able to earn $800. How much will his residual disability benefit provide?

    a. $3,200

    b. $2,000

    c. $1,600

    d. $800

6. The disability buy sell policy is different from other disability policies, in that:
    a. The benefits really are no different, the difference is in how the policy is used
    b. Benefits are paid out in a lump sum amount, once the disability has been established
    c. It usually has a long elimination period and pays out in a lump sum amount
    d. It forces the disabled individual to buy out the other owners

7. The waiver of premium benefit on the disability policy:
    a. Allows the insured to waive their premium regardless of disability status
    b. Waives the premium in the event of premature death
    c. Disregards the premium obligation while disabled
    d. Benefits are waived as the premium comes due

8. Which of the following tax considerations are true for the disability policy?
    a. If the disability policy is paid by the employer the benefits will be taxable
    b. If the disability policy is paid by the individual the benefits will be taxable
    c. If the disability policy is paid by the employer the benefits will be tax free
    d. Benefits will be considered income, and taxed, regardless of who pays the premium

9. Which of the following would be used by a business to pay the overhead expense to keep a business operating while the owner is disabled?
    a. Key employee
    b. Business overhead
    c. Buy sell agreement
    d. Reducing term disability

Answers: 1.c 2.d 3.b 4.b 5.c 6.c 7.c 8.a 9.b

PROFESSIONAL TRAINING INSTITUTION

Chapter 15

Accidental Death and Dismemberment (AD&D) Policies

Accident policies have been around for many years. This policy is designed to assist the insured for those unexpected events in life.

Accidents are **sudden and unexpected events**. Accident policies are designed to pay over and above other insurance in the event of an accident. These policies may be sold as a rider or a standalone policy. They may be sold individually or as a group product. Today's accident policy will pay for a variety of accidental issues. One of the original accident policies was the accidental death and dismemberment policy. This policy was very specific in what it would pay for. The terms and definitions in a health policy are always important. The terms and definitions of the accident policy is no exception.

ACCIDENTAL MEANS

Different policies may use different definitions of an accident. **Accidental means looks at the originating cause of the accident.** It is not just the unintended result, but the means of the accident. If the cause as well as the result was accidental, then the event qualifies as an accident.

Jeff makes a bet that he can stand on a ball. While making the attempt, the ball rolls out from under him. Jeff reaches out to catch himself and breaks his arm in the attempt. Under accidental means definition, the policy would look at the cause of the accident. Since a reasonable person would understand that standing on a ball will, most probably, result in an injury. This would not be considered accidental.

ACCIDENTAL BODILY INJURY

If the policy defines an accident as accidental bodily injury, then it is the result that determines if the event was an accident. **If the injury was unexpected and unintended, then it qualifies as an accident.** The accidental bodily injury definition is an easier definition to qualify for. Accidental bodily injury is said to be less restrictive than accidental means. Accidental means is more restrictive, which means it is more difficult for an insured to qualify for a benefit under this definition.

In our above example, what Jeff did may not have been the most intelligent act; he did not anticipate the result. The broken arm was unexpected and unintended. Under accidental bodily injury, this would qualify as an accident.

PRINCIPAL SUM

The principal sum is **the amount paid for accidental death**. It is also the maximum amount that the policy will pay in a lifetime. Regardless of the number or the type of accidents that occur, once the policy reaches the principal sum, benefits are exhausted.

CAPITAL SUM

The capital sums are the **amounts paid for dismemberment, blindness, or loss of hearing**. Capital sums are typically scheduled in the policy and may be a percentage of the principal sum.

Adam C Dint (or AC for short), buys an accident policy with the following benefits:

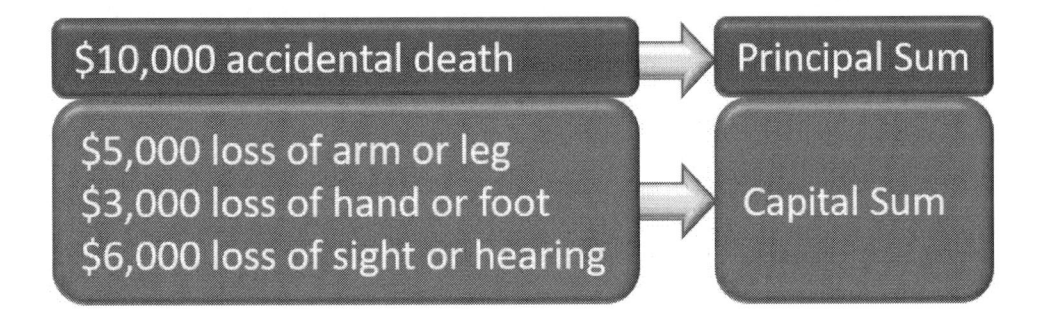

$10,000 accidental death	Principal Sum
$5,000 loss of arm or leg $3,000 loss of hand or foot $6,000 loss of sight or hearing	Capital Sum

AC is in a tragic auto accident and loses a hand. His policy will provide a benefit of $3,000. If later, AC dies in a different accident, he could collect another $7,000.

Multiple Indemnity

Some accident policies may pay a multiple indemnity as a result of specific types of accidents. Double indemnity would pay twice the principal sum when qualified for. An accident policy might double the death benefit due to a transportation accident.

Accidental Death Time Limits

An accident may not result in immediate death. An accidental death and dismemberment policy may allow an amount of time after the death to establish if a death was due to an accident or not. A policy may allow 30, 60, or 90 days in order to establish if the occurrence was an accident.

Chapter Review

TERMS TO KNOW

Accidental means

Accidental bodily injury

Principal sum

Capital sum

Multiple indemnity

Sample Questions

1. Accidental means:
   a. Looks at the end result of the accident to determine qualification for benefits
   b. Is less restrictive than "accidental bodily injury"
   c. States that the injury must be unexpected and unintended
   d. Looks at the originating cause of the accident

2. The amount paid out for death is referred to as the:
   a. Capital sum
   b. Principal sum
   c. Indemnity sum
   d. Residual sum

3. The amount paid out as a result of dismemberment is referred to as the:
   a. Capital sum
   b. Principal sum
   c. Indemnity sum
   d. Residual sum

Answers: 1.d 2.b 3.a

PROFESSIONAL TRAINING INSTITUTION

Chapter 16

Limited Health Policies

Some policies are created with a very specific purpose in mind. The limited policies are products that are very limited in coverage with a very limited purpose.

The following limited lines products are usually offered in addition to other insurance. Since these policies cover a very specific need, they will usually not conflict with an individual's group or individual medical insurance. Benefits are usually paid over and above other policies. These policies will not typically include an "other insurance clause." The limited policy is commonly sold as a supplemental coverage to other insurance. These policies will cover areas of specific concern or areas that may not be adequately covered by the other coverages.

HOSPITAL INDEMNITY POLICIES

The hospital indemnity policy is designed to pay a daily benefit for each day the insured is confined in the hospital. The term indemnity means to make financially whole. Obviously, a policy that pays $100 or $200 per day while in the hospital, will not fully indemnify the hospital expense incurred. The primary purpose of this policy is not to pay the hospital bill, but to indemnify the insured for the financial loss as a result of not being able to work. This policy intends to replace lost income. The hospital indemnity policy is basically a disability policy with a strict definition of disability based upon confinement to the hospital. This policy will provide extra cash, to assist the insured while confined in the hospital.

PRESCRIPTION DRUG POLICY

A prescription drug policy is a policy which reimburses the insured for prescription drug expenses.

Dread Disease Policies

A dread disease policy is a policy that limits coverage to a particular disease that is usually associated with extreme expenses. Probably the most common dread disease policy that has been sold is the cancer policy. Cancer is a disease that is dreaded and feared by most people. Cancer is also associated with experimental treatment, extreme prolonged expenses, and extra costs that may not be covered by other policies. Dread disease policies may provide protection for more than one disease. When it does pay, it will pay directly to the insured, over and above other coverages.

Dental Expense Policies

Dental costs can be quite expensive. The dental policy is designed to assist with these costs. The dental policy is usually divided into three categories of coverage:

- Routine preventive services – Prevention has been found to be very effective in limiting the expenses of future dental care. To encourage prevention, this coverage usually comes with immediate first dollar coverage. Maximum amounts may be limited. Coverage may include full coverage for an annual dental exam and cleaning.

- Routine restorative services – This coverage will come with a deductible and separate limit. Some examples of routine restorative include the filling of cavities, caps, or pulling wisdom teeth.

- Orthodontic – Due to the unique nature and cost of orthodontics, this coverage is separated from the rest. Orthodontics will have its own limit, as well as a higher deductible.

Vision Care Policies

Vision care policies help pay the cost of eyeglasses, contact lenses and regular eye exams.

Travel Accident Policies

Travel accident policies cover the insured while traveling. This policy typically is sold to cover a specific trip, by means of a specific mode of transportation. Coverage is provided while traveling to or from a specific destination. It is sold at airport terminals, bus stations and other places of public transportation.

Credit Insurance

Credit insurance is sold by the institutions providing loans, for the purpose of paying off the debt in the event of death or disability.

Chapter Review

TERMS TO KNOW

Hospital indemnity policy

Prescription drug policy

Dread disease policy

Dental expense policy

Vision care policy

Travel accident policy

Credit insurance

SAMPLE QUESTIONS

1. The primary purpose of the hospital indemnity policy is to:
    a. Pay room and board in the hospital
    b. Pay directly to the provider
    c. Replace lost income while in the hospital
    d. Reimburse the insured for the hospital expense

2. John has a policy that pays specifically if he develops cancer. What type of policy does John have?
    a. Indemnity policy
    b. Dread Disease policy
    c. Basic medical expense plan
    d. Major Medical

3. Which coverage, under the dental policy, does not have a deductible?
    a. Orthodontic coverage
    b. Routine restorative services
    c. Routine preventive services
    d. All areas will have a deductible

Answers: 1.c 2.b 3.c

PROFESSIONAL TRAINING INSTITUTION

Chapter 17

Uniform Individual Health Policy Provisions

Provisions are the sections or clauses of an insurance policy that communicate specific rules and guidelines within the policy.

Provisions are the rules and guidelines of the policy. They are either required or optional. A provision that is required to be included in the policy is required by the state. The state is responsible for the protection of the public. **Required provisions are required by the state because they protect the public from the company.** Since the insurance policy is a contract of adhesion (written by the insurance company), the company may be hesitant to include a rule that benefits or protects the rights of the consumer. **An optional provision is optional because it protects the insurance company from the insured.** Since the insurance companies write the contracts, it is their choice to include the optional provisions or not.

REQUIRED PROVISIONS

The following provisions are required:

#1 ENTIRE CONTRACT & CHANGES

The entire contract provision clarifies what constitutes the complete agreement. **The entire contract includes the policy itself, the application and any attachments.** No other documents will be considered as part of the contract. The entire contract is what the agreement between the two parties is based upon. Any discrepancies or misunderstandings will be clarified based upon the wording of the entire contract. This guarantees that the insured will have access to the full agreement.

The changes portion of the provision states that **any changes made in the contract can only be made by an executive officer of the company**. Since the insurance company is responsible for the wording of the contract, only the company can alter the wording. An agent or the insured cannot make any changes in the wording of the agreement.

#2 Time Limit on Certain Defenses or Incontestable Clause

The time limit on certain defenses clause gives the insurance company a 2 years (3 in some states) to challenge or contest the information on the application. After 2 years, the policy is incontestable. The insurer cannot void the contract because of misstatements on the application. The only exception to the 2 year time limit is fraud. The insurer can void the contract due to fraud. Fraud is not limited to 2 years.

#3 Grace Period

The grace period is the period of time that the insured has to pay the premium after the policy comes due. In health insurance, the insured has 7 days grace to pay the premium if the payment is being made on a weekly basis. The insured has 10 days if the payment is being made monthly. There will be a 31 day period for any other method of payment. If the insured were to have a claim during the **31 day grace** period, **coverage still continues.** Since the premium has not been paid for the new term and since the insurer is required to provide coverage according to the contract, **the insurer may deduct any premium obligation owed from the claim** if the payment of a claim is required.

#4 Reinstatement

The reinstatement clause provides the opportunity for the insured to reinstate a policy in a way that is both fair to the insured, as well as the insurer. If an insured has allowed a policy to lapse beyond the grace period, the company can collect, no more than **60 days of back premium**. The insurer will have up to **45 days to accept or reject the application**. The insurer can place a **10 day waiting period for sickness**. Once a policy has been reinstated, the insured will have all the rights of the original agreement.

#5 Notice of Claim

The notice of claim provision requires that the insured be given at least **20 days (60 in some states) to inform the insurer of a claim or as soon as reasonably possible.** Notice to the agent qualifies as notice to the insurer.

#6 Claim Forms

Once the notice of claim has been received from the insured, the **insurer has 15 days to supply its claim form to the insured.** If the insurer does not provide a claim form within the time allotted, the insured will be required to submit the necessary claim information detailing the information necessary for the claim to be processed.

#7 Proof of Loss

The proof of loss consists of the information necessary to process the claim. Most typically it would be the completed claim form with any necessary receipts or information. Once the insured receives the claim form from the insurer, **the insured has 90 days after the date of loss to submit a proof of loss.** If 90 days is not a reasonable period of time for the insured, proof may be submitted no later than one year from the time proof is otherwise required.

#8 Time of Payment of Claims

This provision states that once proof of loss has been received, the insurer must pay the claim in a timely fashion. **Payment of claims must be paid immediately.** Most state laws define immediately as within **60 days** (30 in some states).

Payments made periodically, as in a disability policy must be made at least **monthly**.

#9 Payment of Claims

Payment of claims provision **specifies to whom claims should be paid**. The provision deals with several different situations. It basically includes the following:

- Any death benefit will be paid out to the named beneficiary. If the beneficiary designation is not listed, then any benefits owed after a death are paid to the insured's estate.

- Any indemnity owed after a death, other than a specified death benefit, will be paid at the insurer's option to either the listed beneficiary or the estate.

- If the insured is alive, any benefit owed will be paid directly to the insured unless otherwise specified in the policy.

This provision may include further language that would allow one or both of the following:

- A facility of payment clause allows the insurer to pay a benefit, of less than $1,000, owed a minor or a beneficiary who is legally incapacitated to any relative; by blood or marriage who is deemed entitled to the money.

- Wording that would allow the insurer to pay claims directly to the hospital or medical provider.

#10 Physical Exam and Autopsy

This provision allows the insurer the right and opportunity to examine the insured as often as it may reasonably be needed. Any expense of an exam or autopsy will always be the responsibility of the insurer. If the insured is alive and receiving benefits, he or she could be required to submit to physical exams to verify the status and qualifications of the benefits.

In the event of death, an autopsy may be needed to determine the cause of the death and the benefits owed. Autopsies can be performed at the expense of the insurer, as long all state laws are complied with and the autopsy is not forbidden by law.

#11 Legal Action

An insured may feel the need to take legal action against the insurance company. Before an insured can take any legal action against an insurance company, the insured must give the company an adequate period of time to respond to the claim. **The insured must allow the insurer 60 days after filing a written proof of loss, before any action can be instigated against the insurance company.**

If the insured is going to take action against the company, **the suit must be filed within 3 years after the time that written proof of loss** has been required to be furnished.

#12 Change of Beneficiary

The policyowner, who is usually the insured, will have the right to designate and change the beneficiary designation, unless an irrevocable designation has been named. Most designations are revocable. A revocable designation can be changed at any time by the insured. The insured maintains the right to choose and change the designation. If an irrevocable designation is named, the insured relinquishes the right to change the designation.

#13 Guaranteed Renewability

In compliance with the federal Health Insurance Portability and Accountability Act of 1996, renewability is guaranteed.

Optional Policy Provisions

The following provisions will be included in the policy at the option of the insurer. Optional provisions are written to protect the insurer.

#1 Change of Occupation

The occupation of the insured may be a critical factor in the rate that is charged for the coverage. Occupation is a major factor in determining the rate for the disability policy. When an insured changes occupation, it is sometimes the insurer that is the last to find out. **The change of occupation provision is written to protect the insurer in the event that the insured changes occupation while the policy is in effect.**

R.V. Wrinkle has just purchased a disability policy that provides a benefit of $1,000 per week. R.V. works at the local mattress factory and has the job of sleep testing each new mattress that the company creates. Since his job is considered low risk, his rate is very reasonable. R.V. has a $600 annual premium. After several years of extensive mattress testing, R.V. has decided to expand his horizons and branch out to something more challenging. He has left the mattress factory and taken a new job at the police department working with the bomb squad. R.V. is the individual that gets to decide whether to pull the red or the yellow wire. Soon after taking the new job, R.V. discovers to his dismay that he is color blind.

Since R.V. has moved from a low risk occupation to a high risk occupation his premium does not cover the exposure of the high risk occupation. The insurance company will lower his benefit and provide a benefit amount, based upon the premium rate of the new, high risk occupation.

Had R.V. moved the other way, from a high risk occupation to a low risk occupation, then the company would have refunded a portion of his premium and provided the benefit expected. In this case, the insurer would say that R.V. overpaid based upon the new occupation.

Whichever direction R.V. moves, **the correction is made by reducing something**. The insurer will either reduce the premium paid or the benefit to be received.

#2 Misstatement of Age

To correct a misstatement of age, **the benefit will be adjusted to provide a benefit based upon what the premium paid would have purchased at the correct age.**

Pat's age is 44. The age that has been given to the insurance company is 39. Since the age is understated, the appropriate rate has not been charged. If the correct age is not provided, once the insurer receives the correct age, benefits will be adjusted to correspond with the premium. In this case the benefit will be reduced. If the age had been overstated, the benefits would have been increased.

#3 Other Insurance with this Insurer

The goal of insurance is to indemnify the insured, but not to over indemnify, based upon insurable interest. An insured who is over indemnified would actually profit from being disabled or sick. This could encourage fraud. Insurers will always try to avoid this situation.

The next three provisions deal with the problem of having more insurance than might be needed to properly indemnify the insured. In this first provision, **the insured has more than one policy with the same insurance company and as a result is over insured.** The insured may have more insurance than the company will pay based upon the insured's average weekly wage and the limitations payable by the company. Or the insured may have two major medical policies, which would pay out a total of more than the cost of the health care.

This provision states that the insurer will pay no more than the benefit the insured qualifies for. Any excess coverage will be refunded. Or, it may state that the insurer will only pay the benefits under one of the two policies. A full refund of the second policy will be paid to the insured.

In either case, the insurer will never over indemnify the insured. The goal is to make the insured whole, no more or no less.

#4 & #5 Insurance with Other Insurers

Both of these provision deal with being over insured with another insurer. In this case, the insured has similar coverage with two different insurance companies. Again, the goal is to indemnify, and to avoid creating the opportunity for the insured to profit from disability or sickness. In these cases, **each insurer will pay on a pro rata or proportionate basis**. The difference between provision 4 and 5 is the type of policies that have been duplicated.

#4 Insurance with other Insurers: Expense Incurred – deals with two expense incurred, or major medical, policies.

#5 Insurance with other Insurers: Other Insurance – deals with two similar policies, disability income, other than expense incurred.

Bob purchased a disability policy with company A. His policy provides a benefit of $1,000 per week if he becomes disabled. After a few years, Bob is earning a higher income and decides to buy a new policy that will provide a better benefit. The new policy is bought from company B and is for $2,000 per week. Since the first policy is due in two months, Bob does not cancel his coverage with company A. Three weeks later, Bob is in an accident and finds himself totally disabled. Since Bob has paid the premium on both policies, he decides to file a claim on each. Bob's average weekly wage limits his coverage to $1800 per week. How will the companies pay this claim?

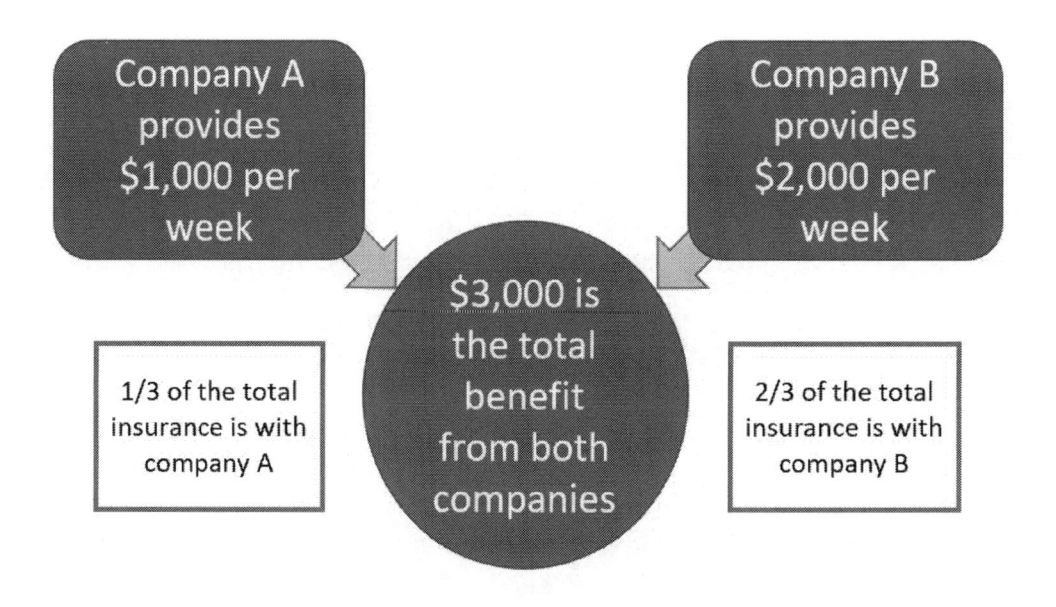

```
Company A provides $1,000 per week        Company B provides $2,000 per week
                    ↓                                        ↓
                        $3,000 is the total benefit from both companies
1/3 of the total insurance is with company A              2/3 of the total insurance is with company B
```

Since 1/3 of the total insurance is with company A, company A will be responsible for $600 per week, or 1/3 of his eligible benefits. Company B will be responsible for $1,200 of the weekly benefit, the other 2/3 of the claim. Bob receives 100% of his eligible benefit.

Typically, there is no advantage to being over insured. Bob is better off with one policy that is designed to meet his needs.

#6 Relation of Earnings to Insurance: Average Earnings

This provision is designed to see that the insured is properly indemnified. Since a disability policy is designed to pay a benefit to replace income, the goal is to provide a fair and adequate benefit, but not to over indemnify the insured. To determine the insured's average earnings, the insurer will **average out the earnings over the last 24 months**. If 24 months of income is not available at the current job, then the company will average out the income based on the number of months of employment.

If the average income is exceeded by the total benefit available, then **the insurer will not pay a benefit that exceeds the average earnings.** The minimum benefit paid will be $200 per month, regardless of the minimum average earnings.

#7 Unpaid Premium

Upon the payment of a claim, this provision allows any unpaid premiums due to be deducted from any amount owed. This provision is essential for companies if they are to deduct any premiums from a claim which continues beyond the due date or begins in the grace period.

#8 Conformity with State Statutes

Any provision of the policy which, on the effective date, is in conflict with the statutes of the state, in which the insured resides, will be amended to conform to the minimum requirements of the state. This provision keeps the insurer and the wording of the contract legal with the state.

#9 Illegal Occupation

The insurer will not be responsible for any loss to which a contributing cause was the insured's commission of or attempt to commit a felony or which a contributing cause was the insured's being engaged in an illegal occupation.

#10 Intoxicants and Narcotics

The insurer will not be responsible for any loss sustained as a result of the insured's being under the influence of any narcotic, unless administered by a physician.

#11 Cancellation

The cancellation provision establishes the right for the company to cancel a policy, once it is in place. This is an optional provision and a company may choose not to include this provision. If the policy is cancellable, the policy can be cancelled with just 5 days notice.

When a policy is cancelled, this provision will state how the unearned premium will be refunded. Who is doing the cancelling will determine the method used to refund any unearned premium.

If the insured requests a midterm cancellation of the policy, the insurer will refund the unearned premium on a **short rate basis**. This means that the insurer will be allowed to "short change" the insured to cover the expense of the request.

If the insurer requests the refund, the unearned premium will be refunded on a **pro rata basis**. The insured will refund a full proportion of percentage of the annual premium owed.

Chapter Review

TERMS TO KNOW

Provision

Required provisions

Optional provisions

Entire Contract & Changes

Time Limit on Certain Defenses

Incontestable

Grace Period

Reinstatement

Notice of Claim

Claim Forms

Proof of Loss

Time of Payment of Claims

Payment of Claims

Physical Exam and Autopsy

Legal Action

Change of Beneficiary

Change of Occupation

Misstatement of Age

Other Insurance

Relation of Earnings to Insurance

Unpaid Premium

Pro Rata Refund

Conformity with State Statutes

Illegal Occupation

Intoxicant and Narcotics

Numbers and Time Periods

2 *(or 3) years – Incontestability

31 days – Grace period

45/60/10 – Reinstatement

20 *(or 60) days – Notice of Claim

15 days – Claim forms

90 days – Proof of Loss

60 *(or 30) days – Time of Payment of Claims

60 days/3 years – Legal Action

24 months – Average earnings

*KY listed in parenthesis

SAMPLE QUESTIONS

1. Why are "required provisions" required and who are they required by?
    a. They are required by the state and protect the insurer from the insured
    b. They are required by the federal government and protect the insured from the insurer
    c. They are required by the insurer to protect the insured
    d. They are required by the state and protect the insured from the insurer

2. Which statement is true concerning changes made to the agreement between the insurer and the insured?
    a. Agents can make changes in the policy if the applicant requests and approves them
    b. Agents can only make changes in applications with consent of the insured
    c. Only an executive officer of the company can make a change in the policy language
    d. The insured may make changes, if they initial any change made

3. Which of the following constitute the "entire contract?"
    a. Offer and acceptance
    b. Policy issued by the company
    c. Policy and endorsements
    d. Policy, attachments and application

4. The "incontestability clause" is:
    a. A three year time period that the insurer has to challenge the statements made on the application
    b. A two year time period that the applicant has to challenge the statements made on the application
    c. A two year time period that the insurer has to challenge the statements on the application
    d. A two year time period before preexisting conditions must be covered

5. Janice told the agent that she was 29 when in fact she was actually 39. When the insurer discovers this misstatement:
    a. Since Janice misrepresented her information on the application, the policy will be voided
    b. It will not affect coverage, since age is not material
    c. Janice will be required to pay the difference in the premium based upon the correct age
    d. *The insurance company will pay a lesser benefit, based upon the premium actually paid*

6. John has a policy that is due the first of the month. John's premium is 30 days past due when he has a heart attack and enters the hospital.
    a. John is not covered, since he has not paid his premium on a timely basis
    b. *The insured will deduct John's premium from the claim and cover him for the benefit period, even if it exceeds the grace period*
    c. John will be covered, but only for one day
    d. John must reinstate his policy to be covered

7. All of the following statements pertaining to the reinstatement provision are true, EXCEPT:
    a. The insurer has 45 days to accept or reject an application
    b. There is a 10 day waiting period for sickness
    c. Companies may collect up to 60 days in back premiums
    d. *Reinstatement is guaranteed insurability*

8. All of the following statements are true, EXCEPT:
    a. *Notice of claim requires that the insured be given at least 90 days to inform the insurer of a claim*
    b. Claim forms must be provided within 15 days of notice
    c. The insured has 90 days to submit proof of loss
    d. Payment of claims must be immediately

9. If an insured is dissatisfied with the insurer's performance and chooses to take legal action against the company, action must be:
    a. No sooner than 30 days and no later than 2 years
    b. *No sooner than 60 days and no later than 3 years*
    c. No sooner than 30 days and no later than 3 years
    d. No sooner than 60 days and no later than 2 years

10. If Jim changes occupation from a more hazardous occupation to a less hazardous one, how will the change affect his disability coverage with the company?

    a. Jim will receive a refund of premium and coverage remains the same
    b. Jim will qualify for a higher benefit
    c. The insurer will pay on a pro rata basis
    d. The insurer will maintain the coverage at the original premium

11. The purpose of the "other insurance" clauses

    a. Is to pay based on a coinsurance basis
    b. Is to properly indemnify the insured
    c. Is to require full payment when over insured
    d. To protect the insured from the insurer

12. "Conformity with State Statutes" provision:

    a. Voids the policy if the language of the contract does not conform with state law
    b. Requires the state to conform to policy language
    c. States that if the language of the policy is in conflict with state statutes, the policy will conform
    d. Is one of the required provisions

Answers: 1.d 2.c 3.d 4.c (a in KY) 5.d 6.b 7.d 8.a 9.b 10.a 11.b 12.c

PROFESSIONAL TRAINING INSTITUTION

Chapter 18

Medicare (Title 18) & Medicare Supplements

In 1965, it was decided that our country would provide health care for the senior population and for the early disabled. Medicare is our country's form of <u>national health care</u> for the senior and the early disabled.

Medicare is designed to provide protection for the elderly and early disabled. In these two situations, the qualification and ability to afford proper coverage is extremely difficult, if not impossible, for a majority of people. The government created a program that would assist individuals as they find themselves in this difficult situation. As much as the Medicare program covers, it is not designed to pay for everything. Medicare comes with deductibles, co-payments and coinsurance gaps. These gaps are typically provided by purchasing a Medicare supplement policy from private insurance companies designed to fill in many of the gaps left behind by Medicare. Between a Medicare supplement and Medicare, the senior can obtain good coverage for a very reasonable rate.

MEDICARE ELIGIBILITY

There are several ways in which a person may become eligible for Medicare benefits. The following is a list of the different ways to qualify for Medicare benefits.

- The most common way is if a person is elderly and over age **65**.
  - Individuals qualify automatically if they are eligible for Social Security benefits.
  - If an individual does not qualify for Social Security benefits, but is willing to pay an additional monthly premium, Medicare benefits can be received.
- A person of any age can qualify for Medicare under the following circumstances.

- The individual is disabled and has received **24** months of Social Security disability benefits.

- Those who have **end stage renal disease or kidney failure**.

ENROLLMENT INTO MEDICARE

There are two primary parts of Medicare, Part A and Part B. **Enrollment in Part A is automatic and free** for individuals entitled to Social Security benefits. Coverage begins the first day of the month in which they turn 65.

Part B enrollment requires a premium payment, which will be deducted from the individual's Social Security monthly check. Because there is a payment, **Part B is considered voluntary**. Enrollment in Part B is assumed when one qualifies for Part A, but Part B could be rejected.

If Part B is rejected after it has been initially offered, the individual may sign up for Part B later, during an annual general enrollment period. The general enrollment period for late enrollments, occurs January 1st through March 31st. Coverage for late enrollments will not begin until the July 1st after the general enrollment period.

Part B enrollment can be delayed without penalty if the senior is working and eligible for credible group insurance coverage through the employer. In this case, the senior could sign up for Medicare Part B when leaving group coverage. The senior would be eligible for open enrollment and would not be required to pay a higher rate for Medicare.

FOUR COVERAGE PARTS OF MEDICARE

Medicare comes in four parts. Each part is unique and has a unique purpose with different methods of funding and payment obligations.

PART A

Part A is funded through payroll or FICA taxes. Since it is funded through payroll taxes, when a senior qualifies for Part A, **there is not a premium obligation for the senior**.

Part A provides four different coverage's:

- **Inpatient hospital care** – This coverage is designed to pay the reasonable expenses incurred when confined in the hospital. It provides coverage for most hospital confinement expenses, including room and board, meals, operating room, nursing expenses and other miscellaneous expenses charged by the hospital.

  holes in coverage

  Once the entrance fee is met, Medicare pays 100% of the covered services for the first 60 days. For the next 30 days, Medicare pays all but a specified daily coinsurance. After 90 days, Medicare provides an additional 60 lifetime reserve days. This gives the senior 150 days of coverage for each benefit period. A new benefit period would begin after 60 days free from care.

- **Skilled Nursing Facility Care** – Medicare provides up to 100 days of coverage for confinement in a skilled nursing facility. Medicare specifically covers skilled care in a skilled facility. Many stays will not qualify for Medicare payment due to Medicare's limited definition. Medicare does not provide coverage in an intermediate facility or for intermediate or custodial care.

  If Medicare does pay, it will provide full coverage for the first 20 days. The next 80 days will require the senior to pay a daily copayment.

- **Home Health Care** – The home health care benefit pays for health care assistance in the home. This benefit is limited and does not pay for all types of home health needs.

- **Hospice Care** – Hospice benefits are designed to meet the needs of the terminally ill. Benefits provided include: medication for pain relief and symptom management, patient and caregiver counseling, in or outpatient care, and medically necessary equipment. Hospice does not provide curative treatment.

  Hospice also provides a respite benefit. Respite care is care designed to provide relief for the caregiver. Hospice will provide up to 5 days of care in a hospice facility.

Part A covers most of the needs of the senior citizen, but it does not cover everything. Some of the services that **Part A will not cover include**:

- Private duty nursing

- Private room, unless medically necessary

- Personal conveniences (telephone, television, etc.)

- The first three pints of blood for each calendar year.

PART B, MEDICAL

Part B is financed partially by the general taxing authority of the federal government. The other part of the cost is paid monthly by the recipient and is most typically deducted from Social Security check.

Part B is designed to pay three primary areas of care:

- Doctor services

- Home health care (if not covered by Part A)

- Outpatient medical services

Most physician services will be covered by Medicare. Part B covers physician services in the hospital, the doctor's office or elsewhere. Other services covered by Part B include: lab tests, x-rays, therapy, surgery, anesthesia, medical supplies furnished by the physician, blood transfusions and many other services.

After an annual deductible, Medicare pays 80% of the reasonable or approved charges. What is considered **reasonable** is determined by Medicare. Any charge over what Medicare considers reasonable is **excess**, and is not covered by Medicare. A doctor may agree to only charge what Medicare says is reasonable. If a doctor only charges what Medicare says is reasonable, the doctor is said to take **assignment**. A doctor might sign a **participating agreement** with Medicare in which he agrees to take assignment for all patients.

PART C, ADVANTAGE

Medicare Advantage plans, or Part C, are **health plans offered by private companies approved by Medicare.** If you join a Medicare Advantage Plan, the plan provides all your Part A (hospital) and Part B (medical) insurance coverage.

Advantage plans always cover emergency and urgent care. They must cover all the services that original Medicare covers, except hospice care. Advantage plans may offer extra coverage, such as vision, hearing, dental, and/or health and wellness programs. Most plans also include Medicare prescription drug coverage.

Advantage plans must follow rules set by Medicare. However, each plan can charge different out of pocket costs and have different rules for how you get services (like whether you need a referral to see a specialist or if you have to go to only doctors, facilities, or suppliers that belong to the plan).

You usually pay one monthly premium to the Medicare Advantage plan, in addition to your Part B premium.

The different type of Medicare Advantage plans include:

- Health Maintenance Organization (HMO) Plans
- Preferred Provider Organization (PPO) Plans
- Private Fee-for-Service (PFFS) Plans
- Medical Savings Account (MSA) Plans
- Special Needs Plans (SNP)

Part D, Prescription Drug

Medicare prescription drug coverage is available to everyone with Medicare. To get Medicare drug coverage, you must join a Medicare drug plan. Plans vary in cost and drugs covered. Drug plans are sold by private insurance companies. The senior chooses a plan and a partial payment is made by Medicare to the selected insurer.

To join a Medicare Prescription Drug plan, you must have Medicare Part A and/or Part B.

The minimum prescription drug benefit begins with an annual deductible. After the deductible has been met, the policy will pay 75% of the bill up to an annual cap. At this point, if the senior's drug expense continues, they enter the donut hole. While in the donut hole the senior will receive a 60% discount on prescription drugs. Once a second cap has been reached the policy will provide 95% coverage for the rest of the year.

The discount will increase to 65% in 2018, 70% in 2019 and level off at 75% in 2020.

Medicare Benefits

Part A Costs for Covered Services and Items

Blood – In most cases the hospital gets blood from a blood bank at no charge and you won't have to pay for it or replace it. If the hospital has to buy blood for you, you must either pay the hospital costs for the first 3 units of blood you get in a calendar year or have the blood donated.

Home Health Care – You pay $0 for home health care services and 20% for durable medical equipment.

Hospice Care – You pay $0 for hospice care. A copayment of up to $5 per prescription for outpatient prescription drugs for pain and symptom management. 5% of the Medicare approved amount for inpatient respite care (short term care given by another caregiver, so the usual caregiver can rest).

Hospital Stay – In 2017 you pay $1,316 deductible and no coinsurance for days 1-60 each benefit period. $329 per day for days 61-90 each benefit period. $658 per "lifetime reserve day" after day 90 each benefit period (up to 60 days over your lifetime).

Skilled Nursing Facility Stay – In 2017, you pay $0 for the first 20 days each benefit period. $164.50 per day for days 21-100 each benefit period. All costs for each day after day 100 in a benefit period.

PART B COSTS FOR COVERED SERVICES AND ITEMS

Part B Deductible – In 2017, you pay the first $183 yearly for Part B covered services or items.

Blood – In most cases the hospital gets blood from a blood bank at no charge and you won't have to pay for it or replace it. If the hospital has to buy blood for you, you must either pay the hospital costs for the first 3 units of blood you get in a calendar year or have the blood donated.

Clinical laboratory – You pay $0 for Medicare approved services.

Home Health Services – You pay $0 for Medicare approved services. You pay 20% of the Medicare approved amount for durable medical equipment.

Medical and Other Services – You pay 20% of the Medicare approved amount for most doctor services (including most doctor services while you are a hospital inpatient), outpatient therapy, most preventive services, and durable medical equipment.

Mental Health Services – You pay 45% of the Medicare approved amount for most outpatient mental health care

Other Covered Services – You pay copayment or coinsurance amounts.

Outpatient Hospital Services – You pay a coinsurance or copayment amount that varies by service for each individual outpatient hospital service. No copayment for a single service can be more than the amount of the inpatient hospital deductible.

Medicare Supplements (Medigap Policies)

The **purpose** of the Medicare Supplement policy is to work with Medicare and to cover the expenses that are not covered by Medicare. Although Medicare does cover many of the expenses that the senior will encounter, there are deductible and copayments that are left for the senior. If a senior purchases a Medicare Supplement policy, most of these gaps can be filled in.

To be **eligible** for a Medicare Supplement, the senior must first qualify for parts A and B of Medicare. A senior can apply for a Medicare Supplement with a private insurer after qualifying for Medicare A and B.

STANDARDIZATION

At one time, there were numerous supplements on the market. Seniors were easily confused on the differences between one product and another. In order to make comparisons and choices easier for the consumer Medicare supplements were standardized. Originally, there were only 10 different plans that could be offered. Companies could not deviate from these original 10. As the years have progressed, the 10 standard plans have been reviewed and updated. Some plans have remained basically the same and some have been eliminated and replaced with new options. As of June 1, 2010, the following 10 plans are currently being offered for sale.

Medigap Plans Effective 2017										
Medigap Benefits	A	B	C	D	F*	G	K	L	M	N
Medicare Part A Coinsurance hospital costs up to an additional 365 days after Medicare benefits are used up	X	X	X	X	X	X	X	X	X	X
Medicare Part B Coinsurance	X	X	X	X	X	X	50%	75%	X	X***
Blood (1st three pints)	X	X	X	X	X	X	50%	75%	X	X
Part A Hospice Care Coinsurance	X	X	X	X	X	X	50%	75%	X	X
Skilled Nursing Facility Care Coinsurance			X	X	X	X	50%	75%	X	X
Medicare Part A Deductible		X	X	X	X	X	50%	75%	50%	X
Medicare Part B Deductible			X		X					
Medicare Part B Excess Charge					X	X				
Foreign Travel Emergency (Up to Plan Limits)			X	X	X	X			X	X
Medicare Preventive Care Part B Coinsurance	X	X	X	X	X	X	X	X	X	X
Out of Pocket Limit**							$5,120	$2,560		

*Plan F also offers a high-deductible plan of $2,200 as of 2017.

**Out of pocket limit is the maximum amount you would pay for coinsurance and copayments

***Plan N pays 100% of the Part B coinsurance except up to $20 copayment for office visits and up to $50 for emergency department visits.

CORE BENEFITS

The "core benefits" are the minimum benefits available in a Medicare Supplement plan. **Plan A is the core benefits. All companies selling Medicare Supplements must offer Plan A.** A company would then have the option to choose which other plans to offer to the senior. One company could offer plans A, C, & F. Another may offer A, G, and N. All companies selling supplements will offer A.

GUARANTEED RENEWABILITY

All Medicare supplements must be at least guaranteed renewable. Since this is a group that will be using and needing the benefits provided in the policies, it is important that the senior will be able to maintain coverage throughout life, regardless of age or health. As long as the senior pays the premium, **the policy is guaranteed to be renewable. Seniors may not be singled out for a premium increase.** Premiums may only be increased based upon class. Renewability must be properly labeled and stated on the front of the policy.

NONDUPLICATION OF COVERAGE

Medicare supplements cannot be written in a way that would allow them to pay a benefit already being covered by Medicare. The Medicare Supplement is designed to pay what Medicare does not pay. With the standardization of the policy, the different plans approved for sale have been established with this in mind.

Agents may not duplicate another supplement that is already in place. If a senior has a supplement in place, the agent must replace the current supplement if a new one is written. This is to keep the senior from being over insured.

POLICY SUMMARY (OUTLINE OF COVERAGE)

Once an agent has sold a Medicare Supplement, it may take an additional month before the policy is issued and delivered. In the meantime, the customer has paid a premium and has not had the opportunity to have seen the purchased contract. The Policy Summary is a **detailed outline of the coverage** purchased by the applicant. It is **written by the insurance company** and is **required to be left behind by the agent at the time the application is taken.** The agent is required to obtain a signature from the applicant that verifies receipt of the summary.

BUYERS GUIDE

The Buyers Guide is a document **developed by the NAIC** (National Association of Insurance Commissioners) to assist the senior in the purchasing process. The Medicare Supplement Buyers Guide is written in **general language** to provide basic information to the senior. It is designed to help the senior understand the different options available. Except in the case of direct response, **the guide must be delivered at the time of**

application. As in the case of the outline of coverage, the agent must obtain verification of the delivery of the Buyers Guide, in the form of a signature.

RIGHT TO RETURN (FREE LOOK PROVISION)

The Medicare Supplement policy provides the applicant with a 30 day right, from the date of delivery, to return (free look) the policy for a full refund. The Free Look provision must also be stated and properly labeled on the front of the policy.

OPEN ENROLLMENT

Once qualified and signed up for Part B of Medicare, the individual has 6 months to purchase a supplement on a guaranteed issue basis. During this time, the applicant cannot be rejected or rated due to health or age.

PRE-EXISTING WAITING PERIODS

Medicare supplement policies cannot have a waiting period for pre-existing conditions any longer than 6 months. In addition, if a senior switches from one supplement to another, any time met under the original supplement for pre-existing conditions may be applied to the new supplement.

REPLACEMENT OF MEDICARE SUPPLEMENTS

Agents cannot sell a Medicare Supplement in addition to another supplement. If an agent is writing a supplement, any existing supplements must be replaced. In a replacement transaction the agent must:

- Ask about other insurance that is currently in place and is the current policy intended to replace an existing policy?

- If the current policy is intended to replace an existing policy, a "notice regarding replacement" form must be signed by both the agent and the applicant. Copies must be left with the applicant and submitted to the insurer with the application.

Chapter Review

TERMS TO KNOW

Medicare

Part A

Part B

Part C

Part D

Assignment

Participating agreement

Reasonable or approved charges

Advantage

Medicare Supplement

Standardization

Core plan

Policy Summary

Buyers guide

NAIC

Open enrollment

Replacement rules

NUMBERS AND TIME PERIODS

65 – Elderly

24 months – Medicare eligibility on Social Security

80% - Medicare Part B coverage after deductible

10 – Original standard supplements

30 days – Free look

6 months – Open enrollment

6 months – Preexisting conditions

PROFESSIONAL TRAINING INSTITUTION

SAMPLE QUESTIONS

1. All companies selling Medicare supplements are required to offer Plan A, along with any other standard plan of their choice. Plan A is also referred to as:

    a. The core benefits

    b. The standard benefits

    c. The basic benefits

    d. The minimum benefits

2. All Medicare supplements must be, at least:

    a. Noncancellable

    b. Guaranteed renewable

    c. Conditionally renewable

    d. Guaranteed insurable

3. Which of the following rules, concerning Medicare enrollment, are correct?

    a. Enrollment in Part B is automatic and free

    b. Enrollment in Part A requires an additional premium payment that will be deducted from the individuals Social Security check

    c. If Part B enrollment is delayed, due to the senior working and having credible group coverage, a penalty will be applied at time of enrollment

    d. If Part B is initially rejected, the individual may sign up for Part B later, during an annual general enrollment period

4. All of the following are ways to qualify for Medicare EXCEPT:

    a. Over 65 and eligible for Social Security benefits

    b. Disabled and having received 12 months of Social Security disability benefits

    c. End stage renal disease or kidney failure

    d. Over 65, unable to qualify for Social Security benefits, but willing to pay an additional monthly premium

5. Which of the following is true, concerning the financing of Medicare?

    a. Part A is funded through state income tax

    b. Part A requires an additional payment from the recipient

    c. Part B is financed partially by the general taxing authority of the federal government

    d. Part B does not require an additional payment from the recipient

6. Part C, Advantage plans:
    a. Are health plans offered by private companies approved by Medicare
    b. Are Medicare Supplement policies designed to work with Medicare
    c. Are HMO or PPO supplemental plans
    d. Is the prescription drug coverage of the Medicare program

7. Agents are required to leave certain information behind, at the time of the application. All of the following disclosure rules are correct, EXCEPT:
    a. The agent must leave behind a Policy Summary and the Buyers Guide
    b. The Buyers Guide is written and developed by the NAIC
    c. The Policy Summary is written by the insurance company and includes specifics of the policy
    d. The Buyers Guide includes a detailed outline of coverage

8. In a Medicare supplement replacement transaction, the agent must do all of the following:
    a. Ask about other insurance and its replacement.
    b. Ask about other insurance and its replacement. Complete a "notice regarding replacement" form.
    c. Obtain the proper signatures and leave copies behind
    d. All of the above

9. The free look provision for the Medicare Supplement policy:
    a. Is 10 days beginning with the delivery of the policy
    b. Is 30 days beginning with the date of application
    c. Is 30 days beginning with the delivery of the policy
    d. Is 10 days beginning with the date of application

10. Open enrollment for the Medicare Supplement:
    a. Is a 6 month period that allows the senior to sign up for Medicare, with no health questions asked
    b. Gives the senior 6 months to enroll in a Medicare supplement on a guaranteed issue basis
    c. Is a 3 month time period, in which Seniors will be allowed to purchase any supplement on the market, no health questions asked
    d. Allows the senior to enroll in Part A and Part B Medicare coverage on a guaranteed issue basis

Answers: 1.a 2.b 3.d 4.b 5.c 6.a 7.d 8.d 9.c 10.b

Chapter 19

Long Term Care Insurance

Individuals are living longer than ever before. With longer life expectancies comes a need for a different type of health care than covered by traditional policies. Long Term Care policies are designed to cover the insured after or as opposed to a hospital stay.

edicare and the supplement are both designed to provide restorative treatment. Long term care goes beyond restorative. Today, seniors may find themselves needing assistance with daily activities and observation as well as restorative treatment like therapy. Most of these treatments are performed outside of the hospital setting. Care is provided in the home, the nursing facilities, assisted living facilities and adult day care centers. The purpose of the LTC (long term care) policy is to provide financial assistance to those being treated for these situations outside of the hospital.

BENEFIT TRIGGERS

There are two types of plans that can be sold, a qualified or a non-qualified plan. Most plans today are qualified plans. **The trigger is the event that determines qualification for payment of the benefit**. On a qualified plan, the benefit can be triggered one of two ways.

- A need for assistance in at least 2 out of 6 ADL's (eating, toileting, transferring, bathing, dressing or continence) for at least 90 days, or

- Severe cognitive impairment

TYPES OF BENEFITS

The LTC policy is more than just a nursing home policy. The policy is designed to protect the insured in the event of nursing home confinement, but it is also designed to provide benefits outside of the nursing home. The following are common benefits available under a LTC policy.

Nursing Home Care

The nursing home benefit pays a daily benefit as a result of confinement in a nursing facility. There are three levels of care provided in a nursing facility. **The LTC policy must pay full benefits for all three levels of care.** The **levels of care include**:

Skilled Nursing Care – Skilled care is the highest level of care provided in a nursing facility. Skilled is professional care that is provided on a daily basis. It is rehabilitative in nature. Examples of skilled include: therapy for a broken hip or stroke, changing sterile dressings, or treating bedsores. The only care that is provided for under Medicare is skilled care.

Intermediate Nursing Care – Whereas intermediate care is professional care, some patients may not need constant or daily care. Intermediate care is a lower level of care than skilled. Patients receiving intermediate care may be stable, but still in need of professional assistance.

Custodial Care – Custodial care is care that could be administered by a lay person. Typically it involves assistance with the **activities of daily living** (eating, dressing, bathing, transferring, toileting, and continence). Someone with cognitive disorder (Alzheimer's) may also need constant attention.

Home Health Care

The home health care benefit provides financial assistance for those who receive treatment and need **care in the home**. Home health care would typically include care provided by a licensed home health care agency. It could include professional treatment as well as oversight and maintenance.

Adult Day Care

Adult day care centers are **day care centers for adults**. This is a place where caregivers can drop off their loved ones for a limited period of time. The facility will provide care and oversight for the individual. This allows the at-home caregiver the time to run errands, go to work, or relax and have personal time.

Respite Care

Respite care **provides respite (relief) to the one providing the care**. Caregivers need time from the full time responsibilities of caring for a loved one, for their own physical and mental health. This benefit allows the caregiver some personal time by providing for a temporary sitter or allowing the loved one to be dropped off at an adult day care center.

Minimum Benefit Period

The LTC policy must provide a minimum of **12 months** worth of benefits. When a LTC product is purchased, the applicant must choose a term of coverage. Benefit periods can be as short as 12 months or as long as a lifetime plan. A lifetime plan would pay benefits regardless of the length of time spent in a nursing home. Companies offer benefits in between the two extremes also. A company could offer a 2, 3, 4, 5, or 10 year benefit package as an example.

Preexisting Condition Limits

Preexisting waiting periods must be clearly marked and labeled on the front of the policy. LTC insurance cannot deny a claim for a preexisting condition once the policy has been in effect for **6 months**. A preexisting condition is defined as a condition for which medical advice or treatment was recommended by a physician within 6 months of the effective date.

LTC policies cannot add an exclusion to the policy on specific conditions beyond the 6 month period.

When one LTC policy replaces another, any time spent meeting the preexisting waiting period from the first policy can be applied to the second policy.

Free Look Provision

The LTC policy is required to provide a **30 day** free look period. This is the period of time, beginning after delivery of the policy, for the insured to review the policy purchased and request a refund if dissatisfied for any reason.

INFLATION PROTECTION

When selling the LTC product the agent **must offer** an option that would provide a benefit that is designed to keep pace with inflation rates. The applicant can reject the inflation protection in writing.

RENEWABILITY

The LTC policy must be at least **guaranteed renewable**. Guaranteed renewable provisions guarantee the right of the insured to renew the product when it comes due. The insurer cannot cancel or nonrenew the insured. Premium can be increased, but only on a class basis. The renewability provision must be listed and labeled on the front of the policy.

MARKETING THE LTC PRODUCT

The following are some of the marketing requirements that the agent should be aware of if selling the LTC product.

SUITABILITY

Prior to selling the LTC product, the agent is required to establish whether the product is appropriate for the applicant. It is the agent's responsibility to make a reasonable effort to determine the product's suitability for sale or replacement.

OUTLINE OF COVERAGE (POLICY SUMMARY)

The outline of coverage is a **detailed** explanation of the policy purchased. **It must be left behind at the time of application.** It is **written by the insurance company** and given to the applicant in order to review the purchased product. A signature must be obtained to verify that the outline of coverage was received.

LTC SHOPPERS GUIDE

The LTC shoppers guide is a document that is **written by the NAIC** (National Association of Insurance Commissioners). This document gives the consumer **general** information concerning the LTC product and assists them in understanding the product. The LTC shoppers guide must be left behind by the agent and a signature must be obtained to establish that the guide was left behind.

Replacement

Agents must determine if the current sale will replace any existing policies. If the current sale is intended to replace an existing policy, then the agent must follow the correct procedures in order to do a proper replacement.

- Ask about other insurance that is currently in place. If a policy exists, is the current policy intended to replace an existing policy?

- If the current policy is intended to replace an existing policy, a "notice regarding replacement" form must be signed by both the agent and the applicant. Copies must be left with the applicant and submitted to the insurer with the application.

Partnership Plans

In a partnership plan, Medicaid partners with the insurance companies to provide the consumer protection against asset depletion.

The partnership plan is a program that gives the insured the opportunity to obtain coverage for future long term care needs while protecting their current financial assets from Medicaid spend down requirements. It is a "partnership" between the state (Medicaid) and private industry (insurance companies). The program allows one to qualify for Medicaid assistance without depleting all of one's assets.

PROFESSIONAL TRAINING INSTITUTION

Chapter Review

TERMS TO KNOW

Benefit triggers

Activities of Daily Living (ADL's)

Skilled nursing care

Home health care

Adult day care

Inflation Protection

Suitability

Outline of coverage (Policy summary)

LTC Shoppers Guide

Partnership plans

NUMBERS AND TIME PERIODS

12 months – minimum benefit period

6 months - preexisting condition

30 days – free look

Sample Questions

1. The Partnership plans:
    a. Are a partnership between the state and federal government
    b. Are a partnership between the federal government and the insurer
    c. Are a partnership between the state and private industry
    d. Are a partnership between the state (Medicare) and private industry (insurance companies)

2. Which of the following is NOT TRUE, concerning the long term care policy?
    a. Policies can exclude preexisting conditions up to 6 months, but not beyond
    b. The minimum benefit period that can be offered is 12 months
    c. Policies must pay full and equal benefits for all three levels of care; skilled, intermediate, and custodial
    d. The agent must leave the "Policy Summary" and "Outline of Coverage" forms behind at the time of delivery

3. Which of the following could trigger a qualified long term care policy?
    a. 2 out of 6 ADL's
    b. 2 out of 5 ADL's for at least 60 days
    c. 2 out of 6 ADL's for at least 60 days
    d. 2 out of 6 ADL's for at least 90 days

4. When selling a long term care policy:
    a. Offering inflation guard is at the option of the agent
    b. The agent must offer the inflation guard, but the applicant can reject it in writing
    c. Inflation guard must be included as a benefit within the policy
    d. The insurer, not the agent, will decide to include or not include inflation coverage in the product

5. The Partnership plans are designed to:
    a. Pay beyond Medicaid coverage
    b. Protect the consumer against asset depletion
    c. Pay along with Medicaid
    d. Encourage asset reallocation

Answers: 1.c 2.d 3.d 4.b 5.b

PROFESSIONAL TRAINING INSTITUTION

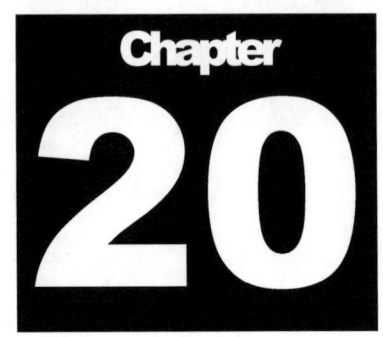

Chapter 20

Group Health

Health insurance can also be sold on a group basis. Purchasing health insurance through a group has many advantages to the individual. It makes health insurance available to those who may not qualify otherwise. When employers participate in the funding of the plan, insurance is easier and more affordable to more people.

Group insurance has many unique characteristics to it. It is defined as one policy written on several individuals. The following chapter will look at the concepts and characteristics unique to the group health concept. These include the policy itself, underwriting, eligible groups and conversion privileges.

THE NATURE OF GROUP COVERAGE

REDUCED ADVERSE SELECTION

Adverse selection occurs when the insurance company has too many poor risks. In order to protect the insurer from an adverse situation, the insurer:

- Requires that purchasing insurance for the group is **incidental to the formation of the group.** It must be a natural group. This group did not formulate for the purpose of buying insurance. If insurance was the primary purpose of the group's formation, then an adverse group could be created to avoid the asking of health questions.

- The insurer will require **a percentage of participation**. The insurer is interested in getting the majority of the group **(contributory 75% or non-contributory 100%)**. The insurer knows up front that there will be some high risk participants, but by requiring the majority of the group's participation, the insurer also knows there will be some healthy participants to offset the risk.

- By limiting enrollment to a specified **enrollment period**, this restricts the employee from last minute participation based upon a new health situation. New employees may be required to meet a probationary period before being eligible for enrollment. The **probationary period is the period of time, chosen by the employer, prior to eligibility for enrollment**. Once the probationary period is met, the employee will typically be given one month to enroll with little or no health questions. This period of time is referred to as the **enrollment period**.

- The **nature of the group itself** is a protection against adverse selection.

    o Groups typically enroll younger healthier individuals and older individuals retire and leave the group. This **turnover** becomes a natural protection against adverse selection.

    o In an employer group, the employees exhibit a certain level of health simply by being able to get up, get out, and work a full day.

REDUCED ADMINISTRATIVE COSTS

One of the advantages of the group concept is lower overall administrative costs. Administrative costs are lower for several reasons:

- Since the underwriting process looks at the group as a whole, as opposed to evaluating each individual, the cost of underwriting is significantly reduced.

- One contract is issued as opposed to multiple policies helps to keep overall costs down. By working through the employer, persistency of the business is more stable.

- The commission structure on the group sale is typically lower than that of the individual sale.

ELIGIBLE GROUPS

The primary purpose of the formation of the group must be for some reason other than the intent to buy insurance. Insurance must be incidental to the group. This concept helps protect the insurer from adverse selection. The insurance company is looking for a natural group. Natural groups can be formed for many reasons.

Single Employers – Single employer groups are one of the most common groups purchasing insurance.

Labor Union – occasionally members of the union may be able to purchase group health through their union under certain circumstances.

Associations – For associations to offer group coverage, they must have a minimum of 100 members and be established for some purpose other than to buy insurance.

Credit Unions – Credit unions can offer credit insurance to their members as a group product.

Creditors (Credit Health Insurance) – Credit life is used to cover the loan being made and is a form of group. The creditor is the owner and beneficiary. The debtor pays the premium. The death benefit is used to pay off the loan. The creditor can only collect up to its insurable interest.

Multiple Employer Trusts (METs) – A MET is a group of **small employers** from a common industry, coming together and **purchasing insurance** through a trust. Earlier we said that purchasing insurance must be an incidental reason for the formation of the group. In this case, the small employers are a part of the same industry, and therefore share a common bond. This allows small employers to come together and create a group large enough to negotiate a better policy.

Multiple Employer Welfare Arrangement (MEWA) – A MEWA is similar to a MET, but the main difference is that the group comes together to self-insure instead of purchasing insurance. By coming together, the small employers can create a group large enough to self-insure. Usually the group will have a third party administrator who oversees the group by calculating premiums, establishing the coverage and paying claims.

Master Policy & Certificates of Insurance

In group insurance, there is only one policy issued. The contract is an agreement between the insurer and the employer; therefore, the employer holds the policy. The policy is referred to as the **master policy**.

Each employee then receives proof of coverage. The employee's proof of coverage comes in the form of an **individual certificate of insurance**.

Premium Rating Factors

The rating of the group policy takes different factors into consideration.

Group Underwriting

Underwriting is the process of gathering information to evaluate the risk to be assumed, processing and categorizing the risk, and then placing a price on the risk if it is to be assumed. One of the primary responsibilities of the underwriter is to avoid adverse selection. Adverse selection is an unhealthy mix of risk. In group health insurance, the employees do not have to prove insurability; therefore, no health questions are asked. The insurance company must use other tools to avoid adverse selection.

The **group risk selection** process is different than that of the individual product. In group, the insurer is looking at the group as one complete unit. This means that the group underwriting process will take into consideration the average age of the group, the mix of male and female in the group, the geographical area and the occupation of those that make up the group.

Experience vs. Community Rating

Experience rating basis the future rates of the group product directly on the groups claim experience. The more claims the group experiences, the greater the impact will be on the group's renewal rate. If the group experiences few claims, rate increases will be limited. This method works best for the larger groups. The larger the group, the more control and influence the employer may have on the health issues and lifestyle issues. Many companies will install a wellness program, stop smoking drives, or exercise programs. Healthy employees mean manageable rates.

For the smaller group, it may be more costly and difficult to provide these extra wellness programs. If one person experiences a significant claim in a small group, it would be a significant portion of the group. Experience rating may not be ideal for the smaller group. Community rating is a better fit for smaller groups. Community rating bundles the group with others of the same size and location. By creating a larger pool of participants in the group, the insurer can provide a more stable, less volatile, premium scenario.

Establishing a Group Plan

Probationary Period

When a group is first established, the employer will choose a probationary period. The probationary period is the period of time that the employee must work for the employer before becoming eligible for group benefits. Employers may choose a long or short probationary period.

Eligibility Period

Once the probationary period is satisfied, there will be a period of time in which the employee will be able to enroll into the group plan without proving insurability.

Open Enrollment

Some employers give the employee the choice of group plans. An employer that provides multiple choices for the employee will have an annual open enrollment time at the end of the calendar year. During this time, an employee will have the opportunity to switch plans without having to prove insurability.

Contributory vs. Non-Contributory

It is essential that a majority of the employees participate in the plan. If not, the insurer could find themselves in an adverse selection situation. The participation requirements will be dependent on how the employer funds the plan.

In a **contributory plan, the employee makes a partial contribution** to the cost of the coverage and the employer pays part. If the plan is a contributory plan, at **least 75% of the eligible employees must participate** in the coverage. This allows for some employees who will not want to pay even a small part for coverage.

In a **non-contributory plan, the employer pays the full cost of the plan** and the employee will not pay anything. Since it is fully funded by the employer, the insurer will require **100% participation** from the eligible employees.

Key Concept of Group Insurance

Group insurance is different than an individual policy. The government is much more involved in protecting the rights of the individual within the group. The majority of people insured for health needs are covered by a group policy.

Occupational Losses

Since most groups are sold as employer groups, the group benefits will typically work with workers compensation benefits to avoid duplication of coverage. Occupational losses may be excluded because workers compensation benefits are expected to provide coverage needed as a result of a work related injury.

Maternity Benefits

Pregnancy is required to be treated as any other sickness if the group consists of **15** or more employees. Pregnancy coverage includes health care needs of the woman before, during and after the delivery. It also includes other covered expenses associated with the pregnancy.

Maternity benefits may be covered by the group insurance plan or it could be provided by the employer.

Discrimination in general is prohibited, whether it is based on pregnancy, disability or age. Group insurance must be available to all eligible employees.

Rights of Dependent Children

Group insurance can also provide coverage for the dependents of the member. Dependents include the spouse and children under certain circumstances.

As plans renew after September 23rd 2010, children can be covered whether or not they are dependents or in school, **up to age 26**. This includes married and out of the household. It does not cover the dependents of the child.

If a child is financially dependent on the parents because of physical or mental impairment, he or she may stay on the parents' plan beyond age 26. The insurer will require proof of dependency within **31** days from the time that the child would normally be required to leave the plan. Insurers can request proof of dependency as often as is reasonable for the first two years. After 2 years, the insurer can ask no more than once per year to prove dependency.

Changing Insurance Companies

There are times when an employer may see the need to change from one insurer to another. In order to protect the members of the group and to allow employers the option to shop around, laws have been established for this situation.

Coinsurance and Deductible Carryover

This allows the insured to carry over any deductible or coinsurance credit earned from the original plan to the new plan. By allowing the carry over, the insured will not be required to meet a second deductible within the same coverage year. It also allows the employer to shop around without harming the coverage of a member.

No Loss/No Gain

With the no-loss no-gain rules, if the insured is in the midst of a claim, coverage will continue even if the employer switches to a new plan. Coverage will continue under the new plan regardless of preexisting conditions.

Coordination of Benefits Clause

The situation commonly occurs in group coverages, in which the family finds themselves over insured with two different insurers.

Ted works at a company that provides health insurance for him and his family. Sallie, Ted's wife, works at a company that also provides benefits for herself and her family. Ted and Sallie have a daughter, Hillary. In this case, the family finds themselves over insured between the two insurers. The concept of indemnity says that the goal of the insurance is to bring them back to whole but not to let them profit from insurance.

Group insurance uses **primary/secondary** rules to determine which company will pay and how much. If Ted goes to the hospital, his insurance will be primary for him. If after his policy pays, there is still an amount left unpaid, he can file the balance with the second insurer. If Sallie uses her insurance then her insurer would be primary and Ted's secondary.

If Hillary goes to the hospital, who will be primary? Under older rules, primary status would be based on gender. Today, a different method is used that is more fair and equitable. This newer method if referred to as the **birthday rule**. **The parent whose birthday falls first in the year will be the primary for the children.** Since Sallie's birthday is in February and Ted's is in July, Sallie's insurance will be primary for Hillary. Even though Ted is older, it is based upon the birthday month not age.

Preexisting Conditions Limitations

A preexisting condition is defined as a condition for which one has received medical advice, diagnosis, or treatment for within the last **6 months**. Waiting periods for preexisting conditions can be for as long as 12 months.

Portability Issues

When an employee leaves a group, coverage may be hard to obtain on an individual basis. Both state and federal governments have passed laws that are designed to help the individual maintain coverage after leaving a group.

COBRA

COBRA (Consolidated Omnibus Budget Reconciliation Act of 1985) allows an employee to maintain group coverage after leaving the group. Employers with **20** or more employees are required to offer COBRA to their employees. If the employee comes off of the group because of a qualifying event, the employee can maintain the group coverage, but must pay the premium. A qualifying event would include:

- Voluntary termination of employment
- Termination for reasons other than gross misconduct
- Employment status change, from full to part time

In these situations, the employee would be given an **election period of 60 days** to continue coverage. Coverage can be maintained for up to **18 months**.

Under the following conditions, COBRA would be available for up to **36 months**:

- Death of the covered employee
- Divorce from the covered employee
- Covered employee becomes eligible for Medicare
- Dependency status is lost

This second set of circumstances provides protection for dependents coming off the group independently of the covered employee. Whereas in the first set of examples, it was the employee that was continuing coverage.

In the event of disability, COBRA benefits can be maintained for **29 months**.

Regardless of the reason for going on COBRA, the employer may charge an extra 2% for administration expenses. Now that the employee has left the group, the full cost of the program must be paid by the insured. The full cost will be 102% of the original premium.

The real advantage of COBRA is that the **benefits will be the same** as they were when the insured was on the group.

HIPAA

The Health Insurance Portability and Accountability Act of 1996 (HIPAA) makes it possible for an individual to move from one employer to another and receive immediate coverage for preexisting conditions.

Elmer has worked for the last 5 years at B&B Hunting Supplies. Elmer has been recruited to a higher paying more prestigious position at the animal control center. Elmer has had a history of heart disease. His previous plan had a preexisting waiting period of 6 months, which he satisfied 4 ½ years ago. The new plan has a waiting period for preexisting conditions for 12 months. Under the HIPAA rules, if Elmer maintains coverage from one plan to another with **no more than a 63 day gap in coverage**, any time met under the original (creditable) coverage will be applied to the new plan.

Since Elmer received a **certificate of prior creditable coverage** from the original plan, the HIPAA rules will apply. Elmer was insured for over 12 months with the previous plan; this time can be applied to his new waiting period. Elmer will be covered immediately under the new plan.

Miscellaneous Group Issues

501(c)(9) Trusts

A MET is a group of **small employers** from a common industry, coming together and **purchasing insurance** through a trust. Earlier we said that purchasing insurance must be an incidental reason for the formation of the group. In this case, the common bond is that they are part of the same industry. This allows small employers to come together and to create a group large enough to negotiate a better policy.

Third Party Administrators

A third party administrator is a firm that has been hired to administer a self-insured plan for a company. Even though a business has the finances to self-insure, it may not have the "know how" to see it through. The third party administrator handles the details: establishing the coverages, handling claims, record keeping and any other needs required by the plan.

Blanket Policies

A blanket policy is a policy that covers multiple individuals without listing the names of those covered. It is designed to cover a particular group while engaged in a specific activity or at a particular location. A blanket policy may cover a sports team or passengers on a bus.

Chapter Review

Terms to Know

Adverse selection

Contributory

Noncontributory

Enrollment period

Probationary period

Multiple Employer Trust (MET)

Multiple Employer Welfare Arrangement (MEWA)

Master policy

Certificate of insurance

Experience rating

Community rating

Open enrollment

Portability

COBRA

HIPAA

Creditable Coverage

Third party administrators

Blanket policy

Numbers and Time Periods

75% - Contributory plan

100% - Noncontributory plan

100 – Association group

15 – Maternity benefits

26 – Children

31 days – Payment for newborns

20 – COBRA available

60 days – COBRA election

18/29/36 months – COBRA terms

102% - COBRA premium

63 days – HIPAA portability

SAMPLE QUESTIONS

1. Which of the following situations help control against adverse selection:
    a. A group established for the purpose of buying health insurance
    b. A large group that is allowed to insure a select few
    c. A specified enrollment period
    d. No health questions asked for new enrollees

2. In group insurance, only one policy is issued. The individual participants will receive a separate proof of coverage. The policy and proof are referred to as:
    a. Primary policy and secondary certificate
    b. Master policy and servitor certificate
    c. Group policy and Employee policy
    d. Master policy and certificate of insurance

3. Companies may use different rating procedures when writing group coverage. Which of the following statements would be true?
    a. Experience rating is preferred by smaller companies
    b. Community rating is preferred by smaller companies
    c. Most companies prefer community rating regardless of size
    d. Most companies prefer experience rating regardless of size

4. Open enrollment is the period of time in which:
    a. The employee may choose a group plan without proof of insurability
    b. Occurs one time, after the probationary period
    c. Occurs immediately, once the employee is first hired
    d. The employer may change the group coverage without consequence to the employee coverage

5. A group plan is either contributory or non-contributory. What are the participation requirements for the group:
    a. 75% for both contributory and non-contributory plans
    b. 100% for both contributory and non-contributory plans
    c. 75% for contributory and 100% for non-contributory
    d. 100% for contributory and 75% for non-contributory

6. In a group plan, maternity benefits must be offered to groups over:
    a. 10
    b. 15
    c. 20
    d. 30

7. If Ted and Sallie both carry a group policy that covers themselves and their families, how will the two policies work together to insure the different members of the family?
    a. Each will work on a primary/secondary basis. Children's coverage will be prioritized based upon the birthday rule
    b. Each will pay on a pro rata basis. Children will then be treated the same as the parents
    c. Each insurer will co-insure with each other to provide full coverage for all family members
    d. Each will work on a primary/secondary basis. Children's coverage will be prioritized based upon head of the household rules

8. COBRA benefits are required to offer:
    a. A 63 day election period if the group is 20 or more
    b. A 60 day election period if the group is 15 or more
    c. A 63 day election period if the group is 15 or more
    d. A 60 day election period if the group is 20 or more

9. Regardless of the reason for going on COBRA, the full cost of the program must be paid by the insured. The full cost will be:
    a. 100% of the original premium
    b. 2% of the original premium
    c. 102% of the original premium
    d. 92% of the original premium

10. HIPAA rules state that if creditable coverage is maintained with a gap in protection of no more than _____ days, any waiting periods met under the original plan may be applied to the new plan.
    a. 20
    b. 31
    c. 60
    d. 63

Answers: 1.c 2.d 3.b 4.a 5.c 6.b 7.a 8.d 9.c 10.d

PROFESSIONAL TRAINING INSTITUTION

Chapter 21

Miscellaneous Government Healthcare Programs

There are several different government sponsored health care programs. We have already looked at Medicare. Other programs include: Medicaid, Social Security, Tricare and other various programs.

MEDICAID (TITLE 19)

Medicaid is a **federal/state health care program** for the needy. Minimum requirements are established by the federal government. The specific benefits, guidelines and qualification rules are set by the states. The states administer the program. Funding is provided partially by the federal government and partially by the state.

ELIGIBILITY

To become eligible for Medicaid benefits the **first requirement is based upon financial need.** Each state sets the net worth and income eligibility requirements. Once financial need has been established, an individual can qualify for Medicaid benefits when one of the following requirements has been met:

- Over age 65

- Caring for children while receiving welfare benefits

- Blind

- Permanently and totally disabled

Benefits

Federal Medicaid guidelines require that states offer a minimum of:

- Physician services
- Inpatient hospital care
- Outpatient hospital care
- Skilled nursing home services
- Laboratory and x-ray services
- Home health care services
- Rural health clinic services
- Periodic health clinic services
- Family planning services

Different states may offer additional services such as: prescription drugs, dental, private duty nursing, eyeglasses, checkups, and medical supplies and equipment. If the recipient of the Medicaid benefit is eligible for Medicare, Medicare and Medicaid will work together to cover the recipient.

Funding

Medicaid is partially funded by the state and local governments. The other part is funded by the federal government.

Administration

Medicaid is administered by the state governments through the states department of Welfare.

Spousal Impoverishment Rule

The spousal impoverishment rule was established to protect the at-home spouse from financial devastation as a result of a spouse's confinement in a nursing facility. The spousal impoverishment rule sets different "spend down" limits for the at home spouse. It allows the spouse to maintain an income, some assets and the home.

Social Security Disability Income Benefits (SSDI)

Not only does social security provide a retirement benefit for the elderly, it also provides an income for those who become disabled at any age.

Definition of Total Disability

Social Security uses an "**any occupation**" definition. In order to qualify for benefits, the insured must be unable to perform the duties of any occupation. More specifically, the definition states;

*The inability to engage in any gainful work that exists in the national economy. The disability must result from a medically determinable physical or mental impairment that **is expected to result in early death within 12 months**, or is **expected to last for a continuous period of 12 months**.*

If the benefits are qualified for, there will be a **5 month waiting period**. If after 5 months, the individual qualifies under the disability definition, benefits will be available.

After receiving **24** months of disability benefits from Social Security, Medicare will become available.

Eligibility

Eligibility for disability benefits is based upon the individual's "insured" status. There are three primary areas of benefits:

- Retirement benefits
- Survivor benefits
- Disability benefits

A worker who is "**fully insured**", is eligible for all three areas of benefit. To be fully insured, a worker must have **40** quarters of coverage, or one quarter of coverage for each year since age 21, with a minimum of six quarters.

A worker who is "currently insured" is eligible for some survivor benefits only.

Primary Insurance Amount (PIA)

The primary insurance amount is the amount of benefit the recipient receives. The PIA is based upon how much has been contributed over a person's lifetime. Since Social Security is deducted from payroll taxes, the more a person earns, the more that person pays into the program. The more one pays into the program, the higher the PIA. The PIA benefit is based upon your average indexed monthly earnings.

Tricare

Tricare is a healthcare program managed regionally for active duty and retired members of the military. Not only does it cover the military, it covers the family of the military. Tricare offers three different choices of health care.

Chapter Review

TERMS TO KNOW

Medicaid

Fully insured

Primary insurance amount

NUMBERS AND TIME PERIODS

5/12 months – Qualifying for early disability

24 months – Qualifying for early Medicare

40 quarters – Fully insured

PROFESSIONAL TRAINING INSTITUTION

Final Test I

1. Which of the following is not an essential component of a legal binding contract?
   a) Competent Parties
   b) Consideration
   c) Agreement
   d) Incompetent Parties

2. Which of the following is gross premium?
   a) Net Premium + Investment Return
   b) Chance of a loss – Interest + Load
   c) Mortality – Load + Interest
   d) Risk – Load + Investment Return

3. Which of the following is not considered an insurance company?
   a) Lloyds
   b) Stock
   c) Mutual
   d) Fraternal

4. In the insurance transaction, unequal values are exchanged; one side of the contract receives more. This characteristic describes which type of contract?
   a) Aleatory
   b) Adhesion
   c) Unilateral
   d) Conditional

5. Not official authority that is assumed by the client based upon circumstances created by the principal is called:
   a) Express Authority
   b) Implied Authority
   c) Apparent Authority
   d) Binding Authority

6. The answers the applicant gives on the application are called:
   a) Misrepresentations
   b) Representations
   c) Warranties
   d) Concealment

7. Which type of insurance company is owned by its policyholders?
    a) Lloyds
    b) Stock
    c) Mutual
    d) Fraternal
8. When a client withholds important information crucial to the underwriting process, it is called:
    a) Misrepresentation
    b) Concealment
    c) Fraud
    d) Representation
9. Which law is used to accurately predict losses?
    a) Law of Adverse Selection
    b) Law of Large Numbers
    c) Law of Underwriting
    d) Law of Accurate Predictions
10. All of the following are true concerning convertible term, EXCEPT:
    a) The insured does not have to prove insurability
    b) The insured is able to convert from term to permanent
    c) The insured is able to convert from permanent to term
    d) This is a good product for those people who develop a health condition after taking out a life policy
11. In life insurance, when must insurable interest exist?
    a) At the time of the sale and at the time of the loss
    b) At the time of the sale
    c) At the time of the loss
    d) At the time of the beneficiary's death
12. When the insurance company makes the insured whole, no more, no less, this is the concept of:
    a) Insurable Interest
    b) Adverse Selection
    c) Insurance
    d) Indemnification
13. Which type of life insurance policy provides temporary coverage for a temporary need?
    a) Universal Life
    b) Term
    c) Permanent
    d) Whole Life

14. All things being equal, which of the following policies would be the most expensive assuming that death occurred one year after purchase?

    a) Straight whole life

    b) 20 pay whole life

    c) 20 year level term

    d) 20 year decreasing term

15. Two postings are made to the universal life product cash value account. The insurer will:

    a) Debit premium payment; Credit cash value

    b) Debit the cost of protection; Credit guaranteed interest rate

    c) Credit cost of protection; Debit current interest rate

    d) Debit cost of protection; Credit current interest rate

16. Which universal life death benefit has a death benefit that automatically increases with the cash value accumulation?

    a) Option A

    b) Option B

    c) Both Option A and B

    d) Neither Option A or B

17. Greta is 50 years of age. Several years ago she paid $50,000, which she received as a life insurance settlement, into an annuity. Her account balance is now $75,000. Greta must withdraw $10,000. What will be the IRS consequences of this withdrawal?

    a) Greta will have to pay taxes on the whole $10,000

    b) Greta will pay taxes on a portion of the $10,000

    c) Not only will Greta pay taxes on the $10,000, she will also pay a $1,000 penalty on the withdrawal

    d) Greta will have to pay a 10% penalty on the withdrawal

18. Which of the following would be accurate concerning the cash value accumulation and the risk assumed by the traditional whole life policy?

    a) Cash value accumulation accelerates the longer the policy is in effect; Risk reduces over time

    b) Risk increases over time; Cash value is greatest initially

    c) Risk is greater at the end of the policy; Cash value is greatest at the beginning

    d) Risk and cash value both increase over the term of coverage

19. What protects option A of the universal life policy from early maturity?

    a) Risk corridor

    b) Reduction of the death benefit

    c) Additional payments required by the insurer

    d) Early maturity will not be possible prior to age 100

20. The policy that will provide permanent protection, but offer a premium structure that increases for five years and then levels off, would be:

    a) Graded premium policy
    b) Modified life policy
    c) Increasing term
    d) Convertible term

21. One policy that may pay out multiple death benefits would be:

    a) Universal life
    b) Family protection policy
    c) Joint life
    d) Survivorship policy

22. Hanze has an annuity that allows him to make payments of differing amounts. He does not plan on annuitizing the product until he reaches age 65. At that point, he would like to establish an income that will last as long as he lives. He will probably want to guarantee a minimum amount. Hanze has:

    a) A life with period certain
    b) A deferred annuity
    c) An immediate annuity
    d) A variable annuity

23. Jack and his wife Jill will receive an income until the first one dies. After which, the survivor will continue to receive an income for half of the original payment. This is:

    a) A straight life with 50% certain
    b) A joint annuity
    c) A joint and 50% survivor
    d) A refund life annuity

24. Taxes prior to annuitization will be paid based upon:

    a) Exclusion ratio
    b) FIFO
    c) LIFO
    d) LIPO

25. In life insurance, once the insured's premium is due, the company gives the insured a ___ day grace period to make a payment.

    a) 30
    b) 31
    c) 20
    d) 10

26. If an insured commits suicide within the first 2 years of the policy, the insurance company:
    a) Pays the death benefit to the beneficiary
    b) Pays half of the death benefit to the beneficiary
    c) Returns the premiums paid to the insured's heirs
    d) Pays double the death benefit to the beneficiary

27. A policy that has become a MEC has violated the:
    a) Cash value accumulation test
    b) 5 pay test
    c) LIFO test
    d) 7 pay test

28. The irrevocable beneficiary designation means:
    a) The owner can change the beneficiary at any time
    b) The owner can only change the designation with the beneficiary's permission
    c) The beneficiary can change the designation at any time
    d) The agent can change the designation at any time

29. The per stirpes designation means:
    a) Equally distributing the benefit to surviving beneficiaries
    b) The benefit is paid through the root
    c) The designation cannot be changed
    d) The designation can be changed

30. Which of the following dividend options allows the dividend to accumulate in a separate account?
    a) Cash
    b) Reduction of Premium
    c) Accumulate at Interest
    d) One-Year Term

31. John would like to maximize his death benefit, without increasing his annual premium. He is more interested in receiving the death benefit early, while his children are home, than later. Which option would you recommend?
    a) Reduced paid up
    b) Extended term
    c) Paid up additions
    d) One year term

32. Which dividend option allows the insured to purchase smaller whole life policies over and above the original?
    a) Reduction of Premium
    b) Paid-Up Additions
    c) Paid-Up Life
    d) Reduced Paid Up

33. Which nonforfeiture option allows the insured to purchase a permanent policy with the cash value, but with a lesser death benefit amount?

    a) Reduction of Premium

    b) Extended Term

    c) Paid Up Insurance

    d) Reduced Paid-Up

34. Which of the following riders pays double indemnity if the insured dies due to an accident?

    a) Payor Rider

    b) Accelerated Death Benefit Rider

    c) Multiple Indemnity

    d) Viatical Settlement

35. If an insured becomes disabled, which rider allows the premium to be waived?

    a) Guaranteed Insurability Rider

    b) Waiver of Premium Rider

    c) Cost of Living Rider

    d) Payor Rider

36. Which of the following is false concerning a key employee life policy?

    a) The key employee must give consent

    b) The business has insurable interest in the key employee

    c) The key employee does not give consent

    d) The policy protects the business in the event the key employee dies.

37. Which of the following is NOT an advantage of a qualified plan?

    a) Tax deductible business expense

    b) Tax deferred contributions for the employee

    c) Tax deferred growth for the employee

    d) Qualified plans have no tax advantages

38. Which type of retirement plan is specifically for the self-employed?

    a) Keogh

    b) SIMPLE

    c) 403b

    d) 401k

39. Which of the following is NOT an eligible group?

    a) MET

    b) MEWA

    c) An association with 50 members

    d) An association with 200 members

40. What is a MEWA?

    a) A labor union purchasing group insurance

    b) A group of small employers in the same industry coming together to purchase group insurance

    c) A credit union offering benefits to its members

    d) A group of small employers coming together to self-insure

41. A fully insured individual has worked:

    a) 40 quarters

    b) 21 quarters

    c) 20 quarters

    d) 13 quarters

Health

42. If Jay has a $1,000 calendar year deductible with 80/20 coinsurance. His policy has a stop loss at $10,000. If Jay has a medical bill for $8,000, how much will Jay have to pay?

    a) $1,000

    b) $1,400

    c) $1,600

    d) $2,400

43. What is the purpose of an "impairment rider?"

    a) Exclude coverage on a specific impairment

    b) Add coverage for a specific impairment

    c) Temporarily exclude coverage on a specific impairment

    d) Cover an impairment for an additional premium

44. The "elimination period:"

    a) Begins on the policy effective date

    b) Is the period of time in which preexisting conditions are not covered

    c) Are common on major medical policies

    d) Is defined as a deductible of time

45. All of the following are true about the guaranteed insurability rider, EXCEPT:

    a) It can be used to help the policyholder keep pace with inflation

    b) The rider will cause premiums to increase, based upon attained age rates, as options are utilized

    c) The insured will be allowed to increase their coverage at certain times without having to prove insurability

    d) Options can be utilized whenever the insured chooses, based upon their individual circumstances and needs

46. What is the standard "free look" period for health insurance?

    a) 10 days from the date of the application

    b) 10 days from the date of policy delivery

    c) 10 days from effective date

    d) 20 days from delivery date

47. The second injury fund is designed to:
    a) Pay for pain and suffering in gross negligence cases
    b) Discourage discriminatory hiring practices of the previously disabled
    c) Penalize the employer for repetitive injuries
    d) Help the employer meet their financial obligation for work related injuries that affect multiple employees

48. Several employers coming together for the purpose of buying insurance, would be a:
    a) MEWA
    b) MET
    c) MMA
    d) HSA

49. All the following are true concerning Blue Cross Blue Shield, EXCEPT:
    a) Blue Cross Blue Shield is a nonprofit organization
    b) Blue Cross Blue Shield pays directly to the provider rather than the individual
    c) Blue Cross Blue Shield is a reimbursement health care program started and created by a group of Doctors
    d) Blue Cross Blue Shield is a service organization with membership participation instead of policyholders

50. All of the following statements are true, EXCEPT:
    a) A primary care physician is the physician that will be responsible for the oversight of the patients care
    b) The gatekeeper system is designed to control the use of specialists and other expensive services
    c) Emergency care will be provided in network only, in a Health Maintenance Organization
    d) A co-pay is designed to encourage the use of a primary care physician

51. Medical benefits:
    a) Are taxed as ordinary income
    b) Are tax deductible
    c) Will not be taxed as income
    d) Taxed over 7.5% of AGI

52. Arlo has a policy with a $500 calendar year deductible, 80/20 coinsurance with an out of pocket limit of $2500. Arlo experiences the following medical bills. How much will his insurance policy pay?
    - **February $300**
    - **May $1,400**
    - **October $200**
    a) $720
    b) $1,020
    c) $1,120
    d) $1,520

53. Managed care could include all of the following EXCEPT:
    a) Case management
    b) Second surgical opinion
    c) First dollar coverage
    d) Pre-admission testing

54. Basic plans differ from major medical plans, in that:
    a) Basic plans are low limit policies with first dollar coverage
    b) Basic plans usually have high deductibles
    c) Basic plans are designed to cover catastrophic needs
    d) Basic plans are comprehensive in nature unlike the major medical policy

55. Newborns or adopted children must be included on a family policy:
    a) From moment of birth at no extra cost
    b) From moment of birth with additional payments due immediately
    c) From moment of birth with payment made within 31 days
    d) At the option of the insurer

56. Presumptive disability is:
    a) A type of partial disability
    b) The inability to sustain employment
    c) Typically defined as a disability caused by and occupational disease
    d) Typically defined as loss of two limbs, permanent blindness or loss of speech or hearing

57. John earns $5,000 per month. He chose to purchase $2,000 in disability benefits. After John's disability, his employer is willing to bring him back on a part time basis. He will be able to earn $1500. How much will his residual disability benefit provide?
    a) $3,500
    b) $2,000
    c) $1,500
    d) $1,400

58. Accidental means:
    a) Looks at the end result of the accident to determine qualification for benefits
    b) Is less restrictive than "accidental bodily injury"
    c) States that the injury must be unexpected and unintended
    d) Looks at the originating cause of the accident

59. John has a policy that pays specifically if he develops cancer. What type of policy does John have?
    a) Indemnity policy
    b) Dread Disease policy
    c) Basic medical expense plan
    d) Major Medical

60. Which of the following constitute the "entire contract?"
    a) Offer and acceptance
    b) Policy issued by the company
    c) Policy and endorsements
    d) Policy, attachments and application

61. The "incontestability clause" is:
    a) A three year time period that the insurer has to challenge the statements made on the application
    b) A two year time period that the applicant has to challenge the statements made on the application
    c) A two year time period that the insurer has to challenge the statements on the application
    d) A two year time period before preexisting conditions must be covered

62. John has a policy that is due the first of the month. John's premium is 30 days past due when he has a heart attack and enters the hospital.
    a) John is not covered, since he has not paid his premium on a timely basis
    b) The insured will deduct John's premium from the claim and cover him for the benefit period, even if it exceeds the grace period
    c) John will be covered, but only for one day
    d) John must reinstate his policy to be covered

63. In health, if an insured is dissatisfied with the insurer's performance and chooses to take legal action against the company, action must be:
    a) No sooner than 30 days and no later than 2 years
    b) No sooner than 60 days and no later than 3 years
    c) No sooner than 30 days and no later than 3 years
    d) No sooner than 60 days and no later than 2 years

64. Which of the following rules, concerning Medicare enrollment, are correct?
    a) Enrollment in Part B is automatic and free
    b) Enrollment in Part A requires an additional premium payment that will be deducted from the individuals Social Security check
    c) If Part B enrollment is delayed, due to the senior working and having credible group coverage, a penalty will be applied at time of enrollment
    d) If Part B is initially rejected, the individual may sign up for Part B later, during an annual general enrollment period

65. All companies selling Medicare supplements are required to offer Plan A, along with any other standard plan of their choice. Plan A is:
    a) The core benefits
    b) The standard benefits
    c) The basic benefits
    d) The minimum benefits

66. The Partnership plans:
    a) Are a partnership between the state and federal government
    b) Are a partnership between the federal government and the insurer
    c) Are a partnership between the state and private industry
    d) Are a partnership between the state (Medicare) and private industry (insurance companies)

67. Which of the following is NOT TRUE, concerning the long term care policy?
    a) Policies can exclude preexisting conditions up to 6 months, but not beyond
    b) The minimum benefit period that can be offered is 12 months
    c) Policies may pay different benefits for each level of care; skilled, intermediate, and custodial
    d) The agent must leave the "Policy Summary" and "Outline of Coverage" forms behind at the time of delivery

68. If Ted and Sallie both carry a group policy that covers themselves and their families, how will the two policies work together to insure the different members of the family?
    a) Each will work on a primary/secondary basis. Children's coverage will be prioritized based upon the birthday rule
    b) Each will pay on a pro rata basis. Children will then be treated the same as the parents
    c) Each insurer will co-insure with each other to provide full coverage for all family members
    d) Each will work on a primary/secondary basis. Children's coverage will be prioritized based upon head of the household rules

69. Companies may use different rating procedures when writing group coverage. Which of the following statements would be true?
    a) Experience rating is preferred by smaller companies
    b) Community rating is preferred by smaller companies
    c) Most companies prefer community rating regardless of size
    d) Most companies prefer experience rating regardless of size

70. COBRA benefits are required to offer:
    a) A 63 day election period if the group is 20 or more
    b) A 60 day election period if the group is 15 or more
    c) A 63 day election period if the group is 15 or more
    d) A 60 day election period if the group is 20 or more

71. HIPAA rules state that if creditable coverage is maintained with a gap in protection of no more than _____ days, any waiting periods met under the original plan may be applied to the new plan.
    a) 20
    b) 31
    c) 60
    d) 63

Answers: Final 1

1. D
2. B
3. A
4. A
5. C
6. B
7. C
8. B
9. B
10. C
11. B
12. D
13. B
14. B
15. D
16. B
17. C
18. A
19. A
20. A
21. B
22. B
23. C
24. C
25. A
26. C
27. D
28. B
29. B
30. C
31. D
32. B
33. D
34. C
35. B
36. C
37. D
38. A
39. C
40. D
41. A
42. D
43. A
44. D
45. D
46. B
47. B
48. B
49. C
50. C
51. C
52. C

53. C
54. A
55. C
56. D
57. D
58. D
59. B
60. D
61. C
62. B
63. B
64. D
65. A
66. C
67. C
68. A
69. B
70. D
71. D

Final Exam, II

1. An insurance company is able to insure:

   a) A pure risk only

   b) A speculative risk only

   c) Either a pure or speculative risk

   d) Neither the pure or speculative risk

2. Which of the following companies typically sell participating policies?

   a) Stock

   b) Mutual

   c) Lloyd's

   d) Fraternal

3. Who typically makes the offer in an insurance transaction?

   a) The applicant

   b) The agent

   c) The insurer

   d) The policyholder

4. In the law of agency, the agent represents:

   a) The insured

   b) The broker

   c) The principal

   d) The insurance agency

5. Under contract law, coverage does not begin until the transaction is complete. What is typically used, to speed up coverage for the applicant?

   a) Coverage always begins the date of the application, nothing needs to be changed

   b) Coverage will begin the date of the application, as long as the premium is paid up front with the application

   c) An interim insuring agreement can be used to speed up the effective date

   d) Coverage will begin the date of the physical. The sooner the physical the sooner coverage goes into effect

6. Upon delivery of the policy the agent may be required to check the health status one last time. This would be a:

   a) Delivery receipt

   b) Statement of good health

   c) Conditional receipt

   d) Condition of coverage

7. All the following would be sources of insurability, EXCEPT:
    a) Application
    b) Producers report
    c) MIB
    d) Fair Credit Reporting Act
8. When must insurable interest exist?
    a) At the time of the sale
    b) At the time of the claim
    c) Both, time of sale and claim
    d) With consent, interest is not a factor
9. In life insurance, the peril covered is death. A peril is defined as:
    a) The chance of a loss
    b) Increases the chance of a loss
    c) The cause of a loss
    d) The chance and cause of a loss
10. Which type of insurance company is owned by its shareholders?
    a) Lloyds
    b) Stock Company
    c) Mutual Company
    d) Fraternal
11. Cash value in a permanent life insurance policy is considered:
    a) Tax deferred
    b) Tax free
    c) Tax free above its cost basis
    d) Taxable as withdrawn
12. The juvenile policy typically includes:
    a) Payor rider and waiver of premium rider
    b) Guaranteed insurability benefit and waiver of premium
    c) Payor benefit and guaranteed insurability benefit
    d) Accidental indemnity with a term rider
13. If a policy is a MEC, all of the following would be consequences, EXCEPT:
    a) All loans and withdrawals will be taxed on a LIFO basis
    b) 10% penalty on anything withdrawn above the cost basis, prior to 59 ½
    c) Death benefits will be taxed above the cost basis
    d) Loans will be taxed above their cost basis, regardless of age

14. Marlin and Margaret have purchased a policy that covers both of them, but will only pay once (when the last one dies). What did they purchase?
    a) Joint life
    b) Joint and survivor
    c) Family policy
    d) Family maintenance policy

15. The difference between a withdrawal and a loan on a universal life policy is that:
    a) They both must be repaid, but withdrawals will not be charged interest
    b) Withdrawals do not have to be repaid and will not be charged interest
    c) Only one withdrawal may be made per year; Loans can be made an indefinite number of times
    d) Loans will be taxed above their cost basis; Withdrawals will not

16. Which term is defined as "the chance of a loss?"
    a) Risk
    b) Peril
    c) Hazard
    d) Loss

17. All of the following would be characteristics of a variable product, EXCEPT:
    a) A variable product require dual licensing
    b) The investment risk is assumed by the insurer
    c) The variable product uses a separate account for investing
    d) The specific investment strategy must be decided by the insured

18. A limited pay whole life policy:
    a) Provides a limited death benefit with a limited premium paying period
    b) Provides a limited paying period with lifetime protection
    c) Provides limited protection with a lifetime premium obligation
    d) Limits the payment of the whole life death benefit in the event of early death

19. Which of the following would be best suited for level term insurance?
    a) John needs protection for life, but wants to keep his premiums as low as possible
    b) Jill owns a thriving business and needs a significant amount of insurance protection
    c) Joe has 3 children and is just beginning a new career with great future possibilities for advancement
    d) Jim just purchased a house and needs insurance to protect the house for his family in the event of early death

20. The traditional whole life policy matures and endows:
    a) At age 100
    b) At age 95
    c) At completion of premium payments
    d) Any time after a 7 year payment period

21. Joey has an income that will pay regardless of how long he lives. If he dies within 20 years the income payments will continue to his wife for the remainder of the 20 year period. Joey has:
    a) A life with period certain annuity
    b) A joint annuity
    c) A joint and survivor annuity
    d) 20 year certain annuity

22. The estate may be the recipient of the death proceeds in all of the following situations EXCEPT:
    a) The estate could be listed as the beneficiary
    b) No beneficiary is listed on the application
    c) All listed beneficiaries have predeceased the insured
    d) The insured's trust is listed as the beneficiary

23. Betty is planning for her future retirement. She is trying to figure out, how much it will cost her to create the income needed for retirement. All of the following factors need to be considered, EXCEPT:
    a) The income amount desired and any guarantees that she chooses to include
    b) Her current age, sex and life expectancy
    c) Interest rate that the insurer will use to generate the income amount
    d) Company expenses to establish the plan

24. The maximum loan value on a permanent life insurance policy is:
    a) Equal to the cash value within the product
    b) Equal to the face amount of the policy
    c) Is slightly less than the face amount of the policy
    d) Is equal to the cash value less interest for that year

25. The exclusion ratio:
    a) Is used prior to annuitization and states that a portion of each payment will be taxed
    b) Is used after annuitization and states that growth is withdrawn first
    c) Is used prior to annuitization and states that withdrawals will be treated on a LIFO basis
    d) Is used after annuitization and states that a portion of each payment will be taxed as received and a portion will not be

26. An application can be backdated up to:
    a) 6 months
    b) 12 months
    c) 3 months
    d) 1 month

27. Which of the following premium modes will charge the highest premium per year?
    a) Annually
    b) Monthly
    c) Quarterly
    d) Semi-Annually

28. If an insured lies about age on the application, the insurer will:
    a) Void the policy
    b) Cancel coverage
    c) Reinstate the policy
    d) Adjust the death benefit

29. Jay needs an income over the next ten years. At that point his social security will kick in and he will take his retirement income. The best product for Jay might be:
    a) Life with 10 years certain
    b) Fixed amount annuity
    c) Fixed period annuity
    d) Variable annuity

30. All of the following are true about reinstatement EXCEPT:
    a) Reinstatement must be within 3 years
    b) Proof of insurability must be established
    c) Reinstatement must be within 5 years
    d) Back premiums must be paid

31. John has a whole life policy. He did not pay his premium when it came due. What will happen to John's policy?
    a) It will lapse
    b) The premium obligation will be paid out of the cash value and coverage will continue
    c) After 30 days if the premium has still not been paid, it will go on extended term
    d) It will go through a 30 day grace period, and then lapse

32. Which of the following is NOT a settlement option?
    a) Cash
    b) Interest
    c) Annuities
    d) Reduction of Premium

33. Which nonforfeiture option allows the insured to use the cash value to purchase a term policy with the same face value as the original policy?

    a) Extended Term

    b) One-Year Term

    c) Paid-Up Life

    d) Term

34. The free look time period on life insurance is:

    a) 5 days

    b) 30 days

    c) 15 days

    d) 10 days

35. Which of the following is NOT a reason accelerated death benefits may be paid out?

    a) Confinement in a nursing facility

    b) Diagnosis of a terminal condition

    c) The insured needs the money to buy a new car

    d) Diagnosis of a dread disease

36. Which rider would typically be included on a juvenile policy?

    a) Accelerated Death Benefit Rider

    b) Term Rider

    c) Waiver of Premium Rider

    d) Payor Benefit Rider

37. The policy owner of the stock purchase plan is:

    a) The business entity

    b) The key employee

    c) The employer

    d) The individual owners

38. Which rider allows the premium to be paid out of the cash value account if the premium is past due?

    a) Automatic Premium Loan Rider

    b) Payor Benefit Rider

    c) Accelerated Death Benefit Rider

    d) Guaranteed Insurability Rider

39. Which type of retirement plan was established for nonprofit organizations?

    a) Keogh

    b) 401k

    c) 403b

    d) SEP

40. Joe has a $100,000 policy with double indemnity. Prior to an accidental death, Joey had borrowed $10,000. How much will Joey's beneficiaries receive?

    a) $90,000

    b) $180,000

    c) $190,000

    d) $200,000

41. The guaranteed insurability rider allows the insured:

    a) To purchase additional amounts of insurance at certain times without proving insurability

    b) To convert from term to permanent

    c) To convert from permanent to term

    d) To increase the death benefit based upon the CPI

42. Which type of retirement plan is designed for small business owners?

    a) SIMPLE

    b) SEP

    c) Roth IRA

    d) 401k

43. In group insurance, who holds the master policy?

    a) The employer

    b) The employee

    c) The insurer

    d) The agent

44. With regards to the blackout rule, the surviving spouse does not receive a benefit after the youngest child turns ____ and until the surviving spouse turns ____.

    a) 18, 60

    b) 16, 60

    c) 16, 65

    d) 15, 55

45. With a contributory plan, how much participation is required?

    a) 100%

    b) 50%

    c) 75%

    d) 25%

Health

46. Guaranteed renewable policies:
    a) Guarantee the right to renew, but may limit renewability up to a designated age
    b) Lock in the premium and guarantee the renewability of the policy
    c) Are sometimes referred to as "guaranteed renewable and noncancellable"
    d) May raise the individuals rate based upon claims experienced

47. All of the following are true concerning a "mutual" company EXCEPT:
    a) Mutual companies are owned by the policyholders
    b) Mutual companies sell nonparticipating products
    c) Mutual company profits are paid out in the form of a policyholder dividend
    d) A mutual company is sometimes referred to as a participating company

48. Coinsurance is:
    a) The portion the insured must pay prior to the insurer paying
    b) A minimum payment designed to encourage preventive care
    c) Coverage that typically follows the stop loss in the policy
    d) A way of sharing the cost of a medical bill between the insured and insurer

49. The primary purpose of a deductible is to:
    a) Avoid larger claims
    b) Create easier access to healthcare
    c) Control against over utilization
    d) Encourage physician participation

50. A noncancellable policy:
    a) Guarantees the right to renew a policy when it comes due
    b) Does not allow the insured to cancel the policy, midterm
    c) Does not allow the insurer to cancel coverage, midterm and at renewal, and locks in the premium
    d) Guarantees issue of the policy and locks in the premium

51. Which of the following would be the full consideration of the insured?
    a) The promises in the contract.
    b) The premium paid
    c) The statements made in the application
    d) Both b & c

52. Which of the following, best describe a Health maintenance Organization:
    a) A prepaid service organization that provides both the protection against healthcare expenses as well as the healthcare providers themselves
    b) A healthcare program that has negotiated special discounts from the providers, that can then be passed on to the consumer in the form of lower premiums
    c) A major medical reimbursement program that specializes in preventive care
    d) A prepaid healthcare program that provides the greatest amount of flexibility for the consumer

53. The best description of a Preferred Provider Organization would be:
    a) A service organization that provides the health care services as well as the protection
    b) A reimbursement plan that provides the greatest amount of options for the customer
    c) A physician network organized for the purpose of marketing and negotiating for their services
    d) A reimbursement plan that has negotiated a prearranged discount with physicians and can offer better protection within their network

54. A Health Savings Account is an account:
    a) That is primarily used for retirement purposes
    b) Is a "use it or lose it" account
    c) Is used in conjunction with a "high deductible health plan"
    d) Does not receive special tax advantages

55. Usual, necessary and customary charge is defined as:
    a) The usual cost for care in that geographical area
    b) The medical providers actual charge
    c) What an individual provider charges
    d) The usual cost for care for the insurer

56. Tim purchased a basic surgical policy with a $1,000 surgery schedule. The schedule states that it will pay $200 for a gallbladder surgery. Tim has 10 units. How much will his policy pay?
    a) $200
    b) $1,000
    c) $1,200
    d) $2,000

57. Benefits from a medical expense policy:
    a) Will be taxable as income
    b) Will not be taxable as income
    c) Will only be taxable if it exceeds 7.5% of your adjusted gross income
    d) Is tax deductible

58. Workers Compensation was designed to be:
    a) A "no fault" system
    b) Exclusive remedy
    c) Both a and b
    d) Neither a nor b

59. Children may stay on their parents policy up till age:
    a) 19
    b) 21 if a full time student
    c) 26 if dependent
    d) 26

60. All the following are characteristics of major medical coverage EXCEPT:
    a) Comprehensive coverage
    b) Catastrophic coverage
    c) Collision coverage
    d) Coinsurance or cost sharing

61. Jay's disability policy defines recurrent disability based upon a 60 day time period. After 6 months of disability, Jay returns to work for 45 days and reinjures his back. As a result, this second disability:
    a) Will require a new elimination period, but will begin a new benefit period
    b) Will begin where benefits left off without a new elimination period
    c) Will begin where benefits left off without a new elimination period, but will receive a new benefit period
    d) Will require a new elimination period, and will not begin a new benefit period

62. An "own occupation" definition:
    a) Is more restrictive than the any occupation definition
    b) Is less restrictive than the any occupation definition
    c) Is not any more or less restrictive than the any occupation definition
    d) Is less advantageous to the policyholder

63. Which of the following tax considerations are true for the disability policy?
    a) If the disability policy is paid by the employer the benefits will be taxable
    b) If the disability policy is paid by the individual the benefits will be taxable
    c) If the disability policy is paid by the employer the benefits will be tax free
    d) Benefits will be considered income, and taxed, regardless of who pays the premium

64. Which coverage, under the dental policy, does not have a deductible?
    a) Orthodontic coverage
    b) Routine restorative services
    c) Routine preventive services
    d) All areas will have a deductible

65. Why are "required provisions" required and who are they required by?
    a) They are required by the state and protect the insurer from the insured
    b) They are required by the federal government and protect the insured from the insurer
    c) They are required by the insurer to protect the insured
    d) They are required by the state and protect the insured from the insurer

66. Which statement is true concerning changes made to the agreement between the insurer and the insured?
    a) Agents can make changes in the policy if the applicant requests and approves them
    b) Agents can only make changes in applications with consent of the insured
    c) Only an executive officer of the company can make a change in the policy language
    d) The insured may make changes, if they initial any change made

67. The amount paid out for death is referred to as the:
    a) Capital sum
    b) Principal sum
    c) Indemnity sum
    d) Residual sum

68. The waiver of premium benefit on the disability policy:
    a) Allows the insured to waive their premium regardless of disability status
    b) Waives the premium in the event of premature death
    c) Disregards the premium obligation while disabled
    d) Benefits are waived as the premium comes due

69. Janice told the agent that she was 29 when in fact she was actually 39. When the insurer discovers this misstatement:
    a) Since Janice misrepresented her information on the application, the policy will be voided
    b) It will not affect coverage, since age is not material
    c) Janice will be required to pay the difference in the premium based upon the correct age
    d) The insurance company will pay a lesser benefit, based upon the premium actually paid

70. All of the following statements are true, EXCEPT:
    a) Notice of claim requires that the insured be given at least 90 days to inform the insurer of a claim
    b) Claim forms must be provided within 15 days of notice
    c) The insured has 90 days to submit proof of loss
    d) Payment of claims must be immediately

71. All of the following are ways to qualify for Medicare EXCEPT:
    a) Over 65 and eligible for Social Security benefits
    b) Disabled and having received 12 months of Social Security disability benefits
    c) End stage renal disease or kidney failure
    d) Over 65, unable to qualify for Social Security benefits, but willing to pay an additional monthly premium

72. Which of the following is true, concerning the financing of Medicare?
    a) Part A is funded through state income tax
    b) Part A requires an additional payment from the recipient
    c) Part B is financed partially by the general taxing authority of the federal government
    d) Part B does not require an additional payment from the recipient

73. Which of the following could trigger a qualified long term care policy?
    a) 2 out of 6 ADL's
    b) 2 out of 5 ADL's for at least 60 days
    c) 2 out of 6 ADL's for at least 60 days
    d) 2 out of 6 ADL's for at least 90 days

74. All of the following statements pertaining to the reinstatement provision are true, EXCEPT:
    a) The insurer has 45 days to accept or reject an application
    b) There is a 10 day waiting period for sickness
    c) Companies may collect up to 60 days in back premiums
    d) Reinstatement is guaranteed insurability

75. When selling a long term care policy:
    a) Offering inflation guard is at the option of the agent
    b) The agent must offer the inflation guard, but the applicant can reject it in writing
    c) Inflation guard must be included as a benefit within the policy
    d) The insurer, not the agent, will decide to include or not include inflation coverage in the product

76. Which of the following situations help control against adverse selection:
    a) A group established for the purpose of buying health insurance
    b) A large group that is allowed to insure a select few
    c) A specified enrollment period
    d) No health questions asked for new enrollees

77. In group insurance, only one policy is issued. The individual participants will receive a separate proof of coverage. The policy and proof are referred to as:
    a) Primary policy and secondary certificate
    b) Master policy and servitor certificate
    c) Group policy and Employee policy
    d) Master policy and certificate of insurance

78. A group plan is either contributory or non-contributory. What are the participation requirements for the group:

    a) 75% for both contributory and non-contributory plans

    b) 100% for both contributory and non-contributory plans

    c) 75% for contributory and 100% for non-contributory

    d) 100% for contributory and 75% for non-contributory

79. Regardless of the reason for going on COBRA, the full cost of the program must be paid by the insured. The full cost will be:

    a) 100% of the original premium

    b) 2% of the original premium

    c) 102% of the original premium

    d) 92% of the original premium

80. In a group plan, maternity benefits must be offered to groups over:

    a) 10

    b) 15

    c) 20

    d) 30

Answers, Final II

1. A
2. B
3. A
4. C
5. C
6. B
7. D
8. A
9. C
10. B
11. A
12. C
13. C
14. B
15. B
16. A
17. B
18. B
19. D
20. A
21. A
22. D
23. B
24. D
25. D
26. A
27. B
28. D
29. C
30. C
31. C
32. D
33. A
34. D

35. C
36. D
37. A
38. A
39. C
40. C
41. A
42. A
43. A
44. B
45. C
46. A
47. B
48. D
49. C
50. C
51. D
52. A
53. D
54. C
55. A
56. D
57. B
58. C
59. D
60. C
61. B
62. B
63. A
64. C
65. D
66. C
67. B
68. C
69. D
70. A
71. B

72. C
73. D
74. D
75. B
76. C
77. D
78. C
79. C
80. B

PROFESSIONAL TRAINING INSTITUTION

Glossary

Accelerated Death Benefit - this benefit allows the insured to collect all or part of the death benefit prior to death, under certain defined circumstances

Accident - a sudden and unexpected event, not under the control of the insured, resulting in injury or damage

Accidental Bodily Injury - the result determines if the event was an accident

Accidental Means - looks at the originated cause of the accident

Accumulation Period - the time period in which the annuitant makes payments into the annuity

Activities of Daily Living - eating, toileting, transferring, bathing, dressing, continence

Adhesion - one party (the insurer) is responsible for the wording of the contract

Adjustable Life Insurance - allows the insured to make changes in the contract without purchasing an additional policy (i.e. increasing or decreasing coverage)

Adverse Selection - selection of risks that is higher or more likely to have a claim

Agent - one who represents the insurance company (principal)

Agent/Producer Report - report that allows the agent to share information and observations with the insurance company concerning the applicant

Aleatory - a contract of unequal exchange; one party stands to receive more than the other

Alien Insurer - an insurer organized under the laws of another country

Annually Renewable Term - one year term

Annuitant - the party the annuity is based upon; when the annuitant dies, the policy ends

Annuitize - the process of moving the accumulated money from the accumulation side of the product to the annuity side and beginning the income stream

Annuity Certain - does not guarantee an income for life; the total principal and interest earned throughout the liquidation phase will be paid out by the company

Annuity - the liquidation of an estate

Any Occupation - the inability to perform the duties of any occupation for which the insured has had past experience, training, or education

Apparent Authority - the appearance of authority created by the insurance company; not official authority

Application - the starting point of the application process

Assignment - to give the rights of the policy to another party

Attained Age - the age of the insured at a specific time period throughout the policy

Attending Physician's Report/Statement (APR or APS) - the past notes and observations of the applicant's attending physician

Authorized (Admitted) Insurer - an insurer who has been approved by the Indiana Insurance Commissioner to do business in the state of Indiana

Basic Hospital - plan designed to reimburse the insured for hospital bills incurred (room and board and miscellaneous medical expenses)

Basic Medical - plan designed to cover doctor visits in the office or hospital

Basic Plans - an older health policy that provides first dollar coverage with very low limits

Basic Surgical - plan designed to cover the specific expenses of surgery

Beneficiary - the recipient of the death benefit

Binding Receipt (Binder) - provides temporary, immediate coverage

Blue Cross Blue Shield - nonprofit membership based service organization established primarily for the purpose of providing hospital and medical expense payments directly to the provider

Broker - one who represents the client

Business Overhead Expense Policy - policy designed to pay overhead expenses to keep the business operating, if the business owner is disabled

Capital Sum - the amounts paid for dismemberment, blindness, or loss of hearing

Carry over provision - if the insured uses the policy at the end of the year (usually the last 3 months), the insured can carry over those expenses to apply toward the next year's deductible

Cash Refund Annuity - refund annuity that pays a lump sum balance to the beneficiary after the annuitant dies, if the minimum guaranteed amount has not been paid out

Cease and Desist Order - an order to stop

COBRA - allows an employee to maintain group coverage after leaving a group

Coinsurance - a way for the insured and insurer to share the cost of a medical bill; usually follows a deductible. When the bill exceeds the deductible, the insurer begins to pay a percentage of the bills up to the stop loss

Community Rating - bundles the group with others of the same size and location, creating a larger pool of participants

Concealment - the hiding or withholding of the truth

Conditional Contract - certain events must occur (sickness or death) before the insurance company will pay its claims

Conditional Receipt - states that coverage will begin either on the date of the application or the date of the physical (if required), whichever is last, **if** the applicant was insurable on that date

Consent - the authorization one person gives another to buy life insurance on their life; obtained by signing the application

Consideration Clause - specifies what each party to the contract has exchanged in order to validate the contract

Consideration - the something of value exchanged between the two parties of the contract

Consultant - a person who for a fee, offers advice, counsel, opinion, or service with respect to the benefits, advantages, or disadvantages promised under any policy of insurance that could be issued in Indiana

Continuous Premium (Straight Life Premium) - premiums are paid every year until the insured reaches age 100; this premium option offers the lowest premium to the insured

Contract - an agreement between two parties

Contributory Plan - the employee makes a partial contribution to the cost of coverage and the employer pays part

Controlled Business - insurance written on the interests of: the applicant or licensee, the applicant's or licensee's immediate family, or the applicant's or licensee's employer

Convertible Term - a product that can be converted from term to permanent without proof of insurability

Credit Life Insurance - insurance used to pay off a debt in the event of the insured's death

Current Interest Rate - the insurance company's guaranteed minimum rate plus excess interest

Death Benefit - the amount payable to the beneficiary after the insured's death

Decreasing Term - term insurance in which the death benefit decreases throughout the term

Deductible - the amount of the risk that the insured retains full responsibility for

Deferred Annuity - an annuity in which annuitization is delayed; the owner decides at what time, if ever, to cross the line of annuitization

Disability Insurance - policy designed to replace lost income due to accident or sickness

Dividend - a return of premium

Domestic Insurer - an insurer organized under the laws of Indiana

Dread Disease Policy - policy that limits coverage to a particular disease that is usually associated with extreme expenses

Effective Date - the date the policy goes into effect

Elimination Period - a period of time in which the insured must wait, before coverage is available for sickness or accidents. A deductible of time

Emergency first aid coverage - emergency care is always provided in or outside any network within the plan

Employer Mandate – employers with over 50 full time equivalent employees must provide adequate coverage at an affordable price or suffer a penalty

Entire Contract - includes the policy itself, the application and any attachments

Equity Indexed Life Insurance - a permanent policy that pays interest based upon the change in a particular equity index such as the Dow Jones Industrial Average or the Standard and Poor 500

Essential Health Benefits (EHB) – Benefits that the insurer must include in policies provided to individuals or small goups

Estoppel - to be legally stopped from being able to enforce one's legal right

Exclusion Ratio - the formula used on the annuity side to determine which portion of a payment is taxed and which part is not taxed. (principal/Expected Return)

Expenses - load; cost of doing business

Experience Rating - bases the future rates of the group product directly on the group's claims experience

Exposure - an area in which a loss could occur

Express Authority - powers and authorities expressed in the agency agreement

Fair Credit Reporting Act - federal legislature designed to protect consumer information

Family (Protection) Policy - a single policy that provides multiples death benefits for multiple insureds (covers each member of the family)

First to Die (Joint Life) - single policy intended to insure multiple lives, but only pays one death benefit(after the first insured's death)

Fixed Amount - annuity certain in which the owner determines the amount of income needed per month and the insurer determines how long the funds will last

Fixed Annuity - an annuity in which the insurance company pays an interest to the owner for the use of his/her money

Fixed Period - annuity certain in which the owner determines the period of time that payments are needed and the insurer determines the amount of each income check

Foreign Insurer - an insurer organized under the laws of another state

Fraternal - non-profit entity that offers insurance to its members and is organized under a lodge system

Fraud - an intentional misrepresentation for the purpose of benefiting

Free Look - the amount of time the insurance company gives the insured to review the policy after the policy delivery

Grace Period - the period of time the owner has to pay the premium payment after the policy comes due

Graded Premium - life product that modifies the premium by gradually increasing each year until it levels off after 5 years

Gross Premium - the total amount paid by the policyholder. Risk- Interest + Expenses

Guaranteed Growth Rate - the minimum interest rate guaranteed by the insurance company

Guaranteed Insurability Rider - rider that allows the insured to purchase additional amounts of insurance at predetermined times without proving insurability

Hazard - a situation that increases the chance of a loss

Health Maintenance Organization (HMO) - prepaid service organization that provides both the protection against healthcare expenses as well as the health providers themselves

Health Savings Account (HSA) - an account established for the purpose of paying health care expenses with tax free money

HIPAA - makes it possible for an individual to move from one employer to another to receive immediate coverage for preexisting conditions

Hospital Indemnity - policy designed to pay a daily benefit for each day the insured is confined in the hospital

Immediate Annuity - the owner of the annuity makes a single payment into the plan and requests an immediate income stream

Impairment Rider - a rider that excludes coverage on a specific impairment

Implied Authority - powers allowed by the insurance company but not expressed in the agency agreement

Incontestable Clause - the period of time the company has to challenge the information the insured gave on the application (2 years)

Increasing Term - term insurance in which the death benefit increases throughout the term

Indemnity (Indemnify, Indemnification) – to make whole, no more no less

Individual Mandate – Individuals must maintain Minim Essential Coverage (MEC) or suffer a tax penalty

Inspection - a report concerning the financial, moral, physical or any other relevant information concerning the applicant

Installment Refund - refund annuity that continues payments to the beneficiary until the company's obligation has been met

Insurability - the ability to be insured

Insurable Interest - financial or emotional interest one has in another's life or health

Insurance Guaranty Association - protects policyowners, insureds, and beneficiaries of life, health, or annuity contracts when these insurers fail to perform their contractual obligations due to financial impairment

Insurance - transference of risk from an individual to an insurance company, which then spreads it among its policyholders

Insured - the policyholder

Insurer - the insurance company

Insuring Clause - clause stating the parties to the contract and the company's promise to pay under the conditions stated within the policy

Interest - return on investment

Interest Sensitive Whole Life - a permanent policy with cash value growth, fixed premium, but the cash value account is credited with an interest rate based on the company's investment experience along with the company's guaranteed minimum

Interim Insuring Agreement - an agreement for the insurance company to provide coverage for the client while still completing the underwriting process

Irrevocable Beneficiary - beneficiary designation that may only be changed if the beneficiary agrees to give up the irrevocable designation

Joint and Survivor (Last to Die) - a single policy intended to insure multiple lives, but only pays one death benefit (after the last (survivor) insured's death)

Joint Life (First to Die) - a single policy intended to insure multiple lives, but only pays one death benefit (after the first insured's death)

Jumping Juvenile Life Policy - a policy written on a child up to age 21 and at that time, the benefit jumps (increases) to 5 times its value without increasing the premium

Juvenile Life - a life insurance product designed to provide coverage on the life of a child

Key Employee Disability Income Policy - policy to protect the business, in the event a key employee becomes disabled

Last to Die (Joint and Survivor) - a single policy intended to insure multiple lives, but only pays one death benefit (after the last (survivor) insured's death)

Law of Large Numbers - more numbers used to establish a statistic the more accurate the statistic will be

Level Premium - a fixed premium; the amount is constant, it will not increase or decrease as the years proceed

Level Term - term insurance in which the death benefit does not change throughout the term

Life Annuities - annuity that pays an income stream as long as the annuitant is alive

Life Annuity with Period Certain - guarantees an income for life with a minimum guarantee based upon a period of time chosen by the annuitant

Life Only Annuity (Straight Life) - pays an income stream of both principal and interest until the annuitant dies; at death, the income ends

Limited Pay Whole Life - limits the premium payment to a designated period of years; this premium option offers a higher premium than the straight life premium option, but the advantage is the premiums do not have to be paid for the rest of the insured's lifetime

Living Benefits - any benefit the insured can utilize while alive

Lloyd's - a company that insures risk by spreading risk over a group of investors; not an insurance company

Major Medical - a high or unlimited catastrophic policy with deductibles and coinsurance

Managed Care - managing and overseeing the healthcare being provided, while controlling expenses at the same time

Market Value Adjusted Annuity - pays a fixed interest rate, but if surrendered early, the contract will be recalculated based upon the market performance throughout the policy term

Material Statement - something that had the insurance company been aware of, the information would have affected how or if the policy would have been issued

Maternity Benefits - benefit designed to help pay the cost of pregnancy

Maturity Date - when the death benefit is paid out in a life insurance policy

Medicaid - a federal/state health care program for the needy

Medical Information Bureau (MIB) - a source that subscribing companies use to share application information

Minimum Essential Coverage (MEC) – minimum benefits required by the federal government that must be carried by individuals to avoid being penalized

Mental Infirmity - policy that typically covers a limited number of days in a mental institution

Misrepresentation - mistruth or a lie

Misstatement of Age and Sex Clause - the insurance company adjusts the benefit based upon how much coverage the insured could have purchased paying the same premium, with the correct age or gender

Modified Endowment Contract (MEC) - a permanent policy paid up (overfunded), in less than 7 years

Modified Life - life product that modifies the premium structure; it begins with a low premium and after a period of time, increases, and then levels off

Moral Hazard - a hazard based upon a person's values and ethics

Morale Hazard - a hazard that deals with carelessness or irresponsibility

Multiple Employer Trust (MET) - several small employers of like industry coming together for the purpose of buying insurance

Multiple Employer Welfare Association (MEWA) - several small employers of like industry coming together for the purpose of self insuring

Mutual Company (Participating) - an insurance company owned by its policyholders

Net Premium - the true cost of insurance; Risk-Interest

Non-Contributory Plan - the employer pays the full cost of the plan and the employee pays nothing

Nonparticipating - product or company that does not pay a dividend to its policyholders

Non-qualified - does not get a full tax benefit; the principal is previously taxed, but the growth still qualifies for tax deferral

Original Age - the age of the insured when the policy is initially purchased

Own Occupation - the inability to perform the duties of the insured's own occupation

Owner - the party that controls the policy

Ownership Clause - the owner has all of the rights in a policy

Partial Assignment (Temporary Assignment) - the owner gives up some of his/her ownership rights for a temporary period of time

Partial Disability - encourages the insured to return to work as soon as possible by paying 50% of the total disability benefit

Participating - product or company that pays a dividend to its policyholders

Payor Rider - rider that states if the payor (adult or parent) dies or becomes disabled, the premium will be paid up until the child is old enough to take over the premium payments

Per Capita - beneficiary designation distributes the benefit to the surviving beneficiaries on an equal basis

Per Stirpes - beneficiary designation that distributes the deceased beneficiary's portion of the proceeds to his/her heirs in descending order; through the root

Peril - an event that causes the loss to the insured

Permanent Insurance (Whole Life Insurance) - life insurance product that provides protection throughout one's whole life, or until age 100

Physical Hazard - hazards that are physical in nature; you can see, touch or smell them

Point of Service (POS) - an HMO that allows the member to leave the HMO for treatment outside of the network

Preexisting Condition - a health condition that existed prior to the purchase of the insurance policy. In the Affordable Care Act only Smoking may be considered when factoring premium.

Preferred Provider Organization - a traditional insurance plan covering health care expenses at a prearranged discount

Preferred Rating - better than average risk

Premium Mode - the frequency of payment (Annual, Semi-annual, quarterly, monthly)

Premium Tax Credit – assistance from the federal government to help with premium payments on plans purchased through the Marketplace if household income is between 100% - 400% federal poverty level

Presumptive Disability - a disability so serious, the insurer does not challenge the status

Primary Beneficiary - the first person designated to receive the death benefit

Primary Care Physician - general practitioner responsible for the oversight of the member's care

Principal Sum - the amount paid for accidental death

Probate - the process of determining and transferring ownership of an estate

Probationary Period - a period of time in which the insured must wait, before coverage is available for sickness

Producer - the insurance agent

Pure Risk - a possibility of loss; insurable

Qualified Health Plan (QHP) – Health plans certified by the Affordable Care Act that meet Marketplace standards

Rate up - when the insured charges a higher premium to cover a higher risk

Recurrent Disability - established by a period of time in between disabilities

Reduced - a way to manage risk by decreasing the likelihood of it occurring

Refund Life Annuity - guarantees an income for life with a minimum guarantee based upon the amount the annuitant annuitized

Reimbursement Contract - contract designed to reimburse the insured based upon the extent of the loss

Reinstatement Clause - the insured, after dropping coverage, can get the policy reinstated if the rules set forth by the company are satisfied

Reinsurance - when one insurer, for consideration, assumes the risk or part of the risk of another insurer

Renewable Term - term insurance that can be renewed after a certain amount of time while insurability does not have to be established

Representation - the truth to the best of one's knowledge

Residual Disability - compensates the insured a proportionate of the benefit, based upon the proportion the insured is able to earn

Retained - a way to manage risk by being willing to pay for a loss when and if it occurs

Retirement Income Annuity - annuity that combines the accumulation of retirement funds within an annuity with decreasing term to age 65 life insurance policy

Revocable Beneficiary - beneficiary designation that can be changed by the owner

Rider (Endorsement) - a change in the original policy

Rights of Conversion - a family member coming off of the policy is allowed to convert his or her own coverage to an individual policy

Risk Corridor - designed by the IRS to insure the cash value in a policy does not exceed the death benefit

Risk - the chance or possibility of a loss

Secondary Beneficiary (Contingent) - the party or parties listed to receive the death benefit if the primary beneficiary does not receive the funds

Section 1035 - allows an individual to move proceeds from one plan to another without tax consequence or penalties

Service Contract - prepaid coverages that provide protection in the form of services rather than benefits

Shared - a way to manage risk when an insured assumes a portion of the risk in relationship to his/her invested portion

Single Premium - one premium payment is made into the policy to pay up the protection for life

Speculative Risk - a possibility of loss or gain; not insurable

Sponsor - in a self-insuring organization, one who creates the coverage, manages the premium, pays the claims or administers the plan

Standard Rating - average or normal rating

Statement of Good Health - requested from the company to insure the risk has not changed since the application date

Steerage - encouraging participants in a health plan to utilize certain services or providers

Stock Company (Non-Participating) - an insurance company owned by stock or shareholders

Stop loss - once the medical bills reach this amount (specified in the policy), the insurance company begins to pay 100% of covered services

Straight Life (Life Only Annuity) - pays an income stream of both principal and interest until the annuitant dies; at death, the income ends

Straight Life Premium (Continuous Premium) - premiums are paid every year until the insured reaches age 100; this premium option offers the lowest premium to the insured

Substandard Rating - higher than average risk

Suicide Clause - if the insured commits suicide within the first 2 years of the policy, it is not covered

Supplemental Major Medical - policy that combines the basic plan with the major medical

Surrender Charges - penalty for an early withdrawal on an annuity

Temporary Producer - a license that allows an individual to service, not sell, existing insurance

Term Insurance - temporary life insurance

Total Assignment (Permanent Assignment) - total relinquishment of rights and ownership

Transferred - a way to manage risk by taking the risk and transferring it to another party, who then assumes the risk

Twisting - when one party misrepresents the truth for the purpose of replacing business

Two-Tiered Annuity - annuity product that calculates a different interest rate on funds if cashed in instead of annuitized

Unauthorized (Non-Admitted) - an insurer that has not been approved by the Commissioner to do business in the state of Indiana

Uniform Simultaneous Death Act - in a simultaneous accident, when order of death cannot be established, it will be assumed that the insured outlived the primary beneficiary

Unilateral - only one party in the contract is held to a promise

Universal Life - a form of whole life insurance in which the owner has both a flexible premium and death benefit amount

Universal Life Option A - level death benefit option up to age 95; risk decreases as cash value increases

Universal Life Option B - increasing death benefit option; risk stays constant

Valued Contract - contract that pays a specified amount that may or may not be related to the extent of the loss

Variable Whole Life - product that takes the cash value in the policy and invests it in a separate account chosen by the insured. The insured assumes then investment risk

Waiver of Cost Rider - a rider found in Universal Life policies that maintains the policy in the event that waives the cost of protection being deducted each month from the cash value account in the event that the insured becomes disabled

Waiver of Premium Rider - waives the premium on a policy, in the event of the insured becoming disabled

Waiver - to voluntarily give up a known right

Warranty - a promise or guarantee

Whole life insurance (Permanent Insurance) - life insurance product that provides protection throughout one's whole life, or until age 100

Index

401k Plans, 127
403b Plans, 128
7-pay test, 51
Accelerated Death Benefit, 106, 114
Accidental Bodily Injury, 202
Accidental Death and Dismemberment (AD&D), 201
Accidental Death Rider, 111
Accidental Means, 201
Accumulation, 62
Adhesion, 11
Adjustable Life Insurance, 38
Adult Day Care, 239
Advantage, 228
Adverse Selection, 140, 245
Affordable Care Act, 178
agency agreement, 12
Agent/Producer's reports, 15
Agreement, 7
Aids, HIV, 15
Aleatory, 11
annually renewable term, 34
Annuitant, 62
annuitization, 63
Annuity, 61
Annuity Certain, 69
Annuity Premium, 71
Any occupation, 192
Application, 14
Assignment, 164
Assignment Clause, 83
Assignment of benefits, 170
attained age, 33, 34
Attending Physician's Report (APR), 15
Attending Physician's Statement (APS),, 15
Automatic Premium Loan, 84
Automatic Premium Loan Rider, 115
Backdating, 84
Backdating Policies, 10
Basic Plans, 166
Beneficiary, 62, 85
Benefit Triggers, 238

Binding receipt, 9
birthday rule, 251
Blackout Period, 146
Blanket Policies, 254
Blue Cross Blue Shield, 174
Business Overhead Expense Policy, 196
Buy Sell Agreement, 119
Buyers Guide, 233
Cancellation, 219
Capital Sum, 202
cash refund, 68
cash value, 35
Cash Value, 36
certificate of insurance, 138
Certificates of Insurance, 247
Change of Beneficiary, 214
Change of Occupation, 215
Claim Forms, 213
COBRA, 252
Coinsurance, 164
Community Rating, 139
Competent Parties, 6
. Concealment, 8
Conditional, 10
Conditional receipt, 9
Conformity with State Statutes, 218
Consent, 9
consideration, 149
Consideration, 7
Consideration Clause, 149
contingent beneficiary, 86
Contract Law, 6
Contributory, 139, 249
Convertible term, 34
Coordination of Benefits, 251
Core Benefits, 232
Cost of Living Rider, 113
cost of protection, 41
Counter offers, 7
Credit Insurance, 208
Credit Life, 51
current interest rates, 41

305

Custodial Care, 239
Decreasing term, 31
DEDUCTIBLES, 152, 164
deferred annuity, 63
DEFINED BENEFIT PLANS, 127
DEFINED CONTRIBUTION PLANS, 127
DENTAL EXPENSE POLICIES, 207
direct transfer, 132
DISABILITY BUY-SELL POLICY, 196
Disability Income Insurance, 190
Disability Income Rider, 114
DISCRETIONARY PROVISIONS, 84
dividend, 4
DIVIDEND OPTIONS, 97
DREAD DISEASE POLICIES, 207
ELEMENTS OF A LEGAL CONTRACT, 6
ELIGIBILITY PERIOD, 249
ELIMINATION PERIOD, 150
Employer Mandate, 179
enrollment period, 140
ENTIRE CONTRACT, 211
ENTIRE CONTRACT/CHANGES CLAUSE, 80
EQUITY INDEXED ANNUITIES, 73
EQUITY INDEXED LIFE INSURANCE, 46
Essential Health Benefits (EHB), 178
estate, 87
Estoppel, 11
excess interest, 41
EXCLUSION RATIO, 71
experience rating, 139
Experience rating, 248
EXTENDED TERM INSURANCE, 103
Fair Credit Reporting Act, 15
family policy, 47
Federal Marketplace, 178, 180
Financial Industry Regulatory Authority (FINRA), 39, 45, 72
FIRST – TO – DIE, 46
Fixed Amount, 69
FIXED ANNUITIES, 72
Fixed Period, 69
Fraternal, 5
Fraud, 11
FREE LOOK, 150
FREE LOOK PROVISION, 84, 150, 234, 240
Full Time Equivalent, 179
fully insured, 145, 263
general account, 45, 72, 73
GRACE PERIOD, 82, 212
GRADED PREMIUM, 50

gross premium, 4
Gross premium, 17
Gross Premium, 97
Group, 245
Group Life Insurance, 137
Guarantee insurability rider, 156
GUARANTEED INSURABILITY RIDER, 112
guaranteed insurability rider., 51
GUARANTEED RENEWABILITY, 233
HAZARDS, 3
HEALTH MAINTENANCE ORGANIZATIONS (HMO), 175
HIPAA, 253
Home Health Care, 227, 239
Hospice Care, 227
HOSPITAL INDEMNITY, 206
Human Life Value Approach, 21
ILLEGAL OCCUPATION, 218
immediate annuity, 63
Impairment rider, 156
INCONTESTABLE, 212
INCONTESTABLE CLAUSE, 81
Increasing term, 32
individual mandate, 178
INDIVIDUAL RETIREMENT ACCOUNTS (IRA'S), 129
INFLATION PROTECTION, 241
Inspection reports, 15
installment refund, 68
insurability, 33
INSURABLE INTEREST, 8
Insurance, 1
INSURANCE WITH OTHER INSURERS, 216
insuring clause, 149
INSURING CLAUSE, 81, 149
Interest Adjusted Cost Method, 19
INTEREST SENSITIVE WHOLE LIFE, 45
INTERIM INSURING AGREEMENTS, 9
Intermediate Nursing Care, 239
INTOXICANT AND NARCOTICS, 218
irrevocable, 86
JOINT AND SURVIVOR, 47
JOINT AND SURVIVOR LIFE, 46
Joint and Survivor Life Annuity, 68
JOINT LIFE, 46
jumping juvenile, 50
JUVENILE LIFE, 50
KEOGH (HR-10), 128
KEY EMPLOYEE DISABILITY INCOME POLICY, 196
KEY EMPLOYEE LIFE, 119

LAST – TO – DIE, 47
LAW OF LARGE NUMBERS, 3
LEGAL ACTION, 214
LEGAL PURPOSE, 6
level premium term, 33
Level term, 31
Life Annuity with Period Certain, 67
Life Insurance Policy Options, 97
LIFO (last in first out), 52
Limited pay whole life, 37
LIVING BENEFIT, 106
LIVING BENEFITS, 20
Lloyd's, 4
LOANS, 36, 42
Long Term Care Insurance, 238
LTC SHOPPERS GUIDE, 241
MAJOR MEDICAL, 167
Managed care, 176
MANAGED CARE, 166
MARKET VALUE ADJUSTED ANNUITY, 74
master policy, 138
MASTER POLICY, 247
material, 8
MATERNITY BENEFITS, 250
MEDICAID (TITLE 19), 260
Medical Expense Policies, 163, 174
Medical information and exams, 15
Medical Information Bureau (MIB), 15
Medicare, 225
MEDICARE ELIGIBILITY, 225
Medicare Supplements, 225, 231
Minimum Essential Coverage (MEC), 178
MINORS, 88
Misrepresentation, 8
MISSTATEMENT OF AGE, 216
MISSTATEMENT OF AGE AND SEX CLAUSE, 82
MODIFIED ENDOWMENT CONTRACTS (MEC), 51
MODIFIED LIFE, 49
Multiple Employer Trusts (METs), 138, 247
Multiple Employer Welfare Arrangement (MEWA), 138, 247
MULTIPLE INDEMNITY, 111, 203
Mutual companies, 4, 158
Needs Approach, 20
Net Cost Method, 19
Net premium, 18
No Loss/No Gain, 251
NON-CONTRIBUTORY, 139, 249
NONFORFEITURE OPTIONS, 100

nonparticipating, 4
NONQUALIFIED PLANS, 125
NOTICE OF CLAIM, 212
NURSING HOME CARE, 239
OFFER AND ACCEPTANCE, 7
ONE – YEAR TERM, 100
OPEN ENROLLMENT, 234, 249
Option A, 43
Option B, 44
OPTIONAL POLICY PROVISIONS, 215
original age, 34
OTHER INSURANCE IN THIS INSURER, 216
OUTLINE OF COVERAGE, 233, 241
Own occupation, 192
Owner, 62
OWNERSHIP CLAUSE, 83
PAID – UP ADDITIONS, 99
PAID – UP LIFE, 100
PART A, 226
PART B, MEDICAL, 228
Partial disability, 192
Partial or temporary assignment, 83
participating, 4
PARTNERSHIP PLANS, 242
PAYMENT OF CLAIMS, 213
PAYOR BENEFIT RIDER, 114
payor rider, 50
PER CAPITA, 89
PER STIRPES, 89
PERIL, 3
PERILS, 152
Permanent, 30
PHYSICAL EXAM AND AUTOPSY, 214
POINT OF SERVICE (POS), 177
POLICY SUMMARY, 233, 241
PORTABILITY, 252
POWERS OF AGENCY, 12
PREEXISTING CONDITIONS, 154
Preferred, 17
PREFERRED PROVIDER ORGANIZATION (PPO), 177
PREMIUM MODES, 18
PREMIUM PAYMENT CLAUSE, 81
Premium Tax Credit, 179
PRESCRIPTION DRUG, 229
presumption of agency, 13
Presumptive disability, 192
primary beneficiary, 86
PRIMARY INSURANCE AMOUNT, 145
PRIMARY INSURANCE AMOUNT (PIA), 263

principal, 12
PRINCIPAL SUM, 202
PRIVILEGE OF CHANGE CLAUSE, 91
pro rata basis., 219
PROBATIONARY (WAITING) PERIOD, 150
probationary period, 140
PROBATIONARY PERIOD, 248
PROOF OF LOSS, 213
Provisions, 80
Qualified Retirement Plans, 125
REDUCED PAID-UP, 102
Refund Life Annuity, 68
Reimbursement contracts, 11
REINSTATEMENT, 104, 212
REINSTATEMENT CLAUSE, 82
REINSURANCE, 5
RELATION OF EARNINGS TO INSURANCE: AVERAGE EARNINGS, 218
RENEWABILITY, 241
Renewable term, 32
RENEWAL PROVISIONS, 153
REPLACEMENT, 234, 242
Representation, 8
REQUIRED PROVISIONS, 80, 211
Residual disability, 192
RESPITE CARE, 240
RETIREMENT INCOME ANNUITIES, 74
revocable beneficiary, 86
Riders, 111
RIGHTS OF DEPENDENT CHILDREN, 250
Risk, 1, 2
ROLL-OVERS, 131
ROTH IRA, 130
Securities Exchange Commission (SEC)., 39, 45, 72
separate account, 39, 45, 72
separate investment account, 73
Service contracts, 11
settlement option, 85
SETTLEMENT OPTIONS, 104
SHOP (Small Business Health Options Program)., 180
short rate basis, 219
SIMPLE, 129
SIMPLIFIED EMPLOYEE PENSION (SEP) PLANS, 128
Skilled Nursing Care, 239
Skilled Nursing Facility Care, 227
Social Security, 144

SOCIAL SECURITY DISABILITY INCOME BENEFITS, 262
Special Enrollment Period, 180
SPENDTHRIFT CLAUSE, 91
SPLIT DOLLAR PLANS, 122
Standard, 17
STANDARDIZATION, 231
statement of good health, 10
Stock companies, 4, 158
stock purchase plan, 120
STOP LOSS, 154, 165
straight life annuity, 67
straight life premiums, 37
Substandard, 17
SUICIDE CLAUSE, 85
SUITABILITY, 241
Term, 30
TERM RIDERS, 113
THIRD PARTY ADMINISTRATORS, 253
TIME LIMIT ON CERTAIN DEFENSES, 212
TIME LIMIT ON LAWSUITS, 84
TIME OF PAYMENT OF CLAIMS, 213
Total or permanent assignment, 83
TRAVEL ACCIDENT POLICIES, 207
TRICARE, 263
TRUST, 87
TWO TIERED ANNUITIES, 73
UNDERWRITING, 14
UNIFORM SIMULTANEOUS DEATH ACT, 88
Unilateral, 11
units, 48
UNIVERSAL LIFE INSURANCE, 40
UNPAID PREMIUM, 218
Valued contracts, 11
VARIABLE ANNUITIES, 72
VARIABLE UNIVERSAL LIFE, 45
VARIABLE WHOLE LIFE, 39
vesting, 126
Viatical Settlements, 106
VISION CARE POLICIES, 207
Waiver, 11
WAIVER OF COST, 43
WAIVER OF PREMIUM, 194
WAIVER OF PREMIUM RIDER, 114
Warranties, 8
WHOLE LIFE INSURANCE, 35
withdrawal, 36
WITHDRAWALS, 36, 42
WORKERS COMPENSATION PLANS, 182

Made in the USA
Columbia, SC
06 June 2019